In the Cage

In the Cage

Eyewitness Accounts of the Freed Negro in Southern Society, 1877–1929

Edited with an Introduction by
ALTON HORNSBY, JR.

Chicago
Quadrangle Books
1971

IN THE CAGE. Copyright © 1971 by Alton Hornsby, Jr. All rights reserved, including the right to reproduce this book or portions thereof in any form. For information, address: Quadrangle Books, Inc., 12 East Delaware Place, Chicago 60611. Manufactured in the United States of America. Published simultaneously in Canada by Burns and MacEachern Ltd., Toronto.

Library of Congress
Catalog Card Number: 70-130388
SBN 8129-0164-9

To Anne and Alton III

Acknowledgments

I am grateful for the invaluable help of several persons in the preparation of this book. Special gratitude must go to Miss Donna Johnson of Bishop College, Dallas, Texas, for the French translations; to Barnes F. Lathrop and Robert A. Divine of the Department of History at the University of Texas in Austin; to Ivan Dee of Quadrangle Books; and to my wife, Anne R. Hornsby. Miss Sharon Clayton, who typed the manuscript, and the librarians of the Main Library of the University of Texas in Austin, the Main Library of the City of Atlanta, the Trevor Arnett Library at Atlanta University, and the Morehouse College Reading Room deserve my thanks. Finally, I am grateful to the Danforth Foundation and the Committee on Research in the Humanities and Social Sciences at Morehouse College for a research grant which enabled me to complete this work.

Contents

Acknowledgments · vii

Introduction · 3

One · Pedagogues and Pupils · 16

Two · Making a Living · 83

Three · Life and Leisure · 128

Four · Religion and Superstition · 169

Five · Manners and Morals · 193

Six · Crime and Punishment · 212

Seven · Politics · 235

Retrospect · 260

Index · 263

In the Cage

Introduction

The commentaries of foreign observers who visited the United States must now comprise several hundred volumes and perhaps as many journal and magazine articles. Many of these reports are characterized by misinformation, exaggeration, and hostility. It is not surprising, therefore, that they have provoked a good deal of counter-hostility, if not disdain, from Americans. Yet the idea of how others see us continues to fascinate Americans, who still like to put on their best face for foreign observers. Any new work of outside commentary still attracts much interest. The interest stems also, in part, from the widely held belief that these commentaries enable Americans to make the necessary corrections in their "image."

This book contains not only foreign observations but also those of Americans of one region on the life of another region, and especially of one kind of people—Southern Negroes.

Owing mainly to his physical characteristics, of which skin color is the most obvious, and to the discrimination resulting in part therefrom, the Negro has played a unique role in American life. (His characteristics, to be sure, are not universal; in many cases one is designated a Negro by law, custom, or choice rather than by physical distinction.) This uniqueness makes feasible the investigation here undertaken, and allows the topic unusual interest and importance.

The Southern United States is a good place to begin any study of the American Negro. The first African slaves were deposited in the South, and until the mid-twentieth century a

In the Cage

large majority of the Negro population lived in the Southern states. The system of Negro slavery survived longer and more extensively in the South than elsewhere in the nation, and racial segregation and discrimination which followed it have been more overt in that region than in any other.

It has been generally assumed, often without adequate verification, that the typical Southern white looks upon the Negro as a distinct creature of God, lying somewhere between beast and man, a creature to be hated and pitied or, most often, to be feared. His assigned general characteristics have included immorality and piousness, laziness and industriousness, excessive joviality and constant despair, treachery and loyalty, and ignorance and avidity for education.[1]

Many analysts of American race relations have contended that Southern whites and Southern blacks have seen each other so closely and for so long that their mutual view has been dimmed, leading to misconceptions and misunderstandings which have darkened, and often bloodied, Southern history.[2] "Outsiders," it is presumed, have a different, less biased picture of the situation. What validity these assertions have, if any, will be more evident to the reader after he encounters the impressions which outsiders or non-Southerners have gleaned upon visiting the South.

Although outsiders can be expected to have a certain de-

---

[1] Excellent analyses of Southern attitudes toward the Negro can be found, among other places, in Gunnar Myrdal, *An American Dilemma: The Negro Problem and Modern Democracy* (2 vols., New York: Harper, 1944), I, 42–50, 50–60, 83–113, 380–397; II, 640–689, 768–781; John Dollard, *Caste and Class in a Southern Town* (3rd ed., New York: Doubleday, 1957), pp. 315–390, *passim;* Frank Tannenbaum, *Darker Phases of the South* (New York: G. P. Putnam's Sons, 1924), pp. 165–167; Floyd Hunter, *Community Power Structure: A Study of Decision Makers* (Chapel Hill: University of North Carolina Press, 1953), pp. 144–147, 151–159, 221–226.

[2] This reasoning was partially responsible for the Carnegie Foundation's selection of Gunnar Myrdal, Swedish economist and sociologist, to lead the study which culminated in the publication of *An American Dilemma.*

Introduction

gree of detachment, they too are inevitably open to various influences—from the contemporary historical setting, from prevailing scientific or pseudo-scientific opinions about race, from their own social, economic, and political positions at home, and from the representative or unrepresentative character of the particular persons, places, and reading matter found on their travels. The mere fact they *are* outsiders, sometimes guests, may limit the candor of remarks made to them, or cause them to be reluctant to pursue certain lines of questioning.[3]

In its larger aspect, this book seeks to broaden our understanding of the life of the Southern Negro by assembling eyewitness accounts of his existence. From these outsiders' observations one can determine, for instance, whether or not the Negro's material progress during the period from the end of Reconstruction to the eve of the New Deal was as rapid and significant as is sometimes claimed. These recorded impressions may also help to round out our conception of the Negro's proper role in American culture.

In selecting the writings for this book, I have construed the South to include all of the states that were slaveholding in 1860—Alabama, Arkansas, Delaware, Florida, Georgia, Kentucky, Louisiana, Maryland, Mississippi, Missouri, North Carolina, South Carolina, Tennessee, Texas, and Virginia—plus Washington, D.C. By non-Southerners I generally mean persons who lived outside the South until they were adults, or persons native to the South who became Northern residents before their adulthood and before 1877. Exceptions in the application of these rules will be noted as they occur.

The observers who figure in these pages are almost

---

[3] For a good discussion of the question of observer bias, see Dollard, *Caste and Class in a Southern Town*, pp. 32–40.

equally divided between natives of the United States and natives of foreign countries, a great majority of the foreigners being Western Europeans. I have focused on what the outsiders saw and on what they heard from the blacks. While their views on race relations are inescapably present, the primary interest here is with general impressions of the Negro and accounts of his everyday life—his labor, education, religion, political affairs, and social activities and attitudes.

In order to evaluate intelligently these outside impressions of the Southern Negro, it is important to bear in mind not only the more significant forces and events that influenced Negro life at the time, but contemporary opinion in the world at large as well, especially as represented by scientific or pseudo-scientific learning about the Negro's physical and social character. The lives of Southern Negroes, as Americans, were affected by national and international events and movements, but because they were blacks the effects upon them were quite distinct from the effects upon the general populace. In the period 1877–1900 the newly reunited United States was reaping the fruits of an industrial and technological revolution and setting its feet upon the world stage. For blacks, however, this was a period that Howard University's Rayford Logan has called "the nadir."[4] The Republican party had abandoned Negroes to the "benevolent" hands of former masters and their descendants. Segregation, discrimination, anti-Negro violence, and economic exploitation were on the increase. It is true that Booker T. Washington, in his "Atlanta Compromise" address at the Cotton States International Exposition in 1895, pointed to significant signs of economic and

---

[4] See Rayford W. Logan, *The Negro in American Life and Thought: The Nadir, 1877–1901* (New York: Dial Press, 1954), pp. ix–x, 11.

Introduction

social progress. But others, like W. E. B. DuBois, recently arrived from the North, could see only more lynchings, more exploitation, and more discrimination.

Between 1870 and 1900 the Negro population in the United States almost doubled, while the white population more than doubled. In 1870 nearly 4.5 million of the 4,880,-009 American Negroes were residents of the late slave states and of Washington, D.C.; in 1900, 7,823,786 of 8,833,994 lived in those places. To observe the Southern Negro during these decades was tantamount to seeing the American Negro. In the South the black population was about half the size of the white.[5]

From the time of his famous address at Atlanta in 1895, Booker T. Washington was the most widely hailed Negro in the United States. By 1900 Presidents had called at his door, and when he died in 1915 he had dined with Presidents and princes. He and his so-called "Tuskegee Machine" largely determined the Negro's response to the issues of the day. For the Negro it was, beyond doubt, the Age of Booker T. Washington.

The Washington era in Negro history coincided with the reformist Progressive Era in the nation at large. To Washington and his adherents it seemed that the Negro shared the social and economic improvements wrought by Progressive reformers and politicians. John Hope Franklin gives some small credence to this view, but Rayford Logan insists that Progressivism ignored the Negro. Negroes of the DuBois school, probably influenced by the Statesboro (Georgia) lynchings, and the Atlanta (Georgia) and Brownsville (Texas) riots, were convinced that the "age of recovery" was nowhere at hand.

---

[5] U.S. Bureau of the Census, *Negro Population, 1790–1915* (Washington, D.C.: Government Printing Office, 1918), p. 43.

In the Cage

Booker T. Washington might be at his zenith, but the mass of blacks were still at their nadir.[6]

The "Atlanta Compromise" address, universally hailed by Washington's supporters, and even by many of his critics, as a gem of public oratory, set the stage for the long, often bitter conflict between the Washington and the DuBois schools over Negro goals and policies in economics, politics, race relations, and education. Washington's formula, outlined in the Atlanta speech, was to accept the status quo in areas of "social equality" and political power in return for white assistance in economic and educational development. The best kind of training to implement this policy would be the agricultural and industrial education emphasized at Hampton and Tuskegee.

W. E. B. DuBois, who labeled Washington's address a "Compromise," and black intellectuals from Harlem to Washington, Nashville, and Atlanta clamored for racial integration in all aspects of American life, and for power at the highest political levels. Because they would need more than farmers and blacksmiths to accomplish their goals, they steadfastly demanded academic-classical training. The outcome of the debate between these two schools, and the progress, if any, made by the Negro during this period, were to be seen in the South. In 1910, 89 per cent of all American Negroes remained there, and by 1920, when the effects of the first great wave of Negro migration to the North were being felt, 85.2 per cent of all blacks were still in the region.[7]

---

[6] John Hope Franklin, *From Slavery to Freedom: A History of American Negroes* (2nd rev. ed., New York: Alfred A. Knopf, 1965), pp. 377–405, 426–444; Rayford W. Logan, *The Negro in the United States: A Brief History* (Princeton: Van Nostrand, 1957), p. 67. Franklin has a good discussion of the incidents mentioned here. See *From Slavery to Freedom*, pp. 431–436.

[7] See U.S. Bureau of the Census, *Negroes in the United States, 1920–32* (Washington, D.C.: Government Printing Office, 1935), p. 3.

Introduction

American participation in World War I sets the stage for the last period of this study. More than 100,000 blacks—most of them undoubtedly Southerners—served in Europe during the war. Most of these were in labor battalions which unloaded ships and sent supplies to the front, but more than ten thousand were in the 93rd Infantry Division, largely black, which saw combat duty. The war produced its share of Negro heroes, recipients of the *Croix de guerre* and Distinguished Service Medals and Crosses, and its share of Negro wounded and dead.

The spilling of Negro blood in the pursuit of democracy did not, however, have the favorable results many had anticipated. Even during the war, white soldiers, particularly in France, circulated rumors among Europeans to the effect that Negroes were sexual maniacs who endangered the safety of white women. At home, black soldiers from Camp Logan, Texas, were harassed by the Houston police. A full-fledged race riot resulted, in which seventeen whites were killed, thirteen blacks were hanged, and forty-one Negroes sentenced to life imprisonment. At Spartanburg, South Carolina, a similar outbreak was prevented only by sending the Negro troops stationed there to Europe.[8]

Once the war was over, hopes that the races could live more peacefully at home because they had served together in the military were severely disappointed. During the first postwar year both Northern and Southern newspapers reported rumors of plots, revolts, and insurrections by "French-woman ruined" black veterans. The first great wave of Negro migration to the North, which had accompanied the war, helped also

---

[8] For good general discussions of the Negroes' role in the First World War, see Franklin, *From Slavery to Freedom*, pp. 447–468, and George B. Tindall, *The Emergence of the New South, 1913–1945* (Baton Rouge: Louisiana State University Press, 1967), pp. 150–151.

In the Cage

to inflame Northern white opinion. The result was "the greatest period of interracial strife the nation had ever witnessed." Most of the violence occurred during the summer of 1919, beginning with a racial incident at Longview, Texas, in July. By October twenty-five cities and towns, North and South, had seen bloodshed—mostly Negro blood—in what James Weldon Johnson called the "Red Summer."[9]

As the Springfield, Brownsville, and Atlanta riots a decade earlier had led to the formation of the National Association for the Advancement of Colored People, the "Red Summer" sparked the establishment of the South's first successful interracial civil rights group—the Commission on Interracial Cooperation. Organized by prominent Southerners at Atlanta in 1919, it set out to still the "deadly menace" of race antagonism and to help the Negro improve his economic, political, social, and physical condition. But whatever progress this and similar groups might make was handicapped by the recession of 1919–1920, and practically wiped out by the Great Depression which began in 1929. The disposition of many blacks to turn, in despair, to a Marcus Garvey type of black nationalism and pseudo-religious cults strongly suggests that even the roaring twenties did not roar for them.

Presumptions about Negroes which outsiders brought with them to the South throughout the years from Reconstruction to the New Deal were unlikely, as far as they were based upon studies of the Negro's physical and mental traits before World War I, to have advanced much beyond the ideas of the seventeenth and eighteenth centuries.[10] Anthropologists, eth-

---

[9] The "Red Summer" is discussed at length in Franklin, *From Slavery to Freedom*, pp. 469–477, and Tindall, *The Emergence of the New South*, pp. 151–156. See also the reports on Negro migration to the North in U.S. Bureau of the Census, *Negroes in the United States, 1920–32*, p. 3.

[10] Adequate summaries of learned views before 1890 on the Negro's physical, mental, and social traits can be found, among other places, conveniently in

Introduction

nologists, and psychologists, writing between 1890 and 1914, generally concluded that physically and mentally the Negro was more animal than man.

Among the better-known works current in the 1890's was *Races and Peoples* (1890) by Daniel G. Brinton, noted University of Pennsylvania ethnologist. Brinton believed there were distinct racial traits, including differences in jaws, teeth, skin color, and "special senses." His studies showed the "projection of the maxillaries, or upper and lower jaws, beyond the line of the face" to be "much more observable in the black than in the white race" and "more pronounced in the old than in the young." Such a condition was "considered to correspond to a stronger development of the merely animal instincts." The Negro's skin color was largely the product of "a congenital disproportion of lungs to liver" which caused the retention of carbonic oxide in the lungs, and hence "an increased tendency to pigmentary deposit of the skin." In musical sense the "native African" excelled the "native American," though the difference was not greater than that between European nations. Brinton's general conclusion respecting black and white was that "the adult who retains the more numerous fetal, infantile or simian traits, is unquestionably inferior to him whose development has progressed beyond them, nearer to the ideal form of the species, as revealed by a study

---

Daniel G. Brinton, *Races and Peoples: Lectures on the Science of Ethnography* (New York: N. D. C. Hodges, 1890), in John C. Greene, *The Death of Adam: Evolution and Its Impact on Western Thought* (New York: Mentor Books, 1961), and in Mark Haller, *American Eugenics: Heredity and Social Thought, 1870–1930* (Ann Arbor: University of Michigan Press, 1959). For the period 1890 to World War I, see, in addition to Haller, George Oscar Ferguson, Jr., "The Psychology of the Negro: An Experimental Study," *Archives of Psychology*, V (1916), No. 36. Works which bring the subject down to recent times include Oscar Handlin, *Race and Nationality in American Life* (Boston: Little, Brown, 1957); Haller, *Eugenics* (New Brunswick: Rutgers University Press, 1963), and Thomas F. Gossett, *Race: The History of an Idea in America* (Dallas: Southern Methodist University Press, 1963; Schocken paperback, 1966).

In the Cage

of the symmetry of the parts of the body, and their relation to the erect stature. Measured by these criteria, the European or white race stands at the head of the list, the African or Negro at its foot."[11]

Francis Galton, sometimes called the founder of the science of eugenics, "studied the relative capacity of the Negro and the white races by dividing each race into sixteen defined grades of ability, eight above and eight below its racial average, and considered that the intervals separating the grades were equal throughout." Galton surveyed eminent men of each race and concluded that the ablest black ranked two grades below the ablest white. Then, "by an application of the 'law of deviation from an average,' he held that Negroes as a race have two degrees of ability less than Europeans."[12] Even though the number of "half-wits" among blacks was very large, the Negro race was "by no means wholly deficient in men capable of becoming good factors, thriving merchants, and otherwise considerably raised above the average of whites." The so-called disabilities placed upon the Negro in America, Galton admitted, made any comparison of his achievements with those of whites difficult.[13]

In discussing "human faculty as determined by race," anthropologist Franz Boas concluded that the physical differences between races made it likely that there might also be differences in faculty. The face of the Negro Boas found larger in proportion to the skull than that of the American Indian or the Caucasian. There was, Boas said, "no denying that this feature . . . represents a type slightly nearer the animal than

---

[11] Brinton, *Races and Peoples*, pp. 24–30, 36, 48.
[12] Quoted in Ferguson, "The Psychology of the Negro: An Experimental Study," p. 8.
[13] Francis Galton, "The Comparative Worth of Different Races," in Charles Dudley Warner, ed., *Library of the World's Best Literature* (New York: J. A. Hill, 1896), XV, 6177–6184.

Introduction

the European type." Despite this, Boas conceded that there was no evidence that the Negro and other "lower" races could not attain a level of civilization attained by most whites.[14]

Gustave LeBon, one of the early modern psychologists, classified Negroes as one of "the primitive and inferior peoples." From measurements of several thousand skulls, he found differences among races in the relative size of the brain. Although the differences were not very great, the "primitive and inferior" races, such as the Negro, "had a relative incapacity to reason or associate, to compare and draw conclusions, ... to observe and reflect, to exercise foresight, to persist in a given line of activity, to hold to a distant rather than a present end." Unfortunately these traits were, according to LeBon, "practically ineradicable and they determine the achievement of races."[15]

Anthropologist E. B. Tylor, basing his conclusions on the testimony of "European teachers," noted that at the age of twelve children of the "lower races," mainly Negroes, fell behind those of the "ruling race," Caucasian. This confirmed what "anatomy teaches of the less developed brain in the ... African than in the European."[16]

The famed psychologist G. Stanley Hall, writing in 1905, claimed that no two races in history differed so much in both physical and psychological traits as the Caucasian and the African. "The color of the skin and the crookedness of the hair" were only outward signs of many far deeper differences, including cranial and thoracic capacity, glands and secretions,

---

[14] Franz Boas, "Human Faculty as Determined by Race," American Association for the Advancement of Science, 43rd Annual Meeting, *Proceedings* (Brooklyn, 1894), pp. 311–327.

[15] Gustave LeBon, *The Psychology of Peoples* (2nd ed., New York: G. E. Stechert, 1912), pp. 233–236.

[16] Quoted in Ferguson, "The Psychology of the Negro: An Experimental Study," p. 4.

"vita sexualis," food, temperament, character, emotional traits, and disease. And because the Negro child stopped developing at about the age of twelve, the "virtues and defects of the Negro through life remain largely those of puberty."[17]

One of the few scholars in the early twentieth century to deny apelike qualities to blacks and significant differences in Negro and Caucasian brain weights was F. P. Mall. In 1909 he stated that the brain weight of "eminent men" was one hundred grams above that of the general run of men, and that the average white man had a brain one hundred grams heavier than that of the average black. But the frontal lobe, as compared with the rest of the brain, had the same relative weight in both races and in both sexes. Mall also found that the configuration of black and white brains was the same. Thus he concluded that "with the present crude methods the statement that the Negro brain approaches the foetal or simian brain more than does the white is entirely unwarranted."[18]

After a survey of the available evidence of racial mental differences, the famed educational psychologist Edward L. Thorndike also urged caution in making racial generalizations. He cited the need for "more actual measurements of race differences, and of intelligence in interpreting them."[19]

In 1913 Joseph Bardin, a little-known psychologist, writing for a larger audience, rejected the cautions of Thorndike and the conclusions of Mall. He agreed that there must be a connection between mental differences and physical differences since both evolved together. It had become increasingly evident, Bardin thought, that blacks and whites differed men-

---

[17] G. Stanley Hall, "The Negro in Africa and America," *Pedagogical Seminary*, XII (1905), 358–362.

[18] F. P. Mall, "Anatomical Characters of the Human Brain," *American Journal of Anatomy*, IX (1909), 20.

[19] Quoted in Ferguson, "The Psychology of the Negro: An Experimental Study," pp. 8–9.

Introduction

tally, therefore it followed that there were corresponding neural differences, "as marked . . . as are the external physical signs of race, such as skin, hair texture and facial angle." Those attempting to "modify" the Negro's mind while yet keeping him "a physical Negro" were undertaking the impossible. The Negro could never measure up to the "ideas and political philosophies" of Caucasians.[20]

In so far as learned estimates of Negro racial traits were concerned, the years following World War I saw a realization "that the facts of human heredity were not as simple as had been portrayed by some eugenicists and that environmental and cultural factors played a much greater part in man's development than earlier eugenicists were willing to admit."[21] Clearly, those intelligent observers who toured the South in the years after the war could bring with them beliefs or expectations quite different from those influenced by nineteenth-century learning which had concluded that the Negro was an inferior being, closer to beast than to man.

---

[20] J. Bardin, "The Psychological Factor in Southern Race Problems," *Popular Science Monthly*, LXXXIII (1913), 374.
[21] Haller, *American Eugenics*, p. 6.

1
Pedagogues and Pupils

Before Reconstruction the educability of the Negro had been a question pondered by Northerners as well as Southerners. Many had concluded that it was an impossibility. But the experience of Freedmen's Bureau schools and the rise of Negro colleges in the South convinced people in both regions that the race could absorb formal academic training. Still, others remained doubtful, and opposition to Negro education continued widespread, reinforced by scientific studies which purported to show that the brain of the Negro was smaller than that of the white and his mental capacity therefore more limited. Almost all outside observers wished to see for themselves how Negroes were doing in school.

At Atlanta in 1895 Booker T. Washington begged the white people in his audience to help and encourage Southern Negroes in the education of their heads, hands, and hearts. In the controversy that followed Washington's speech, many quoted him erroneously as advocating the training of hands over heads—thus adding heat to the debate over educational goals for the freedmen and their descendants. The "Atlanta Compromise" speech did, to be sure, emphasize agricultural and mechanical pursuits rather than the professions, assigning as much dignity to tilling the soil as to writing a poem; and Washington stressed the same means in his policies as head of Tuskegee Institute. He did not, however, condemn academic education nor advocate its exclusion from curriculums for Negroes. Nevertheless, many of those who discussed Negro education, including both supporters and detractors of Washington, spoke as if it were conveniently divided, at all levels, into two warring camps—one exclusively training the head, the other the hand. Outsiders naturally wanted to see which was winning.

> **Laura M. Towne** was born in Pittsburgh. A Unitarian, she studied at the Woman's Medical College in Pennsylvania, became active in Philadelphia abolitionist circles, and volunteered to go to the Sea Islands of South Carolina to help the Negroes there. She arrived in Port Royal in the spring of 1862; she was to remain on the Sea Islands for nearly half a century. From her residence at "Frogmore" and in her classrooms she was well placed to observe the everyday life of the Negro. In the following selection Mrs. Towne describes some of the many and varied activities which occurred at the Penn School. Of special note is her description of the annual school closing activities, taken from her published diary for the year 1879.

The school is crammed, and in the hot weather it is singeing—the closely packed benches, small windows, and sunned roofs accumulating heat. The trees have grown up so as to keep off the stiff breezes that used to moderate the heat. I am so glad we do not teach till July, as we used to.

In the Cage

Our exhibition was a success, as usual. The church was packed, and I think a hundred or more people could not get seats—many could not get in at all. I think we have had more attractive days before, but the people all seemed enthusiastic and well amused. We had no white visitors but Mrs. Davis and her niece, Miss Dennis, and Mr. Macdonald. It was a cloudy day with constant threatening of rain, but cool, and so pleasanter than usual. It is a great trouble, but, as it is the great event of the year on the island,—the day that brings back our old scholars, flocking from Savannah, Charleston, Bull River, and all about, to witness the exercises,—we ought not to feel it a trouble. We are well tired when it is over.

The school is enchanting, and I am happy as the day is long. I did think things disgusting when I first got back, coming as I did from the lap of luxury. . . .

The concert is over. It was not the success the first one was because Kit Green and Robert Smalls divided the attention of the audience. The church was so crammed that the children's voices were smothered (in the pieces) but the singing went well. Robert Smalls is going to Arizona to look at lands, with a view to emigration—not of himself, but of such as will go somewhere. . . .

We are busy hunting out exhibition pieces, making the usual reports, etc., and if I do not write much for a week or two, or till after exhibition, do not be alarmed. It is only hurry, and I will soon send a line or two. We have all the merits and demerits for the year to count out—no joke! . . .

Closing of school is the event of the year to hundreds on the island as well as to ourselves. Our boys come back from Charleston, Savannah, and the "Rock" to be present, and the church was so crowded that there was no standing-room, and there were crowds outside. Miss Botume and Miss Lord did not come, as there was an easterly storm on Wednesday, but we had from Beaufort, Mr. Collins, our senator, Mr. Wheeler, school commissioner, and Mr. Thomas, Editor. The latter took notes, and I think we shall see an account in the paper of the day's exercises. All expressed extreme astonishment at the advancement of the scholars, and Mr. Wheeler said that he thought there was no such advanced school in the state, outside of Charleston. Mr. Collins said it was no wonder Beaufort County was going ahead of any other in the state, when it had such a school, etc., etc.—nuts, of course, to us!

We never had such perfect recitations, such prompt movements, nor such nice singing. "Calm on" went most beautifully —all four parts clear, distinct, and true.

Ellen had for her amusement piece, Columbus, first as petitioner at the court of Spain, then on the ship in the mutiny, and subsequent discovery of land—thus showing how easy it is to find worlds, by the egg. It was well acted and an entire success.

I had a temperance piece—a comic one—which brought down the house in a series of laughs, and ended the performance, except the giving of prizes.

The church was decorated outside by flags at the windows, and inside by wreaths of oleanders, ivy, and cedar, hung on the lamps and pillars. It was very pretty. Ellen's oleander supplied not only enough for that, but also to give every girl and boy a breastknot or a buttonhole flower, and yet you couldn't miss one blossom from the tree, which is like one big red ball in its cool, green corner. . . .

I determined that when school closed I would devote myself for a month to my material property, with a zeal worthy of a better cause, and I am doing it. I am hunting up turkey

In the Cage

and guinea nests, attending to pickles, preserves, and blankets, etc., diligently. . . .

From Rupert Sargent Holland, ed., *Letters and Diary of Laura M. Towne: Written from the Sea Islands of South Carolina, 1862–1884* (Cambridge, Mass.: Riverside Press, 1912), pp. 295–297.

Sir George Campbell, a Scot and a member of the British Parliament, visited the United States in 1878, after long service in India, specifically to observe the Negro and to compare his condition with that of the Indian. Campbell first went to India in 1843 and was in and out of that country for some thirty years as a magistrate, district commissioner, and finally lieutenant-governor. He had a reputation for working in the best interests of the Indians. Campbell wrote a multi-volume *Ethnology of India* (1864–1865). His *White and Black,* from which the following selection is taken, became one of the most widely used travel books about the South. He visited Negro schools and colleges in Virginia and the Carolinas and applauded the efforts being made to educate the blacks.

At the time of emancipation the negroes were destitute of education to an excessive degree. . . . Since emancipation a good deal has been done to educate the negro. Many schools in which a superior education is afforded have been maintained by benevolent Northerners, and the State Governments have set up, and continue to maintain, several colleges in which the more ambitious and aspiring young blacks are educated. For the education of the masses a public school system has been started in all the States, of which the blacks have a fair share. Owing, however, to financial difficulties these schools are extremely imperfect, being open but a small portion of each year —in some States as little as two months on the average. However, this is better than nothing. The negroes show a laudable zeal for education, and upon the whole I think that as much has been done as could be expected under the circumstances.

During the last dozen years the negroes have had a very large share of political education. Considering the troubles and the ups and downs that they have gone through, it is, I think, wonderful how beneficial this education has been to them, and how much these people, so lately in the most debased condition of slavery, have acquired independent ideas, and far from lapsing into anarchy, have become citizens with ideas of law and property and order. The white serfs of European countries took hundreds of years to rise to the level which these negroes have attained in a dozen. Such has been the thoroughness of the measures adopted in America. . . .

I notice that I am now quite in the land of blacks, especially here, where they collected in numbers during the war. In this district they are quite in a majority. They do all the work about the wharves, and most other work. I principally came here to see the 'Hampton Agricultural Institute' for blacks. I went over it under the guidance of General Armstrong, who has charge of it, and has made it what it is. It is not quite an Agricultural Institute, for it is more used to turn out schoolmasters than anything else. . . . Several trades are also taught. I believe that this is the only place in the Southern States where black printers are educated. The Institution is primarily supported by funds subscribed in the North, but is now largely aided by the State of Virginia. It is not a free school, not being looked upon as charitable. The students are expected to pay moderate fees, and by their work to earn something towards their own living. Besides the negro students there are a good many Indians, sent by the United States Government. They are Indians from the Western tribes; and it is intended that, after being civilized and educated, they are to go back, and to improve their countrymen. I was much interested in these Indians. They are not red, but rather yellow, and not at all unlike some of the Indo-Chinese tribes to the east of Bengal.

I had a good deal of talk with General Armstrong about the negroes and about Southern politics. He is the son of a missionary who spent many years in the Sandwich Islands, but was a distinguished Federal soldier in the war. He thinks that the blacks are certainly inferior to the whites in intellect, but they are improvable. The Indians are decidedly stronger in intellect, but much more difficult to manage. . . . He thinks about one-third of the negroes are decidedly good; one-third may be made good by good management; and one-third are bad. Like most of the people I have spoken to, he has not much opinion of the mulattoes. The race is not sterile, but it deteriorates. . . .

Next day I went to see Dr. ———, State Superintendent of Education. I had a good deal of talk with him, and went with him to see some schools, both black and white. . . .

Dr. R—— [sic] thinks the negroes are generally inferior in intellect to the whites, and not capable of sustained or skillful work; but still they are very good within certain limits—they are very well disposed, and much can be made of them.

Of public free schools there are three classes—Primary, Grammar, and Higher—but these seem to run very much into one another when they are in the same building, as was the case at Richmond. . . . In the black schools I noticed some very fair mulattoes—one girl in particular, who would have been very fair for a European, was placed among the blacks, many of whom are very black and hideous. I hardly knew before what an ugly race some of the blacks are.

I visited the Richmond Institute, a philanthropic establishment, for the education of black teachers and preachers. It seemed to be doing very well. Mr. C——, the principal, has a high opinion of the negroes, but he admits that they are not mathematical. He is a Northerner sent by Northern people to carry on this work. He admits that the men of Richmond behave very well to him, but says that the ladies are much more bigoted.

I visited Mr. T——, head of the Shaw Institute, a college maintained by Northern subscriptions to educate black teachers. The buildings are good, and it seems a successful institution. Mr. T—— says his pupils turn out well. He is a Bostonian, served in the war, and is now rather bitter in his political talk. . . . Mr. T—— says he is quite isolated; he has no sympathy from the people here. . . . He has some building work going on; the master-mason is a black, and two white men are among the workmen; but this is an exceptional case. . . . He thinks the blacks are rather slow in intellect and deficient in enterprise, but they are otherwise good. Many of them are very religious, but many others have very little idea of the Christian religion. . . .

I visited Dr. C——, the Northern President of the Benedict Institute for blacks. He seems a very fair and moderate man.

He, too, thinks that the intellect of the black is inferior to that of whites, but among the blacks there are some who are very superior, and the mulattoes are better than the ordinary blacks. He understands that in slave times the slaveholders used to distinguish between different races of blacks, some being intellectually as well as physically superior to others; but

In the Cage

they are now so mixed up that the races can hardly be distinguished.

From Sir George Campbell, *White and Black: The Outcome of a Visit to the United States* (New York: R. Worthington, 1879), pp. 130–131, 275–276, 283–284.

William Wells Brown (1816–1884) was born at Lexington, Kentucky. His mother was a slave, his father probably a white slaveholder. Having escaped into Ohio in 1834, Brown became active in the antislavery and other reform movements. Long afterward, in 1880, he visited Alabama, Tennessee, and Virginia. Brown's reputation as a pioneer Negro historian rests largely on such works as *The Black Man: His Antecedents, His Genius, and His Achievements* (1863) and *The Negro in the American Rebellion* (1867). Brown viewed the education of the Southern Negro as the greatest challenge facing the nation in 1880.

The education of the negro in the South is the most important matter that we have to deal with at present, and one that will claim precedence of all other questions for many years to come.... I have watched with painful interest the little progress made by colored men and women to become instructors of their own race in the Southern States.

Under the spur of the excitement occasioned by the Proclamation of Freedom, and the great need of schools for the blacks, thousands of dollars were contributed at the North ... and some of the noblest white young women gave themselves up to the work of teaching the freedmen....

Pedagogues and Pupils

Upon the foundations laid by these small schools, some of the most splendid educational institutions in the South have sprung up. Fisk, Howard, Atlanta, Hampton, Tennessee Central, and Straight, are some of the most prominent. These are all under the control and management of the whites, and are accordingly conducted upon the principle of whites for teachers and blacks for pupils. And yet each of the above institutions is indebted to the sympathy felt for the negro, for their very existence. Some of these colleges give more encouragement to the negro to become an instructor, than others; but none, however, have risen high enough to measure the black man independent of his color.

At Petersburg I found a large, fine building for public schools for colored youth; the principal, a white man, with six assistants, but not one colored teacher amongst them. Yet Petersburg has turned out some most excellent colored teachers, two of whom I met at Suffolk, with small schools. These young ladies had graduated with honors at one of our best institutions, and yet could not obtain a position as teacher in a public school, where the pupils were only of their own race. . . .

It is generally known that all the white teachers in our colored public schools feel themselves above their work; and the fewest number have any communication whatever with their pupils outside the school-room. Upon receiving their appointments and taking charge of their schools some of them have been known to announce to their pupils that under no circumstances were they to recognize or speak to them on the streets. It is very evident that these people have no heart in the work they are doing, and simply from day to day go through the mechanical form of teaching our children for the pittance they receive as a salary. While teachers who have no interest in the children they instruct, except for the salary they get, are employed in the public schools and in the Freedman's

In the Cage

Colleges, hundreds of colored men and women, who are able to stand for the most rigid examination, are idle, or occupying places far beneath what they deserve.

It is to be expected that the public schools will, to a greater or less extent, be governed by the political predilections of the parties in power; but we ought to look for better things from Fisk, Hampton, Howard, Atlanta, Tennessee Central, and Virginia Central, whose walls sprung up by money raised from appeals made for negro education. . . .

Storer College, at Harper's Ferry, is . . . an institution . . . of whose officers I cannot speak too highly.

I witnessed, with intense interest, the earnest efforts of these good men and women, in their glorious work of the elevation of my race. And while the benevolent of the North are giving of their abundance, I would earnestly beg them not to forget Storer College, at Harper's Ferry.

The other two [Payne Institute, in South Carolina, and Waco College, in Texas], of which I have made mention, are less known, but their students are numerous and well trained. *Both these schools are in the South,* and both are owned and managed by colored men, free from the supposed necessity of having white men do their *thinking,* and therein ought to receive the special countenance of all who believe in giving the colored people a chance to paddle their own canoe.

I failed, however, to find schools for another part of our people, which appear to be much needed. For many years in the olden time the South was noted for its beautiful Quadroon women. Bottles of ink, and reams of paper, have been used to portray . . . these impassioned and voluptuous daughters of the two races,—the unlawful product of the crime of human bondage. . . . Although freedom has brought about a new order of things, and our colored women are making rapid strides to rise above the dark scenes of the past, yet the want of protection to our people since the old-time whites have regained power, places a large number of the colored young women of the cities and towns at the mercy of bad colored men, or worse white men. To save these from destruction, institutions ought to be established in every large city.

Mrs. Julia G. Thomas, a very worthy lady, deeply interested in the welfare of her sex, has a small institution for orphans and friendless girls, where they will have a home, schooling, and business training, to fit them to enter life with a prospect of success. . . .

From William Wells Brown, *My Southern Home, or The South and Its People* (Boston: A. G. Brown and Co., 1880), pp. 213–219.

T. Thomas Fortune was born in Florida, the son of a Reconstruction legislator, and graduated from Howard University. Shortly thereafter he moved permanently to the North, where he entered the newspaper business. He wrote for the *New York Sun*, then edited the Negro-owned *New York Globe* and *New York Age*. Fortune was strongly Caucasian in appearance. At the peak of his career he was the intimate of the best-known Negro business and cultural leaders in the country. He early identified with the principles of Booker Washington, and in later years with some of the ideas of Marcus Garvey. Fortune lived in the South for a considerable period between 1880 and 1884. In this selection he attacks the multiplication of Negro colleges and schools of the academic-classical variety and praises Hampton Institute, an agricultural-industrial school.

In the Cage

It cannot be denied that much of the fabulous sums of money lavishly given for the education of the Freedmen of the South has been squandered upon experiments, which common sense should have dictated were altogether impracticable. Perhaps this was sequential in the early stages of the work, when the instructor was ignorant of the topography of the country, the temper of the people among whom he was to labor, and more important still, when he was totally ignorant of the particular class upon whom he was to operate—ignorant of their temperament, receptive capacity and peculiar, aye, unique, idiosyncrasies. Thus thousands of dollars were expended upon the erection and endowment of "colleges" in many localities where ordinary common schools were unknown. Each college was, therefore, necessarily provided with a primary department, where the child of ten years and the adult of forty years struggled in the same classes with the first elements of rudimentary education. The child and the adult each felt keenly his position in the college, and a course of cramming was pursued, injurious to all concerned, to lessen the number in the college departments. No man can estimate the injury thus inflicted upon not only the student but the cause of education. Even unto today there are colleges in localities in the South which run all the year while the common school only runs from three to eight months.

Indeed, the multiplication of colleges and academies for the "higher education of colored youth" is one of the most striking phenomena of the times, as if theology and the classics were the things best suited to and most urgently needed by a class of persons unprepared in rudimentary education, and whose immediate aim must be that of the mechanic and the farmer—to whom the classics, theology and the sciences, in their extremely impecunious state, are unequivocable abstractions. There will be those who will denounce me for taking this view of collegiate and professional preparation; but I maintain that any education is false which is unsuited to the condition and the prospects of the student. To educate him for a lawyer when there are no clients, for medicine when the patients, although numerous, are too poor to give him a living income, to fill his head with Latin and Greek as a teacher when the people he is to teach are to be instructed in the abc's—such education is a waste of time and a senseless expenditure of money.

I do not inveigh against higher education; I simply maintain that the sort of education the colored people of the South stand most in need of is *elementary and industrial.* They should be instructed for the work to be done. Many a colored farmer boy or mechanic has been spoiled to make a foppish gambler or loafer, a swaggering pedagogue or a cranky homiletician. Men may be spoiled by education, even as they are spoiled by illiteracy. Education is the preparation for a future work; hence men should be educated with special reference to that work.

If left to themselves men usually select intuitively the course of preparation best suited to their tastes and capacities. But the colored youth of the South have been allured and seduced from their natural inclination by the premiums placed upon the theological, classical and professional training for the purpose of sustaining the reputation and continuance of "colleges" and their professorships.

I do not hesitate to say that if the vast sums of money already expended and now being spent in the equipment and maintenance of colleges and universities for the so-called "higher education" of colored youth had been expended in the establishment and maintenance of primary schools and schools of applied science, the race would have profited vastly more than it has, both mentally and materially, while the results would have operated far more advantageously to the State, and satisfactorily to the munificent benefactors....

But already the absurdity of beginning at the apex of the educational fabric instead of at the base is being perceived by those who have in hand the education of colored youth. A large number of colleges are adding industrial to their other features, and with much success, and a larger number of educators are agitating the wisdom of such a feature.

Perhaps no educational institution in the Union has done more for the industrial education of the colored people of the South than the Hampton (Virginia) Normal and Agricultural Institute under the management of General S. C. Armstrong. The success of this one institution in industrial education, and the favor with which it is regarded by the public, augurs well for the future of such institutions. That they may multiply is the fervent wish of every man who apprehends the necessities of the colored people....

The American system of education proceeds upon a false and pernicious assumption; and, while I protest against its application generally, I protest, in this connection, against its application in the case of the colored youth in particular. What the colored boy, what all boys of the country need, is *industrial not ornamental* education; shall they have it? Let the State and the philanthropists answer....

From T. Thomas Fortune, *Black and White: Land, Labor, and Politics in the South* (New York: Fords, Howard, and Hulbert, 1884), pp. 79–82, 86–87, 90–92.

James Bryce won the Arnold Prize at Oxford in 1863 for his essay on the Holy Roman Empire. He

Pedagogues and Pupils

taught civil law there from 1879 until 1893. First elected to the House of Commons in 1880, he was a member of Gladstone's cabinet in 1892; president of the Board of Trade under Lord Rosebury in 1894; administrator in Ireland until 1907; and ambassador to the United States, 1907–1913. He was the author of several books, including *The Relations of the Advanced and Backward Races of Mankind* (1902). His *The American Commonwealth*, from which the following selection is taken, has become one of the most important commentaries on American life by an outsider. Bryce visited the Deep South and the Border states in 1881. He was critical of the Negro's zeal for education.

Looking merely at . . . figures, elementary education would seem to have made extraordinary progress. . . . Between 1877 and 1908, while the white pupils in the common schools of the South increased 156 per cent, the coloured pupils increased 191 per cent. It must not, however, be concluded from these figures that nearly the whole of the coloured population are growing up possessed even of the rudiments of education. . . . But the school-terms are so short in most of the Southern States that a good many of whites and a far larger number of coloured children receive too little teaching to enable them to read and write with ease. . . . The amount of higher education—secondary, collegiate, or university education—obtained by the blacks, is no more than might be expected from the fact that they constitute the poorest part of the population. . . .

These universities are, of course, on a comparatively humble scale, and most of them might rather be called secondary schools. The grants made by the State governments nearly all go to elementary education, and the institutions which provide higher education for the negro are quite unequal to the

In the Cage

demands made upon them. Swarms of applicants for admission have to be turned away from the already overcrowded existing upper and normal schools and colleges; and thus the supply of qualified teachers for the coloured schools is greatly below the needs of the case . . . , though much has been and is being done by Northern benevolence for this admirable purpose. There is something pathetic in the eagerness of the negroes, parents, young people, and children, to obtain instruction. They seem to think that the want of it is what keeps them below the whites, just as in the riots which broke out in South Carolina during Sherman's invasion, the negro mob burnt a library at Columbia because, as they said, it was from the books that "the white folks got their sense." And they have a notion (which, to be sure, is not confined to them) that it is the want of book-learning which condemns the vast bulk of their race to live by manual labor, and that, therefore, by acquiring such learning they may themselves rise in the industrial scale. . . .

From what has been said of the state of education, it will have been gathered that the influence of books is confined to extremely few, and that even of newspapers to a small fraction of the coloured people. Nevertheless, the significance of whatever forms the mind of the small fraction must not be underestimated. The few thousands who read books or magazines, the few tens of thousands who see a daily paper, acquire the ideas and beliefs and aspirations of the normal white citizen, subject of course to the inherent differences in race character. . . . They are in a sense more American than the recent immigrants from Central Europe and from Italy who are now a substantial element in the population of the Middle and Western States. Within this small section of the coloured people are the natural leaders of the millions who have not yet attained to what may be called the democratic American consciousness. And the number of those upon whom books and newspapers play, in whom democratic ideas stimulate discontent with the present inferiority of their people, is steadily, and in some districts, rapidly increasing. The efforts of those who are best fitted to lead have been hitherto checked by the jealousy which the mass is apt to feel for those who rise to prominence; but this tendency may decline, and there will be no reason for surprise if men of eloquence and ambition are one day found to give voice to the sentiments of their brethren as Frederick Douglass did. . . .

The provision for the instruction of the young negroes in any handicraft is still quite inadequate, though such institutions as Hampton and Tuskegee have set admirable examples and the need of means for imparting it is even more urgent than is that of secondary schools. It is satisfactory to know that the necessity is beginning to be recognized, and some effort made to provide industrial training. The first person to point out that it was the thing most needful was the founder of Hampton, one of the noblest characters of his time, the late General S. C. Armstrong. . . .

From James Bryce, *The American Commonwealth* (2 vols., rev. ed., New York: Macmillan, 1912), II, 518–522.

William Edward Burghardt DuBois (1868–1963), the most brilliant of American Negro intellectuals, was born at Great Barrington, Massachusetts, in a community and in a region where Negroes were about as plentiful as sheep among a pack of

In the Cage

wolves. DuBois reportedly had French and Dutch ancestry, but he proudly identified himself with blacks. He received a Ph.D. from Harvard in 1895 with a dissertation on *The Suppression of the African Slave-Trade to America* (1896). Later published as a book, this together with his work on the Philadelphia Negro (1899), his *Atlanta University Studies* (1897–1911), and his *Black Reconstruction* (1935) were his most scholarly publications. *Souls of Black Folk* (1903) established his reputation as a stylist and crystalized the revolt of Negro intellectuals against the compromises of Booker T. Washington. DuBois was, among other things, editor of the NAACP organ, *Crisis,* professor of economics and history at Atlanta University from 1897 to 1910, and head of the department of sociology at Atlanta from 1932 to 1944. He was known as a bitter, eloquent radical with an encyclopedic mind. His first intimate contacts with fellow Negroes came in the fall of 1885, when he journeyed to Nashville to attend Fisk University. Here he describes his first teaching assignment—in the hills of Tennessee.

Once upon a time I taught school in the hills of Tennessee, where the broad dark vale of the Mississippi begins to roll and crumple to greet the Alleghenies. I was a Fisk student then, and all Fisk men think that Tennessee—beyond the Veil—is theirs alone, and in vacation time they sally forth in lusty bands to meet the county school commissioners. Young and happy, I too went, and I shall not soon forget that summer, ten years ago.

First there was a teachers' Institute at the county-seat; and there distinguished guests of the superintendent taught the teachers fractions and spelling and other mysteries,—white teachers in the morning, Negroes at night. A picnic now

Pedagogues and Pupils

and then, and a supper, and the rough world was softened by laughter and song. . . .

There came a day when all the teachers left the Institute, and began the hunt for schools. I learn from hearsay . . . that the hunting of ducks and bears and men is wonderfully interesting, but I am sure that the man who has never hunted a country school has something to learn of the pleasures of the chase. . . . I feel my heart sink heavily as I hear again and again, "Got a teacher? Yes." So I walked on and on,—horses were too expensive,—until I had wandered beyond railways, beyond stage lines, to a land of "varmints" and rattlesnakes, where the coming of a stranger was an event, and men lived and died in the shadow of one blue hill. . . .

. . . There I found at last a little school. . . .

The schoolhouse was a log hut, where Colonel Wheeler used to shelter his corn. It sat in a lot behind a rail fence and thorn bushes, near the sweetest of springs. There was an entrance where a door once was, and within, a massive rickety fireplace; great chinks between the logs served as windows. Furniture was scarce. A pale blackboard crouched in the corner. My desk was made of three boards, reenforced at critical points, and my chair, borrowed from the landlady, had to be returned every night. Seats for the children,—these puzzled me much. I was haunted by a New England vision of neat little desks and chairs, but, alas, the reality was rough plank benches without backs, and at times without legs. They had the one virtue of making naps dangerous,—possibly fatal, for the floor was not to be trusted.

It was a hot morning late in July when the school opened. I trembled when I heard the patter of little feet down the dusty road, and saw the growing row of dark solemn faces and bright eager eyes facing me. . . .

In the Cage

There they sat, nearly thirty of them, on the rough benches, their faces shading from a pale cream to a deep brown, the little feet bare and swinging, the eyes full of expectation, with here and there a twinkle of mischief, and the hands grasping Webster's blue-back spelling book. I loved my school, and the fine faith the children had in the wisdom of their teacher was truly marvelous. We read and spelled together, wrote a little, picked flowers, sang, and listened to stories of the world beyond the hill. At times the school would dwindle away, and I would start out. I would visit Mun Eddings, who lived in two very dirty rooms, and ask why little Lugene, whose flaming face seemed ever ablaze with the dark red hair uncombed, was absent all last week, or why I missed so often the inimitable rags of Mack and Ed. Then the father, who worked Colonel Wheeler's farm on shares, would tell me how the crops needed the boys; and the thin slovenly mother, whose face was pretty when washed, assured me that Lugene must mind the baby. "But we'll start them again next week." When the Lawrences stopped, I knew that the doubts of the old folks about book learning had conquered again, and so, toiling up the hill, and getting as far into the cabin as possible, I put Cicero pro Archia Poeta into the simplest English with local applications, and usually convinced them—for a week or so.

On Friday nights I often went home with some of the children; sometimes to Doc Burke's farm. He was a great, loud, thin Black, ever working, and trying to buy the seventy-five acres of hill and dale where he lived; but people said that he would surely fail, and the "white folks would get it all." . . . They lived in a one-and-a-half-room cabin in the hollow of the farm, near the spring. The front room was full of great fat white beds, scrupulously neat. . . . In the tiny back kitchen I was often invited to "take out and help" myself to fried chicken and wheat biscuit, "meat" and corn pone, string beans and berries. At first I used to be a little alarmed at the approach of bedtime in the one lone bedroom, but embarrassment was very deftly avoided. First, all the children nodded and slept, and were stored away in one great pile of goose feathers; next, the mother and the father discreetly slipped away to the kitchen while I went to bed; then, blowing out the dim light, they retired in the dark. In the morning all were up and away before I thought of awaking. . . .

For two summers I lived in this little world; it was dull and humdrum. . . .

<small>From W. E. B. DuBois, "A Negro Schoolmaster in the New South," *Atlantic Monthly*, LXXXIII (January 1899), 99–102.</small>

Samuel J. Barrows (1845–1909) was born in New York City, studied at the Harvard Divinity School, and was pastor of Unitarian churches in Dorchester and Boston, Massachusetts. He edited the *Christian Register* (1881–1897) and in 1897 was awarded a Doctor of Divinity degree by Howard University, "the capstone of Negro education." He also served a term in Congress, 1897–1899, as a Republican, and was internationally prominent in the movement for prison reform. Barrows visited the South in 1891 and was favorably impressed with Negro progress in the region. This was especially true, as the selection below shows, in the area of education.

The subject of Negro education is vast and absorbing. Among its varied aspects two are of special and correlative interest:

In the Cage

first, What is education doing for the Negro; secondly, What is the Negro doing for education? In this paper I can refer only to the latter topic. But these questions cannot be absolutely separated. No man "receives an education" who does not get a good deal of it himself. The student is not so much inert material; he reacts on the forces which impress him. The Negroes are showing their awakened and eager interest in education by the zeal with which they are embracing their opportunities. Everywhere I found in colleges, normal institutes, and district schools fresh, live interest. In some sections, the eagerness of the colored people for knowledge amounts to an absolute thirst. In Alabama, the state superintendent of education, a former Confederate major, assured me that the colored people in that State are more interested in education than the whites are. Nothing shows better this zeal for education than the sacrifices made to secure it. President Bumstead of Atlanta University, asks, "Where in the history of the world have so large a mass of equally poor and unlettered people done so much to help themselves in educational work?" This challenge will long remain unanswered. The students of Atlanta University pay thirty-four per cent of the expenses of that institution. A letter from the treasurer of Harvard College informs me that about the same proportion of its expenses is paid from tuition fees. If we compare the wealth represented by the students of Harvard with that represented by the colored students of Atlanta, we shall find how large a sacrifice the latter are making in order to do so much. It must be remembered, also, that at Harvard tuition fees and other expenses are mostly paid by parents and guardians; at Atlanta they are paid by the students themselves, and to a large degree by personal labor. President Bumstead calculates that for every million dollars contributed by the North at least a half million is contributed by the colored people for educational purposes.

Pedagogues and Pupils

Though it is difficult to get the material for such large and general totals, it is easy to furnish a vast number of facts illustrating the truth that in the very process of getting his education the Negro is learning the lesson of self-help. Among the denominational colleges, the Livingston Institute at Salisbury, North Carolina, is a good illustration of this capacity for self-help. It receives no state aid. The colored people of the Zion Methodist Episcopal church give $8000 towards the support of this school. The students give towards their own support not less than $6000 more. The president, Dr. Price, one of the ablest colored orators of the South, is a conspicuous example of what the colored man can do for himself.

Another remarkable illustration is furnished by the Tuskegee Normal School. This institution was started in 1881 by a Hampton graduate, Mr. Booker T. Washington, on a state appropriation of $2000. It has grown from 30 pupils to 450, with 31 teachers. During the last year 200 applicants had to be turned away for want of room. Fourteen hundred acres of land and fourteen school buildings form a part of the equipment. While friends of education, North and South, have generously helped its growth, the success of the school is due largely to the executive ability of Mr. Washington and his officers. General Armstrong says, "I think it is the noblest and grandest work of any colored man in the land." All the teachers are colored. Of the fourteen school buildings, eight have been erected, in whole or in part, by the students. The school is broadly unsectarian. It is teaching the colored people the dignity of labor and how to get out of debt. It is an agricultural and industrial school combined. Its stimulating and renovating influence is felt all through the Black Belt.

One of the most important results of the excellent work done by Hampton, Atlanta, and Tuskegee is seen in the radiating influence they exert through the country in stimulating primary education. In most of the communities of the lower Southern States, the money derived from local taxation is not sufficient to keep the school more than three months in the year, and the pay of teachers is poor. The interest of these communities is so quickened by a good teacher that the people raise money to extend the school time and supplement the pay of the teacher. A few examples taken from many will illustrate. In one district in Alabama, the school time was thus extended by private subscription from three months to seven. In Coffee County, the teacher's salary was increased from ten to twenty-five dollars a month. In many cases the raising of this extra sum means a good deal of self-denial. As the State makes no appropriation for school-houses, most of the schools in the Black Belt are held in churches, which gives rise to sectarian jealousy and disturbance. To overcome these difficulties and build school-houses, additional sacrifice is required. In a district of Butler County, Alabama, the children formed a "one cent society." They brought to the teacher a penny a day. About thirty dollars was raised to buy land, and the school-teacher, a colored girl, helped to clear it and burn the brush. In one township, where the school fund is sufficient for seven or nine months, the teachers are paid thirty-five dollars a month. In Lee County, the people "supplement" for an assistant teacher. One district school which I visited, eighteen miles from Tuskegee, taught by a graduate of its institute, well illustrated the advantage of industrial education. Having learned the carpenter's trade at the normal school, he was able, with the help of his pupils, to build a fine new school-house. The girls often do better than the men. One, who teaches about twenty-five miles from Tuskegee, has now a good two story school building with four rooms. She has two assistant teachers, who live with her in the building. She has revolutionized that section of the country. . . .

Pedagogues and Pupils

The interest in education is seen also in the self-denial and sacrifice which parents make to keep their children at school. This sacrifice falls chiefly on the mothers. A student told me that two thirds of the younger scholars at Tuskegee were sent by their mothers. Very often the mother is a widow. She may get twenty dollars a month, or eight, or only four, for her labor. Out of this small sum she sends to college and clothes her boy or girl. "I know mothers," said a student, "who get three dollars a month, and out of that pay one dollar for the rent, and yet send their children to school." To do this they will wash all day and half the night. Said a colored clergyman in Chattanooga: "Sometimes when I go about and see how hard many of these mothers work, I feel almost inclined to say, 'You ought to keep your child at home;' but they hold on with wonderful persistence. Two girls graduated from Atlanta University. Their mother had been washing several years to keep them in school. She came up to see them graduate. She was one of the happiest mothers I ever saw." . . .

From Samuel J. Barrows, "What the Southern Negro Is Doing for Himself," *Atlantic Monthly*, LXVII (June 1891), 810–812.

Ray Stannard Baker was one of the most prominent journalists of the Progressive Era. His principal career as a "muckraker" was with *McClure's Magazine* (1899–1905) and the *American Magazine* (beginning in 1906). Born in Lansing, Michigan, in 1870, and educated at Michigan Agricultural College and the University of Michigan, he began his newspaper career with the Chicago *Record* in 1892. Baker went South in 1906 and toured most of the region, making extensive stops in urban and rural Georgia. He did not feel that enough money was being spent for Negro education in cities like Atlanta, even though the blacks were eager for learning and were willing to make great sacrifices in order to get it.

Every child, white or coloured, is getting an education somewhere. If that education is not in the schools, or at home, or, in cases of incorrigibility, in proper reformatories, then it is on the streets, or in chain-gangs.

My curiosity, aroused by the very large number of young prisoners, led me next to inquire why these children were not in school. I visited a number of schools and I talked with L. M. Landrum, the assistant superintendent. Compulsory education is not enforced anywhere in the South, so that children may run the streets unless their parents insist upon sending them to school. I found more than this, however, that Atlanta did not begin to have enough school facilities for the children who wanted to go. . . . Just as in the North the tenement classes are often neglected, so in the South the lowest class—which is the Negro—is neglected. Several new schools have been built for white children, but there has been no new school for coloured children in fifteen or twenty years (though one Negro private school has been taken over within the last few years by the city). So crowded are the coloured schools that they have two sessions a day, one squad of children coming in the forenoon, another in the afternoon. The coloured teachers, therefore, do double work, for which they receive about two-thirds as much salary as the white teachers.

Though many Southern cities have instituted industrial training in the public schools, Atlanta so far has done nothing. . . .

The eagerness of the coloured people for a chance to send their children to school is something astonishing and pathetic.

Pedagogues and Pupils

They will submit to all sorts of inconveniences in order that their children may get an education. One day I visited the mill neighbourhood of Atlanta to see how the poorer classes of white people lived. I found one very comfortable home occupied by a family of mill employees. They hired a Negro woman to cook for them, and while they sent their children to the mill to work, the cook sent her children to school! . . .

Here is a curious and significant thing I found in Atlanta. Because there is not enough room for Negro children in public schools, the coloured people maintain many private schools. The largest of these, called Morris Brown College, has nearly 1,000 pupils. Some of them are boarders from the country, but the greater proportion are day pupils from seven years old up who come in from the neighbourhood. This "college," in reality a grammar school, is managed and largely supported by tuition and contributions from Negroes, though some subscriptions are obtained in the North. Besides this "college" there are many small private schools conducted by Negro women and supported wholly by the tuition paid—the Negroes thus voluntarily taxing themselves heavily for their educational opportunities. One afternoon in Atlanta I passed a small, rather dilapidated home. Just as I reached the gate I heard a great cackling of voices and much laughter. Coloured children began to pour out of the house. "What's this?" I said, and I turned in to see. I found a Negro woman, the teacher, standing in the doorway. She had just dismissed her pupils for recess. She was holding school in two little rooms where some fifty children must have been crowded to suffocation. Everything was very primitive and inconvenient—but it was a school! She collected, she told me, a dollar a month tuition for each child. Mollie McCue's school, perhaps the best known private school for Negroes in the city, has 250 pupils.

Many children also find educational opportunities in the

In the Cage

Negro colleges of the city—Clark University, Atlanta University and Spellman [sic] Seminary, which are supported partly by the Negroes themselves but mostly by Northern philanthropy.

Even with a double daily session for coloured pupils, nearly half of the Negro children in Atlanta, even in 1903, were barred from the public schools for lack of facilities, and the number has increased largely in the last four years. Some of these are accommodated in the private schools and colleges which I have mentioned, but there still remain hundreds, even thousands, who are getting no schooling of any kind, but who are nevertheless being educated—on the streets, and for criminal lives....

I made a good many inquiries to find out what was being done outside of the public schools by white people toward training the Negro either morally, industrially, or intellectually—and I was astonished to find that it was next to nothing....

A white man or woman, and especially a Northern white man or woman, in Atlanta who teaches Negroes is rigorously ostracised by white society. I visited one of the Negro colleges where there are a number of white teachers from the North. We had quite a talk. When I came to leave one of the teachers said to me:

"You don't know how good it seems to talk to someone from the outside world. We work here year in and year out without a white visitor, except those who have some necessary business with the institution."

Explaining the attitude toward these Northern teachers (and we must understand just how the Southern people feel in this matter), a prominent clergyman said that a lady who made a social call upon a teacher in that institution would not feel secure against having to meet Negroes socially and that when the call was returned a similar embarrassing situation might be created. . . .

From Ray Stannard Baker, *Following the Color Line: American Negro Citizenship in the Progressive Era* (Torchbook ed., New York: Harper and Row, 1964), pp. 52–55.

Albert Bushnell Hart, long-time professor of history at Harvard, was born in 1854 at Clarksville, Pennsylvania, and graduated from Harvard in 1880. He was the author of a number of books on such diverse subjects as the formation of the union, slavery and abolition, and foreign policy; editor of *The American Nation* series (28 vols., 1904–1918), and an officer in both the American Historical Association and the American Political Science Association. Hart made a grand tour of the South in 1907–1908 and gave a comparatively judicious assessment of the condition of the Negro. In this selection he reports the status of some Negro schools he saw.

The mere statistics of negro schools and attendance after all carry with them little information. What kind of pupils are they? What kind of school buildings are provided for them? What is the character of their teachers? Naturally, among both races, many are at work after twelve or fourteen years, but the percentages of enrollment and attendance are so much less than those of the white people that apparently colored children are less likely than white to be sent to school and to be kept there when started. Though every Northern state without exception has some kind of compulsory education, not a single

In the Cage

Southern state, except Kentucky and Missouri, has enacted it.

Some personal knowledge of Southern schools, both in cities and the country, suggests several reasons why attendance is small. Visit this negro wayside school in the heart of the piney woods near Albany, Ga. The building is a wretched structure with six glass windows, some of them broken; the sky visible between the weatherboards. There is one desk in the room, the teacher's, made of rough planks; the floor is rough and uneven. Of the forty-four children enrolled, none of whom came more than about three miles, thirty-two are present on a pleasant day; six of them appear to be mulattoes. They wear shoes and stockings and are quiet and well-behaved but sit in the midst of dirt on dirty benches. The teacher is a pleasant woman, wife of a well-to-do colored man in the neighboring town, but apparently untrained. She teaches five months at $35 a month. Last year there was no school at all in this district.

Enter another school at Oak Grove, Ala. The house is a single room, twenty-five feet square; larger than is needed, like many of the schoolhouses, because it may serve also for church services. There is not a sash in any one of the seven windows, each having a hinged shutter. The teacher has a table, and for the pupils are provided several rude benches with or without backs; the room is furnished with a blackboard and is reasonably clean; the teacher, a young man eager and civil, a graduate of a neighboring school carried on by the Negroes for themselves with some white assistance, for the county commissioners will do no more than offer $100 to a district that will spend about $300 more on a building. The room overcrowded, four or five at a desk; twice as many girls as boys; a good teacher who has had some normal training; a book for each group of three in the reading class; the lesson about a brutal Yankee officer who compels a little Southern girl to tell where the Confederate officer is hiding. The children read well and with expression.

These are probably fairly typical of the rural negro schools throughout the South, and better than some. As a matter of fact, thousands of negro children have no opportunity to go to school, because the commissioners simply refuse to provide a school in their district; perhaps because the number of children is thought too few; perhaps merely because they do not wish to spend the money. In a town with perhaps 2,000 Negroes there is sometimes only one negro teacher. . . .

One reason why the schools are poor is that the pupils are irregular, and one reason why they are irregular is that the schools are poor. The wretched facilities of the rural schools both white and negro tend to drive children out; and the incompetent teachers do not make parents or children fonder of school. As to the Negroes, with few exceptions, every teacher is a Negro, though appointed by and supervised by some white authority; it is doubtful whether half the negro teachers have themselves gone through a decent common school education. Many of them are ignorant and uneducated.

Conditions are not much better in the towns, where many negro teachers earn only $150 to $200 a year; but in the cities the negro teachers are more carefully selected, for they can be drawn from the local negro high schools or the normal schools. But the colored people are said to scheme and maneuver to get this teacher out and that one in. They have been known to petition against a capable and unblemished teacher on the ground that she was the daughter of a white man, and it was immoral for her to be teaching black children.

If the negro common schools are inferior to the white, this is still more marked in their secondary and normal pupils who get a training very like that of the Northern academies,

In the Cage

and some favored cities have public schools for the Negroes. This is the case in Baltimore, and was the case in New Orleans until about 1903. . . .

It must not be forgotten that there are more than a hundred institutions for training the colored people, which draw nothing from the public funds. These schools, in part supported by the colored people themselves, in part by Northern gifts . . . are usually better than the public schools, and have more opportunities for those lessons of cleanliness and uprightness which the Negro needs quite as much as book learning. Those schools are a thorn in the side of the South—so much so that for years it was hardly possible to get any Southern man to act as trustee; they are supposed to teach the negro youth a desire for social equality; they are thought to draw the Negroes off from cordial relations with the Southern whites; above all, they include the higher institutions which are credited with spoiling the race with too much Greek and Latin. To a considerable degree the schools of this type are mulatto schools, probably because the people of mixed blood are more intelligent and prosperous, and more interested in their children's future; but many of them are planted in the darkest part of the Black Belt—such as the Penn School in the Sea Islands. Wherever they exist, they appeal to the ambition and the conscience of the Negro, and help to civilize the race; they are not only schools but social settlements. Along-side the earlier schools and colleges planted by Northerners in the regular academic type, during the last thirty years have arisen first Hampton, then Tuskegee, and then many like schools, built upon the principle of industrial training. . . .

The negro colleges in the South are far from prosperous; planted in the day of small things with limited endowments, frequented by people who have little money to pay for tuition, they have been supported from year to year by Northern gifts which are not sufficient to keep them up to modern demands. Though some of them have tolerable buildings, few have adequate libraries, laboratories, or staff of specialist instructors. The state institutions of this grade open to blacks are nearly all rather low in standards and offer little inducement for academic training; they are either normal or industrial in type. So far from the number of negro college graduates being too great, it is entirely too small for the immediate needs of the race. They must have educated teachers and trained professional men; the negro schools will never flourish without competent teachers and supervisors of the negro race. In many respects the colleges are the weakest part of negro education. One school in which numbers have had good training, Berea College, Kentucky, has now been abandoned under an act of the state legislature forbidding the teaching of Whites and Negroes together, but an industrial school of high grade will be provided exclusively for the colored race.

Many of the academic and normal training schools of various grades are situated in the midst of large colored populations, and take upon themselves a work similar to that of the college settlements in Northern cities. Such is the flourishing school at Calhoun, Alabama, which is in the midst of one of the densest and most ignorant Negro populations in the South, and besides training the children sent to it, it has supervised the work of breaking up the land, which is sold to negro farmers in small tracts, thereby giving an object lesson of the comfort and satisfaction of owning one's own land. Most such schools aim to be centers of moral influence upon the community about them. Here again, they encounter the hostility of their neighbors on the ground that they are putting notions into the heads of the Negroes, and are destroying the labor system of the community. On the other hand, many of the Whites take a warm interest in these schools, although not a single one has ever received any considerable gift of money from Southern white people. . . .

Education will not do everything; it will not make chaste, honest, and respectable men and women out of wretched children left principally to their own instincts. Education is at best a palliative, but the situation is too serious to dispense even with palliatives.

Perhaps the first necessity is to improve the character and training of the negro teachers. Both in the rural and the city schools appointments are in many cases made by white school board men who have little knowledge and sometimes no interest in the fitness of their appointees. The colleges and industrial schools all have this problem in mind. State normal schools for Negroes in many of the Southern states try to meet this necessity, but a great many of the country teachers, some of them in the experience of this writer, are plainly unsuited for the task. Some of them are themselves ignorant, few have the background of character and intellectual interest which would enable them to transmit a moral uplift.

One of the most serious difficulties of negro education is the attendance, or rather nonattendance. Within a few weeks after the beginning of school, pupils begin to drop out; often perhaps because the teacher cannot make the work interesting. . . .

Some of the schools are overcrowded. There have been cases where 6 teachers were assigned for 1,800 children, of whom 570 enrolled, yet the average earnings of the six teachers would not be more than $100 a year. Against these instances must be placed a great number of intelligent, faithful teachers who make up for some deficiencies of knowledge by their genuine interest in their work.

For negro education as for white, but perhaps with more reason, it is urged that the federal government ought to come

Pedagogues and Pupils

in with its powerful aid. . . . Aside from any claim of right, it is true that the problem of elevating the Negroes concerns the whole nation, and is a part of the long process of which emancipation was the beginning. . . .

From Albert Bushnell Hart, *The Southern South* (New York: Appleton, 1910), pp. 311–321.

Sir Harry H. Johnston explored Portuguese West Africa and the River Congo in 1882 and 1883, commanded the scientific expedition of the Royal Society to Mt. Kilimanjaro in 1884, and was British consul-general for Tunis and Uganda. He wrote books on colonization, slavery, and diplomacy. Sir Harry's Southern trip (1908) was confined mainly to Alabama and Virginia. He visited Hampton Institute and Tuskegee Institute.

The grounds of Hampton surround a peaceful, walled, cypressed cemetery, where lie the remains of the soldiers of the North and South, white man and negro, who fell in this part of Virginia fighting over the Slave issue. But Hampton, though attractive and inspiring in its outward appearance—perhaps one of the most beautiful amongst the many beautiful educational institutions in the United States—is thoroughly practical in its teaching resources. Besides a model farm at Shellbank, some five miles distant, there are fields for agricultural and horticultural experiments within the home area, together with greenhouses and hot-houses for the training of negro gardeners, poultry runs to teach the students in the principles of poultry farming; cowsheds and stables and yards for horse and mule breeding or training. There are shops for teaching bricklaying and masonry, waggon, cart, and carriage building, painting and lettering, tailoring and hat-making, millinery and dressmaking, printing and book-binding, architectural designing and surveying. There are iron foundries and electrical engineering works. Such of the students as show aptitude are trained in music, and there is a fine students' band.

To some extent, also, arts of design in addition to architecture are encouraged and stimulated. The Amerindians in this respect at Hampton outvie the negroes; their basketwork and matmaking are exquisite, and some of them have executed remarkable specimens of wood-carving. . . . The negro, however, takes the lead in music.

Indeed, one dimly perceives a musical solution of the Negro-culture problem, a possibility that in music the Aframerican—perhaps even the Negro of Africa—may achieve triumphs not yet attained by the White men. This race is sensitive to rhythm and melody to an extraordinary degree; it almost seems as though they were, or could be, ruled by music. At any rate, at Hampton, as at Tuskegee, music is the main discipline. The big and small children of the Whittier School, moving to and out of their classrooms—a hundred or more at a time—to some inspiring tune, and the adult students entering and leaving the church and lecture-hall in the same manner, hold themselves well, look up with bright, confident faces, and extort one's sympathy by their grace of movement. . . .

Although Hampton and Tuskegee are described as undenominational (Hindu and Muhammadan students are received at both places without question), there is still a great deal of doctrinal religion enforced on the students who beside scarcely ever singing any song or chorus that it not "sacred," are required to attend rather lengthy religious services in the chapel. . . . If a Negro student at Hampton or Tuskegee contributed an article to a review, it would probably be on the subject of Jeptha's daughter—was she sacrificed or not? The righteousness of the fate which overtook the children who mocked Elisha, or the trials of Job; as though any one of these or similar problems are of the slightest practical utility in the Negro world of today, any more than the legends of Iphigenia, of Romulus and Remus, or other stories told in the infancy of history....

That the Negro students would be receptive of the wonderful gospel which has been revealed to us through the books of Darwin, Spencer . . . Huxley, Humboldt . . . Wallace, Agassiz, Lyell . . . and the great astronomers and chemists of the nineteenth and twentieth centuries is evident by the interest shown in the lectures of a Welsh professor directing the research department at Hampton, and those of Professor Carver at Tuskegee (on botany)....

An interesting adjunct of the Hampton Institute is the Whittier School for children, which begins with a kindergarten, and ascends through higher grades of instruction till the child is able . . . to . . . [enter] the Institute as a college student. It is pretty to see these children with their pearly-white teeth and gleaming white eyeballs, plump little bodies, and perfect satisfaction with their own personal appearance, marching into school to a musical drill, and singing . . . "An' befo' Ah'll be a slave, Ah'll be buried in ma grave, and ma spirit shall ascend to God on high."

It is surprising to note amongst these Negro children and students at Hampton, as at Tuskegee, the extraordinary prevalence, with dark eyes and dark skin, of red, blond, or golden hair. There are even examples of blue-eyed, fair-haired Negroids, retaining as the only trace of their African blood, the undulating curl in the hair and the pale olive complexion. Have we here a new race in the making? . . .

In the Cage

During my stay of ten days at Tuskegee I visited in detail all the departments of education. Especially interesting was the kindergarten for the tiny children, in which there were golden-haired, blue-eyed babies; red-haired, brown-eyed children; and brown-black negrolets. . . . These children danced and sang and went through their exercises with a grace and an adroitness which brought them the hearty plaudits of Mrs. Bryce [wife of the British Ambassador] and other visitors. . . .

It is of course the Industrial Education that makes Tuskegee specially worth visiting. There is a School of Agriculture and a chemical laboratory and a museum where specimens of the very varied vegetable products of the South are preserved for illustrative lectures, and where the animals (including insects) of the South-eastern States are illustrated. Attached to this Agricultural School are hot-houses, classes for practical horticulture and floriculture, and even for landscape gardening. On the large farm attached to the Institute, and in the experimental plantations, almost every crop known to the Southern States is cultivated by the students under instruction. Particular attention is given to the cultivation of fruit and vegetables. A department of Bee culture was started in 1887 by Mr. J. H. Washington, the brother of the Principal. . . .

Sound instruction is given in Veterinary science, in the matching of sires (donkeys and horses) and mares for mule-breeding. . . .

In the vast Slater-Armstrong Memorial Trades Building, mechanical industries are taught in an effective and practical manner. . . . I noticed particularly what excellent boots and shoes—shapely and strong—were being turned out by the students of the shoemaking department. It seemed to me, in fact, that in all those sections of the Institute the instruction was of the very best, and of the most-up-to-date character. The schools and shops were supplied with the most recent technical literature on the subjects taught, obtained, not only from the United States, but also the United Kingdom, Germany and France. . . .

With regard to the special instruction for women, there are the "Girls' trades," which are taught in a great, commodious building called "Dorothy Hall." They comprise laundry-work, cooking, dressmaking, millinery, basket-work, mattress-making, and soap manufacture. When passing through the well-equipped dress-making establishment I listened to a part of a lecture on the juxtaposition of colours. The lady professor proved as an article of the Religion of the Modes, that the placing side by side of mauve and heliotrope on a hat was a crime of peculiar heinousness. Personally I could not agree with her diatribes, for the delicious samples of these two exquisite tints which she held up side by side that we might be duly shocked seemed to me to blend as delightfully as they do in many a flower, and the arrangement, together with white, was a fitting contrast to the tawny skin of a handsome mulatto student who was wearing a gown in which they were temporarily combined.

This department was conducted by women of colour; but although the work was exceedingly tasteful, it all seemed to be designed more with reference to a white skin; and no special attempt was made to meet the requirements in shape and colour of a dress appropriate for dark-complexioned, dark-haired women. The models and *mannequins* on which costumes or the hats were fitted all seemed to be dazzling blondes. This it seems to me—the special designing of costumes for educated coloured women—is a point that Tuskegee has not quite grasped, and which it should go into most thoroughly and perhaps lay down the law of taste, to be spread far and wide through America by its pupils. . . .

I never entered a class-room that did not seem faultlessly clean and neat, and with windows always open. Many of these rooms are bright with flowers from the gardens of the Institute. ... Visitors to Tuskegee, both expected and unexpected, have a feeling that the teachers of these classes are ladies and gentlemen in the best sense of these terribly abused words. They may be so "near white" as to be mistaken for teachers borrowed from the white world, or they may be of unmixed Negro race, like Professor Carver, who teaches scientific agriculture, botany, agricultural chemistry, etc. He is, as regards complexion and features, an absolute Negro; but in the cut of his clothes, the accent of his speech, the soundness of his science, he might be professor of Botany not at Tuskegee, but at Oxford or Cambridge. Any European botanist of distinction, after ten minutes' conversation with this man, instinctively would deal with him "de puissance en puissance." ...

From Sir Harry H. Johnston, *The Negro in the New World* (London: Methuen, 1910), pp. 389–399, 404, 406–413, 415–416, 418–419.

William Archer, Scottish critic and journalist (1856–1924), came to the United States in 1908 specifically to study the race problem. He was trained as a lawyer but became a writer for the *Edinburgh Evening News,* then a dramatic critic for London newspapers. He was a lover of travel, languages, literature, and adventure. In the selection below he gives impressions of three "giants" of Negro higher education—Hampton and Tuskegee Institutes, and Atlanta University. His conversation with, and impressions of, DuBois at Atlanta are especially interesting.

Pedagogues and Pupils

It is very difficult to get at the true truth as to public education for the negro in the South. The probability is, in fact, that there are as many truths as there are points of view. One high authority (a negro) told me that for every single dollar expended on a black child about five dollars are expended on a white child. That is very likely true; but it is probably no less true that the sums expended on negro education are large out of all proportion to the sums paid by negroes in taxes. "Let us reduce their education to the scale of their taxation," I have heard it said, "and where would they be?" The true question is: Where would the South be? Probably half-way back to barbarism. . . .

The hostility to negro education has, however, lost much of its former strength. This is apparent from the case of Professor Patterson, head of an excellent State school for negroes in Montgomery. The Professor (a title as lightly accorded in the South as Major or Colonel) is a sturdy Scot. When he first came to the South in Reconstruction days chance led him to a county in the State of Alabama where there was, indeed, already a school, but it was kept by a negro who could neither read nor write. An educator by instinct, if not by training, Mr. Patterson determined to set up a school of his own. For this misdemeanour he was twice shot at, and was finally arrested, and put under a bond of 15,000 dollars to desist from teaching in that county. He went into another county and started a school in the frame building that served as a negro church; but here the negroes themselves had to turn him out, as they were warned that if they did not the church would be burnt. These experiences only stiffened the professor's backbone. He said "I will teach—teach in Alabama—and teach negroes!" And here he is today, head of a fine large school in the State capital, and partially maintained by the State—a school well planned, well built, and with an excellent system of industrial training going on in various annexes in its spacious grounds.

As I passed through one of the senior schoolrooms, a boy had just written on the blackboard, in a fine round hand, a quotation from a recent speech by Senator Foraker on the Brownsville affair—the affair of the negro regiment which President Roosevelt is alleged to have treated with high-handed injustice. The sentence ran: "We ask no favour for them because they are men." Evidently there is no affectation of excluding from the schoolroom the all-absorbing problem.

Tuskegee (pronounced like Righi, but with the first "e" sound lengthened) is about forty miles from Montgomery, situated on an open rolling upland, with many small knolls and sudden gullies. In the course of a short drive from the station to the Institute, one passes a dignified old ante-bellum plantation-house, not without wondering what its owners of fifty years ago would have thought of the Tuskegee of to-day.

I am not going to attempt a minute description of "Booker Washington's City," as it has been called. It is beyond all doubt, a wonderful place. Everywhere one sees the evidence of a great organizing capacity, a great inspiring force, a tireless, indomitable singleness of purpose—in short, a true magnanimity. I did not see Mr. Washington in his principality—I had met him some weeks earlier in the North—but the dominance of his spirit could perhaps be more clearly felt in his absence than in his presence.

Mrs. Washington I did see—a lady with the mien and manner of a somewhat dusky duchess. The observation may (or, rather, it does) seem an impertinence; but such impertinences are forced upon one by the very nature of the inquiry. Not only Mrs. Washington, but other members of the General Staff with whom I was brought in contact—for instance, Mr.

Pedagogues and Pupils

Emmett J. Scott (Mr. Washington's secretary) and Mr. Warren Logan (the treasurer of the Institute)—were far more Caucasian than African in feature, and very light in colour. Indeed, I saw no one in high position at Tuskegee who would not, with a very small lightening of hue, have been taken without question for a white man. I make the remark, however, without suggesting any deduction from it. I believe there is little evidence of any intellectual superiority of the mulatto (in all his various degrees) over the pure negro. It is often assumed as a matter of course; but those who have had the best opportunities for close comparison are quite unconvinced of it. One well-known white educator of the negro told me that for character, if not for intellect, he gave the pure black the preference over the mulatto....

Externally, Tuskegee has none of the orderly design which one finds in the "campus" of a Northern university. It is evidently a place that has "growed." Buildings are dotted here and there over the somewhat rugged site, with small eye to picturesqueness or dignity of general effect. Except the Carnegie Library, with its well-proportioned portico, there is no building of much architectural ambition; but the chapel or general assembly hall of the Institute struck me as showing real originality of design. I was extremely sorry not to hear one of Mr. Washington's Sunday evening "talks" to the students in this fine hall. I had not time even to see an assembly of the whole school, in its neat blue uniform nor to hear its singing of old negro melodies, which is said to be remarkable....

After a far too brief visit, I left Tuskegee with the liveliest admiration for its methods and results. It is beyond all question a radiating centre of materially helpful and morally elevating influences. Mr. Washington is assuredly doing a great and an indispensable work for his race; nor is he doing it in any such spirit of contempt for academic and literary culture as his critics attribute to him.

But two reflections occurred to me as I returned through the red twilight to Montgomery. The first was obvious enough —namely, that the men and women turned out by such an institution cannot possibly be taken as representing the average of negro capacity. They are a select company before they go there—or, rather, in the very fact of their going there. They are impelled by individual and exceptional intelligence, thirst for knowledge, desire for betterment. Some, it is true, are sent by their parents, very much as white boys are sent to school or college; but whereas the white boy's parents are merely following a social tradition, the black boy's parents are taking a clear step in advance, and showing not only ambition but (in all probability) a good deal of self-denial. Almost every one, in short, who enrolls himself at Tuskegee is animated from the outset by some measure of Mr. Washington's own spirit; and not a few show, in the pursuit of knowledge, something of the heroism which marked his early career.

My second reflection took the form of a query. I did not doubt for a moment that Mr. Washington's work was wise and salutary; but I wondered whether the material and moral uplifting of the negro was going to bring peace—or a sword. In other words, do the essential and fundamental difficulties of the situation really lie in the defects of the negro race: May not the development of its qualities merely create a new form of friction? And far beneath the qualities and defects of either race, may there not lie deep-rooted instincts which no "Atlanta Compromise" will bring into harmony?

Tuskegee marks an inevitable stage of the conflict; but is it the beginning of the end? I wonder.

After the daughter, the mother. Being again in America

Pedagogues and Pupils

this year (1909), I stole a few days for a run into Virginia and a visit to Hampton, the fount and origin of the whole movement for the industrial training of the coloured race. It is perhaps well to take Tuskegee before Hampton, just as, in visiting English universities, it would be well to take Liverpool or Birmingham before Oxford or Cambridge.

Hampton is on historic ground, and looks over still more historic waters. It stands at the tip of the peninsula formed (roughly speaking) by Chesapeake Bay to the east and north and the James River to the west and south. . . .

The fundamental contrast . . . between the two institutions lies in the fact that at Tuskegee the organizing and teaching staff is all black (or brown), at Hampton all white. . . .

At Hampton there are now 113 buildings (65 of them of considerable size) and a home farm of 120 acres; while at Shellbank six miles away, the school owns a farm of over 600 acres, with 150 head of cattle, 30 horses and mules, 100 hogs, and fowls by the thousand. The students enrolled in the Institute number 863, while the Whittier Preparatory School has nearly 500 pupils. In addition to all branches of agriculture and horticulture, fifteen trades are taught to boys, while girls are thoroughly trained in every form of domestic industry, laundry-work, dressmaking, etc. The teaching and organizing staff number about 200, or one to every six pupils. It is the deliberate policy of the Institute to seek for increase of efficiency rather than of numbers, and the entrance tests are correspondingly severe. . . .

Hampton was the only negro college or school I ever visited in which I saw no student who could have passed as white. There was, indeed, one singularly beautiful girl with auburn hair, who might have been taken for a European of peculiarly rich colouring; but she was of Indian, not of negro, blood. There must, I think, have been some reason for the absence of

In the Cage

"white negroes" at Hampton; but I had not time to inquire into it. We bade an unwilling farewell to our kind hosts, and departed deeply impressed by the spirit and achievement of this noble institution.

That evening I spent at Atlanta University with Mr. W. E. B. DuBois. Twilight fell as we stood on the eminence which is crowned by University buildings, and looked out over a wide expanse of red Georgian landscape. The sunset had left behind it a delicate rosy flush, and just where it paled off into greenish blue, the slender crescent of a new moon hung in the sky, with a glorious planet above it. Behind us lay the city, with its 60,000 white men ready to "brain" its 40,000 black and brown men on the slightest provocation. . . .

The influence of the immediate surroundings, too, had something to do with my mood. About Atlanta University there is nothing of the cheerful energy and optimism of Tuskegee. This is a home of intellectual culture; and intellectual culture, however necessary, can scarcely be exhilarating to the negro race at this stage of its history. The more you strive to break through the veil (to use Mr. DuBois' favorite metaphor), the more keenly are you conscious of its galling and darkening encumbrance. For assuredly it galls and darkens, whether it be a real barrier or a figment conjured up by the pride and folly of men.

At all events, his culture, which is great, and his genius, which is not small, have not made of Mr. DuBois a happy man. With perfect simplicity, without an atom of pose, he is and remains a singularly tragic figure. He is, perhaps, more impressive than his book, able as that is. In some of its pages we are conscious of a little rhetorical shrillness; but there is nothing of this in the man. He is perfectly urbane and dignified; there is nothing of the apostle, and still less of the martyr about him. He regards and discusses phenomena with the calm of the trained sociologist. But beneath the calm one is conscious of a profound bitterness of spirit. If he is hopeful at all, it is for a day that he will never see; and, in a man still in the prime of life, such hope is not very different from despair.

I met no man in the South with whom I felt more at ease, or seemed to have more in common. And yet, as we talked, there lurked in my mind a sense of hypocrisy, almost of treachery. I could not frankly expose to him my doubts as to whether the stars in their courses did not fight against his racial ideal.

Of his very interesting conversation I shall here record only a few fragments.

"The problem in the South," he said, ". . . is not that of the vagabond or the criminal, but of the negro who is coming forward. That is why even the good people of the South are taking their hands off, saying, 'we can't do anything.'

"The older generation of negroes had friends among the white people of their own age; but the boys and girls now growing up have no white friends. The younger white people have no feeling towards the negro but dislike, founded on utter lack of comprehension."

"The race antipathy is fomented in the schools. The progressive negro is held up as a bugbear to the white child, who is told to 'Look out, or he will get ahead of you!' Fear, jealousy, and hatred are actively taught to the rising generation of whites. But, after all, they are being taught something, and that's more than their fathers were. Where intelligence increases there is always hope."

At one point I did come near to hinting to Mr. DuBois the doubt lurking in my mind. I quoted to him this passage from "The Souls of Black Folk":

"Deeply religious and intensely democratic as are the mass of the whites (in the South), they feel acutely the false position in which the negro problems place them. . . . But . . .

the present social position of the negro stands as a menace and a portent before even the most open-minded; if there were nothing to charge against the negro but his blackness or other physical peculiarities, they argue, the problem would be comparatively simple; but what can we say to his ignorance, shiftlessness, poverty, and crime?"

"Now, tell me, Mr. DuBois," I said, "whatever these people may say, is it not really just the other way about? The ignorance, shiftlessness, etc., are manifestly temporary and corrigible; is it not precisely the 'blackness and other physical peculiarities' that are the true crux of the problem?"

Mr. DuBois smiled. "No," he said! "that is the point of view of the outsider, the foreigner. The Southerner, brought up among negroes, has no such feeling. In using the argument I there attribute to him he is perfectly sincere."

I refrained from pressing the point, but Mr. DuBois' answer did not quite meet my difficulty. I had no doubt of the Southerner's sincerity; what I questioned was rather his self-knowledge; or (perhaps I should say) his reading of race psychology. And that doubt, I own, remains.

If the Ethiopian could but change his skin, how trifling would be the problem raised by his ignorance, shiftlessness, poverty, and crime!

From William Archer, *Through Afro-America: An English Reading of the Race Problem* (London: Chapman and Hall, 1910), pp. 104–119, 125, 140–145.

Rossa Belle Cooley, Northern philanthropist and educator, taught for several years at Penn School on St. Helena Island, South Carolina, before succeeding

Pedagogues and Pupils

Laura M. Towne as principal of the school, a position she held for some twenty years. She describes below some of the varied activities of the rather unique rural school for blacks.

One day an abbreviated dog show held the school spellbound, and if we did not have circus bleachers we had the same effect, for boys and girls in the back rows stood on the benches to see the performance. Speaking first to the point that a dog well bred and well trained was worth owning, explaining what "well-bred" and "pure-bred" meant, I called on Con himself to show the meaning of a well-trained dog. Speaking in my usual conversational tone, I asked him to say "Good morning," to lie down, to die for his country like a good soldier, to catch the bit of cracker on his nose, the audience growing more and more delighted as he went through his repertoire without a miss. . . . Some of the island homes begin to boast of better pups and a generation is springing up to appreciate dog stock. A rural school has as many sides to it as an automobile factory.

Our fields began to change as agriculture settled into the curriculum. The boys marched out to clear new land on the school farm that had not seen a crop since the tasks of overseers had kept their grandfathers on those acres. They cut through the thick tangle of growth . . . ; plow points were broken as men and mules turned the soil. Using big tools has a charm for any well-developed country boy. It was when some rather large stumps had to be dug up by sheer muscle that the first group came in saying that they were "sick in the side." A night's rest and an assurance that they could do a man's job resulted in their return and that was the last of the complaints against the new work. But the beautiful field that has the record of fifty-three bushels of corn and $453\frac{1}{2}$ bushels of sweet potatoes to the acre, still goes by the name of "The Sticks."

In the Cage

Our next move was to carve out seven acres of our best land on "The Sticks" for a study farm. The block was measured off by the agriculture boys and put into crops that an island farm should carry—crops for food, for the home and stock, crops for cash—and for land improvement. Here all the classes have had work during their agriculture periods, following expenditures as well as receipts, and giving the opportunity to our senior boys to serve as supervisors in the group. This put into practice again the principle of our "miniature" farm, but on a larger scale. It opened the way for school agriculture in the field graded as carefully as the classroom subjects are graded. And this grading will be true of all our program of industrial studies, built around the basic nurture of the soil.

A decadence in all handwork on the island had been an unforeseen by-product of emancipation. The strict requirements of the plantation regime had been removed; the freed man . . . longed for the book to take the place of all labor, and in the course of half a century, it had come to pass that practically all the farm repair work was carried to Beaufort, our nearest town on Port Royal Island, or perhaps to Savannah. When soon after my arrival I heard a white friend say of the island boys that he never saw such a total lack of mechanical skill, that nearly all who attempted to unscrew a nut naturally turned it to the right, I wondered why they shouldn't; for they never had an opportunity at home or at school to loosen nuts or struggle with any mechanical appliances except the tiny plows and cultivators which no one taught them to keep in order. If the farms were to come to school, surely the farm tools and home necessities should have a place in the school curriculum. And so the school shops became another main limb of the "various branches" which "hang on de wings ob dis school."

Pedagogues and Pupils

Our Cope Industrial building was the first large structure built by the islanders themselves—built to celebrate the fiftieth anniversary of the founding of Penn School. Under Hampton graduates they worked, the walls of oyster-shell concrete rising to song and laughter. It was a normal development, using their own steer carts to carry sand and oyster shells from nearby oyster factories. And so island resources, muscles, and spirit were utilized and "We Building" took its place in the school's equipment to make possible a larger service to the island.

Into the new building went first of all a class of boys who were learning to "sew" the island baskets. This bit of industrial work is not only a hang-over from the old days but has an African origin. We had found Alfred Graham, one of the plantation craftsmen who had held on to his gift, using rushes that grow in the tide rivers, and sewing them with strips of palmetto. He was an old man, very straight and self-respecting. Often he would come into my office "to git de light on hit" so that he could serve as an interpreter to his people when the new doings at Penn needed so much the native bridge. His loyalty never wavered when our doings were most revolutionary.

He had learned to make baskets from his African uncle and in turn passed his skill on to his grand-nephew. From the first work baskets the shop has taught the boys of today to make scrap baskets needed in every home, clothes hampers which are sometimes beautiful enough for a museum (these were developed from the old cotton baskets), and wood baskets such as we found used on the farms. These last are oval and if "lined with pitch within and without" could have served to conceal the infant Moses in the bulrushes....

From all corners of the island came the farm tools to be mended at the new Cope shops, often the boy who mended the tool taking it home at night. Down the oyster-shell road anew

In the Cage

went closer connections between school and farm and home. Not only did the blacksmith and wheelwright shop mend the tools; the carpenter shop took its important place in the scheme of life.

Autumn on the island, as the children see it when they enter school, is a golden time; there are long stretches of yellow marshes and golden-brown grass in many fields. The brilliant-colored gum trees, the purple asters growing along the roadsides, the flash of the Kentucky cardinals and their charming whistle, the jolly song of the mocking birds and brown thrashers, all these sights and sounds play upon the consciousness of the boys and girls that cover the roads which lead in from the home farms.

Fields left bare of crops tell of summer's work done. The autumn term begins with October. There are three weeks of the usual school studies before the first call of the fields comes to these country children, the call of the sweet potatoes. We turn the children out, the teachers follow them and while the children work beside their parents and harvest the crop which will help them stay on the road of education during the winter months, the teachers meet them there on their own acres during that home week. All across the island the work goes forward by families. The father or big brother plows up the furrows with the family ox, or pony, or mule. The mother and the children follow with the hoes, and the potatoes are dug and placed in piles to be gathered for the storage. Great bens are made of them—layers of earth piled upon layers of potatoes, till sweet-potato pyramids take their place beside the house or barn ready for the winter's demand.

The visits are expected, as regular schedules are followed by each teacher. With few exceptions the whole family are ready to greet her and the household background becomes a part of her equipment. Experiences in school and at home are talked over; not only is the potato crop of interest, but the past and the coming corn crops, the home garden, the children's record in school. A new understanding takes root. When the teacher has spent an hour in driving to a home, she has a clue as to why Emanuel is sometimes languid in school when he has walked the long miles in the hot sun. When she finds adverse conditions, she can see why Elizabeth does things that are irritating at school. She gets into the shoes of her children at sweet-potato harvest....

The acre is measured by the child and the school lessons go home to that particular bit of ground, which often becomes the most interesting plot on the home farm to the parents as well as the children. Results on the farm, in the children, and in the school seem to prove the value of the experiment. In our first years on the island the only crop that was considered worthy of being measured was cotton; and when, under the school lead, corn was measured and valued and prizes won, it meant new horizons for the island culture. The results, put into figures, influenced the whole community. The children's corn crop was valued at over $3,000 the first year, and over two thousand cans of fruit and vegetables from their acres were recently put up for food in the homes.

These home acres have become our best classrooms. You should go out to Frogmore Plantation where the son of one of the boys in my first class in agriculture at Penn has his acre. This was the father who balked at our early efforts at bringing farming into the school work, but now that same father stands back of his boy and his home acre. It lies directly behind the house, has a neat fence all around it, and is raising crops all the year round now.

Just before the children are turned home for "Potato week" they take part in our annual Farmers' Fair, helping to prepare for the exhibits brought in from all the island homes,

In the Cage

and showing their own corn, garden stuff, and pigs, and their own handiwork done at school. One autumn as I was looking at the coops of chickens that had come to be judged, I found a small disheveled bird lying at one side with legs tied together with a calico rag. A small boy stood on the outskirts of the crowd. He had run home, caught his chicken and slipped it in with the others. A sad bunch of feathers it was, but its small owner learned that day something about the better breeding of chickens and how to enter one for an exhibit. The club boys and girls wear a red arm band, front seats are reserved for them, and these farmers-to-be feel their importance on this community feast day. A feast day I call it for always there come to us speakers from the Department of Agriculture in Washington, our own agricultural colleges in South Carolina, or other agricultural schools. . . .

From Rossa B. Cooley, *School Acres: An Adventure in Rural Education* (New Haven: Yale University Press, 1930), pp. 50–55, 68–71.

Edward T. Ware, a white man, was president of Atlanta University during the heat of the Negro debate over educational goals and methods. Ware (1874–1927), son of one of the founders and the first president of the University, was born in Atlanta, attended high school in Hartford, Connecticut, and studied at Yale and Union Theological Seminary. A member of the Congregational Church, he was successively chaplain (1901–1907), president (1907–1922), and president emeritus and trustee (1922–1927) of Atlanta University. He saw early what most enlightened observers now concede, that both industrial and academic training would help the Negro.

The agricultural and mechanical colleges for the Negroes are institutions supported by the Southern States with that portion of their federal land grant funds which they choose to assign to their Negro citizens. As the name implies, these institutions devote their chief energies to industrial and agricultural training. There are also courses for training teachers. The Georgia State Industrial College for Negro youth is of this type. On June 10 eleven pupils were graduated from the academic course and thirty-four from the industrial departments. The Florida Agricultural and Mechanical College gives the degree of B.S. for those who satisfactorily meet the requirements. Some of the Southern States take genuine pride in the state institutions for Negroes and make generous appropriations for their maintenance. In 1912 the Alabama State Normal School received $17,000 and the Florida Agricultural and Mechanical College received $12,000 from state appropriations. The presidents and teachers of the state schools are Negroes and the salaries paid are frequently better than those paid in the institutions supported by Northern philanthropy.

The number of educational enterprises for Southern Negroes which are doing at least some work of college grade is so great as to be bewildering; and calls for some attempt wisely to discriminate among them and to determine the value of the work they are doing. . . .

The whole system of public education in the South from the grammar school to the state college provides for separate education of the two races; and almost without exception the Negro schools are presided over and taught by people of their own race. Most of the private schools of the industrial type and those doing work of secondary grade are also taught by

In the Cage

Negroes. It may be said without question that such measure of success as these institutions have attained has been largely due to the teacher training of the institutions of higher education.

From information recently obtained from fifteen of the Southern state normal and agricultural schools it appears that 142 of their 347 teachers, all of them colored, are graduates of colleges. That is, 41 per cent, or about two-fifths of the teachers in the state schools for Negroes are college graduates. Of the 186 teachers and instructors at Tuskegee Institute 45, or 24 per cent, are college graduates. On the other hand there may always be found in the better Negro colleges graduates of the industrial schools who have proved themselves capable of further study. There are now several Tuskegee graduates studying at Atlanta University and several Atlanta graduates teaching at Tuskegee. This suggests that the two types of education are but branches of the same great work, the work of educating a race.

The question of the relative importance of industrial and higher education for the Negroes has led to much fruitless discussion. The truth is that both types of training are indispensable for the proper education of the people; and neither can fulfill its mission without cooperation with the other. The advantage of such industrial training as that offered by Hampton Institute is established beyond the shadow of a doubt. One of the surest evidences of this is that it is no longer urged as a peculiar method of dealing with Negro youth, but that it has influenced and modified our opinions regarding the whole question of public school training for the children of America, tending to emphasize the organic, vital relationship between education and the problems of everyday life. Hampton has been a pioneer in the campaign for vocational training not of the Negroes alone but of all Americans. As a special type of training adapted to the Negroes, it may have had opponents, but as a type of training making for efficient citizenship and specially adapted to the needs of a multitude of American citizens it has acquired a position where its friends and advocates need fear no opposition. There may be those who would allow vocational training to crowd academic instruction to the wall but the true followers of General Armstrong are not among them. And who would argue that because industrial education of this sort is good for white youth the colleges of New England should be turned into industrial or technical schools?

The higher education of the Negroes is quite a different question today from what it was fifty years ago. Like any question involving so large a number of citizens and containing so many human elements, it is a matter of national rather than sectional concern; still it must affect the Negroes and the South more directly than any other part of the nation. There are elements to deal with today which either did not exist or were practically ignored fifty years ago. At that time we did not ask the Negro if he wanted higher education and we did not consult his former master to know whether it was advisable. Northern philanthropy took the Negro by the hand and said, "I know that you have the ability to learn," and then opened before him the door of opportunity.

There were many who ridiculed the effort, saying that it was foredoomed to failure, and among them were the people of the South who thought they understood the Negro race and knew its limitations. Today we must work with the Negro rather than for him. How shall we know what is best for the race without taking into our counsels the thousands of its college graduates?

Another element which must not be ignored in any educational effort for the Negroes is that growing class of Southern white people who appreciate the educational needs of the colored people as American citizens and who sympathize with their best aspirations. . . .

Of this we may be certain, every Negro who receives a modern college education worthy of the name will be fully aware of the discriminations and injustices that fall to his lot because he is a Negro and lives in America. And it is a question how long he will endure with patience the disabilities under which he lives at present on this account. The answers to the questionnaire make repeated claim to equality before the law, full citizenship rights and privileges, the right to vote and unrestricted educational opportunities. What educated American citizen would demand less?

We cannot expect that all Southern white people, even those who have received the benefits of higher education, will sympathize with the educated Negroes or applaud their sentiments of independence. But there is a growing number who will. . . .

From Edward T. Ware, "Higher Education of Negroes in the United States," *Annals of the American Academy of Social and Political Science*, XLIX (September 1913), 212–213, 215–218.

Jan and Cora Gordon, "observant and shrewd" English artists, drove from Maine to Georgia in 1927 "looking for the picturesque." In Atlanta they stopped at Spelman College, the nation's oldest college for black women, and neighboring Morehouse College, a prestigious school for black men. The Gordons were not very impressed with the intellectual atmosphere at the colleges, though they liked the singing.

Pedagogues and Pupils

No matter how poor a state may be, towns have their pride. A few miles from Atlanta the concrete began again to usher us into the city. The cars meeting us had across their radiators the slogan, "Gate City of the South," a recrudescence of boosting as in the North; since Atlanta aspires also to commercial importance. We passed through the town to a seminary for young coloured women. The new Principal of this college was a lady we had met in New York; she had given us a general invitation to visit her should we come to Atlanta and we arrived just in time to catch her in the act of trying on her inauguration robes.

By tradition the college was religious and strict. To the distress of the pupils it frowned on ostentation in dress, and the girls eagerly watched the first appearance of the Principal to deduce if a weakening was visible in her costume towards the embargo on heels of extra height. But the Principal wore Oxfords and the college heaved a united sigh of resignation. Yet, considering the poverty of many of the homes from which the girls came the church parade was a tribute to what can be done on very little. Like the Scotch, the Negroes put themselves to great privations in order to get education for their children; and in the college itself practically all the homework, kitchen work, etc., was done by poor girls in exchange for classes. The Negro is more eager for education than the poor white. Eighty per cent are now literate although public outlay on coloured education is only one fifth the part per head of that expended on a white child.

They had not yet that touchy sense of white folks' ridicule which has made the northern Negro so self-conscious. They did not know that, because the traditional Mammy wore bright colours, therefore bright colours were taboo; so they wore what colours they liked and made a pretty bouquet as they filed into chapel on a morning; but they did know of the vulgarity of kinky hair, and thus on Inaguration Day the campus smelt persistently of singed hair and of heated vaseline, for with a comb of heated metal and the unguent even the kinkiest of hair can be persuaded, temporarily, to lie straight.

They were at college to learn all sorts of things: Latin and algebra, chemistry and biology; to be taught so that they might teach in turn; thrusting the coloured race sternly upwards into an American society which is far from ready to admit it at any level other than the very lowest, putting themselves into the predicament of Kipling's Tomlinson, fit neither for Heaven nor for Hell, scorned in the one, scorning the other.

The red buildings were spaced round the wide green quadrangle on which the young people loitered in groups, drilled, played basketball or whispered girlish secrets in their suave Afro-American voices. In the evening when the light was shining from the big arched door of the main building the girls, sitting on the steps in banks of coloured raiment, invoked their sad past as their voices swelled into the uncontrollable song of the Negro, into that simple spiritual music which, more easily than words, seems to express the black man's emotions:

There's a li'll wheel a'turning in my heart, O Lord,

A li'll wheel a-turning in my heart,

In my heart, in my heart, in my heart, O Lord,

A li'll wheel a-turning in my heart. . . .

A visitor, unhampered by accident of birth, yet not ignorant of words such as "prejudice" or "problem," might see strange contrasts here, such as the spry little children of the junior classes, just past the pickaninny stage, with a certain perkiness like Californian blackbirds. Or the girls of the senior school, already aware of the social value of tint, knowing that a fair skin is of more worth than virtue and naturally straight hair a passport into the best coloured society. Or the gang of nurses, rollicking plebians of deep hue, over whom hung the threat of an enquiry about their goings on. Or the visiting ex-student, wife of a minister, poor old lady in rusty black whose certificates for Latin or biology had long been foundered under the cares of a family, but who wished dearly to hear a few words of French spoken, and carried away the experience as a treasurable memory. Or the college musician —violinist, pianist, organist—a man of humour and of observation. Or, to touch the highest pitch of the Afro-American scale, the Principal of the boys' college, a coloured gentleman whom it was more of a compliment to address as "Mister" than as "Doctor," since, to a white Southerner, a Negro, even a Doctor of Philosophy, has no right to anything more than a familiar Christian name; as if he were the meanest labourer. In spite of his intellect and his honours, he had schooled himself to hold his hat in both hands when greeting a white man; so that he could avoid any appearance of needing a hand-shake, unless you chose to offer it. . . .

We gave a lecture to the assembled girls, and never has a harder task been set before us. The audience gazed up at us with a masked expression of Stygian gloom. They may have studied all the sciences and arts, but outside of the narrow lines of their studies they knew nothing except their immediate or previous surroundings; cabins and cotton fields, aeroplanes and radios were commonplaces; but of European life, not a thing; nor could any bridge be built in a single hour by which we might cross over into their comprehension. Besides, the only lectures they had attended previously had been those of missionaries, and they had at once shut their minds, in the way one naturally does to such improving talk. They could not realise that we were trying to amuse them, and when the sermon did not come they were left wondering what the talk was

In the Cage

all about. Then again we did not understand at first how difficult our English dialect would be to them. At any rate, talk as best we might, our audience remained as expressionless as the bottom of a blackened pot; not a flash of an eyeball, not one gleam of teeth, could we awaken in that dense blackness. Their minds were strictly circumscribed by five boundaries—domesticity, vanity, lessons, religion and sex—how could we, who were talking of the poetry of humility and the arts of the illiterate, touch them?

But when we began to play, another humour was at once visible. The audience came alive. To music they responded instinctively; it was an international language. Strange Spanish rhythms, which once baffled an educated English colonel, were easy to them. We could feel that audience sway to those fluid rhythms, understanding them as they should be understood, with musically sensitive ears.

After the experience gained here we lectured to the boys' college. But now we interlarded snatches of the music with the talk, and spoke mostly of the sporting element in European life; by analogy with a football match they could understand a bull-fight. Nevertheless, without venturing a wholesale judgment, we estimated the boys as being almost fifty per cent brighter than the girls. But the girls were still under a strict bondage, that protective system built up to give value to one invaluable commodity, virtue; from many of the limitations contingent on this condition the boys were free. But in any case, no matter how individuals may develop, a wholesale sense of responsibility is with difficulty inculcated in two generations. Slavery is bound to cling to a race no matter what aspect it may assume, that of submission or that of revolt. . . .

From Jan and Cora Gordon, *On Wandering Wheels* (New York: Dodd, Mead, 1928), pp. 243–248.

Lance G. E. Jones, a British scholar, received a grant from Oxford in the late 1920's to assess the work of the Jeanes Fund in the South. Founded in 1900 by a Philadelphia Quaker, Anna T. Jeanes, the Fund was the first to deal only with rural public schools for Negroes. It provided Negro teachers and "Jeanes Supervisors" for the schools. Expenditures for this work in twelve Southern states from 1915 to 1920 alone totaled $246,500. Jones carefully examined the condition of these rural schools, especially those in Virginia, in 1927.

First of all we may note that, with few exceptions, the Jeanes Teachers today are women, often married women or widows. Some of those who began work in the early days are still serving and are now between fifty and sixty years of age; the majority are between the ages of thirty-five and fifty, while several of those recently appointed are between the ages of twenty-five and thirty. In almost all cases the Supervisor has had previous experience as a teacher, and about half of them have been educated, either wholly or in part, at State Normal Schools or at private schools like Hampton or Tuskegee. Until recent years this would usually have meant that they had been trained in industrial subjects, but of late there has been an increasing freedom of choice in the curriculum of these schools, with the result that the extent to which their graduates have received such training varies considerably. The remaining Supervisors (that is, about half the total number) have attended only high schools or colleges with purely academic curricula. An increasing number, however, have completed a course of preparation for teaching in elementary schools, while a few have subsequently added special courses in rural school supervision. Indeed, most Supervisors are desirous of improving their academic or professional qualifications and attend summer schools, which as a rule devote particular attention to the problems of teaching in elementary grades. It may safely be claimed, therefore, that the majority of Jeanes Teachers are by education, as well as by training and experience, superior to those whom it is their duty to supervise, although it would be too much to assert that they are all highly qualified.

Secondly, it is important to realize the wide variations in the conditions under which they work. For example, the percentage and also the actual number of Negroes varies greatly from county to county, and so therefore does the number of schools for Negro children, as well as the type and size of school—one-teacher, two-teacher, three-teacher. If we take as our basis of comparison the number of teachers with whom each Supervisor has to co-operate, we find, for example, that in Virginia this ranges all the way from 15 to 116, and in Alabama from 22 to 252, the larger numbers being more usual in the thickly populated counties of the Black Belt, or in the delta sections of Mississippi. . . .

For the Jeanes Teacher the number of months for which she is employed is important because her salary, like that of many American teachers, is on a monthly basis, and she is paid only for the number of months of her engagement. This monthly salary varies from county to county, sometimes because of differences in the number of schools to be supervised, but most usually because of differences in the amount raised from public funds to supplement the contribution made by the Jeanes Trustees. As is to be expected, most salaries today are higher than the $40 a month which was paid to Virginia Randolph [the first Jeanes Supervisor] in the first year of her engagement, and in a normal year the rate of pay would now vary from $70 to $120 a month. Hard times have brought reductions in these salaries, as in many others and another less noticeable economy which has proved equally trying for the Jeanes Teacher has been the cessation of the contribution formerly made by many counties towards her travelling expenses. . . .

Thirdly the reader should know something of the conditions prevailing in the rural schools which the Jeanes Teacher visits and the quality of the teachers whom she tries to advise and help. Statistics are useful in that they enable us to compare the public school systems of various states in respect to certain measurable characteristics, but they fail to convey an idea of the wide variations which are to be seen as the traveller moves from county to county. Here he will find a progressive county with a high proportion of Rosenwald schools [another fund for aiding black education], there a county with almost all its schools housed in churches, lodge halls, or other buildings in no way adapted for the accommodation of children. In one community the school building, whether old or new, will be found in decent repair and well cared for, in another the building will show every sign of local indifference and neglect, even of willful destruction. In one school the pupils will be comfortably housed, carefully classified and reasonably well taught; in another the building will be overcrowded, and because of irregular attendance and poor teaching a large number of over-age pupils will be found in the lower grades. Of teaching equipment there will in some cases be a reasonable sufficiency; often, however, there may be little or none. In the words of an American observer: "To the visitor colored schools seem not a system but a series of incidents: bizarre, heroic, pathetic, romantic." . . .

Such records of visits to rural schools in the poorer and

In the Cage

more backward sections of the South bring out clearly the need for sympathetic supervision. . . . Without leaders whom they could understand the coloured people would have remained uninformed and undirected, and as leaders in the cause of education and social improvement the Jeanes Teachers have played their part well. . . .

>From Lance G. E. Jones, *The Jeanes Teacher in the United States, 1908–1933: An Account of Twenty-Five Years' Experience in the Supervision of Negro Rural Schools* (Chapel Hill: University of North Carolina Press, 1937), pp. 73–78, 84–86, 96–97.

2

Making a Living

The economic fortunes of the Negro have been bound up with both his social ills and his social progress. They have also had profound consequences for the nation. In the main Negroes in the South remained tillers of the soil. By 1877 many of them had become self-sufficient farmers owning their property and sometimes employing fellow Negroes to work sizable acreages. The great majority, however, were either tenants, sharecroppers, or wage- or day-laborers. Often they worked on cotton or other plantations, as they had in the ante-bellum period.

The prominence of sharecroppers and tenants was largely a new feature of Southern agriculture. The end of slavery and the failure after the war of the wage contract system—a failure that M. B. Hammond in *The Cotton Industry* attributed to the ignorance of the Negro—produced a mushrooming of tenancy. The tenant was, to put it simply, a semi-independent farmer, generally owning his implements but renting land for which he paid either money rent or, more often, a portion of his crop. A lower type of tenancy, that of the sharecropper, was more common among blacks. The sharecropper can best be described as half-tenant, half-laborer, in that he owned no implements and substituted labor for rent.[1]

The emancipated Negro, Booker T. Washington asserted, needed the opportunity to earn a dollar more than the opportunity to spend one in an opera house. Wisely used, this dollar, whether the product of farm or factory, would win respect and a degree of power for the race. Social equality Washington would gladly abandon for economic security.

Washington stressed the training of mechanics as well as farmers, but most Southern Negroes remained in the country and would have to look to the soil for their livelihood.[2] Those who did make it to the cities were more likely to become servants than industrial workers, and even mechanics trained at Tuskegee and Hampton found most of the doors to the South's growing industries closed to them. Only a few blacks managed to gain security in the professions or in business.

While American agriculture, as a whole, enjoyed a measure of prosperity in the Progressive Era, the Negro farmer remained largely trapped in the unprofitable tenant system or continued as a subsistence laborer. Tilling the soil, then, is where most observers found blacks trying to make a living between Reconstruction and the Great Depression.

---

[1] Even though his works reflect the racism of the time, U. B. Phillips' *American Negro Slavery* (1918) and *Life and Labor in the Old South* (1929) remain classic studies of the nineteenth-century plantation. Works of value on cotton, tenancy, and the plantation after the war include M. B. Hammond, *The Cotton Industry* (1897); Roger W. Shugg, "Survival of the Plantation System in Louisiana," *Journal of Southern History*, III (1937), 311–325; E. M. Banks, *Economics of Land Tenure in Georgia* (1905); Robert Preston Brooks, *The Agrarian Revolution in Georgia, 1865–1912* (1914); and Fred A. Shannon, *The Farmer's Last Frontier* (1945).

[2] In 1910 the Negro population was 72.7 per cent rural, in 1920, 66 per cent. (United States Bureau of the Census, *Negroes in the United States, 1920–1932*, p. 48.)

Making a Living

Sir George Campbell saw blacks toiling in the fields of Virginia and the Carolinas as well as in urban factories. He thought they were considerably better off than the Indian "coolies."

When we look to practical success in life, appearances seem at first sight less favourable to the blacks. I constantly asked, "Have any individuals among them come to the front and achieved success in industrial pursuits, in commerce, or in the professions?" and I could not learn that they have. . . .

For the rest I have not been able to hear of a successful negro merchant—the shopkeeping business in the most negro districts is almost entirely in the hands of whites. I have scarcely found a negro who has risen in the mercantile world higher than an apple-stall in a market. Certain professions they almost monopolize throughout—waiters and barbers, and in some parts ship-caulkers; but I found very few negro lawyers, and no doctors. All over the world it is curious to notice how ready people are to entrust the care of their souls to very unsafe home-rulers, and how much less trustful they are of their bodies. . . .

What is more disappointing is the failure of the negroes, so far, as superior artisans and in all that requires accuracy and care. As it is expressed, they are not *responsible*—they cannot be depended on. In slavery times some of them were pretty good artisans, and many of them, in the South, are now fairly good carpenters, bricklayers, and blacksmiths. But they seem hardly to have progressed in this respect since emancipation. A man who will do his carpentry so far well enough will not fit the pieces accurately; and in factories which employ black labour they do not rise to the higher posts. In the North the trades unions are so strong, and the jealousy of the negroes on the part of foreigners . . . is so great, that they would not have a fair chance; but in the South they labour under no such disadvantage, and employers rather prefer negro labour; yet in practice they don't seem to be able to trust the blacks beyond a certain point. In mechanical shops the blacks do the manual labour, but are hardly trusted to work engines. . . . In tobacco factories the labour is almost exclusively negro, and many of them are very well paid for labour requiring considerable skill; but I noticed that for certain work, the weighing and making up the packages and such-like, white men were always employed. I was in all these cases assured that no black man could be trusted to be accurate. Yet they make very fair cotton-farmers, and much of their handiwork in various branches of industry is quite good.

On the whole, I think it must be considered that at present, whether from natural defects or from want of cultivation, they are to a certain extent inferior to white men in the qualities which lead to the higher grades of employment. On the other hand, they have a very remarkable good nature and good temper, much docility, and great physical power and endurance—qualities that admirably fit them for labourers. . . .

There is a general concurrence of opinion, and not of opinion only, but of the most practical experience, that the blacks make admirable labourers when they are under sufficient supervision. On public works, and all undertakings carried on under professional superintendence, nothing can be better or more effective than their labour. They are physically exceedingly fine men; they can stand any climate and any weather, and are quite ready to do a good day's work for a

Making a Living

moderate day's pay, provided it is fairly and regularly paid. I heard of no case in which when such work had been offered to them they have preferred to squat down in idleness; that allegation against the negro character seems to me quite disproved by experience. The worst said is that they cannot always be depended on, and sometimes after labouring for a time will go off for a time. There may be some cases in which, work not being readily available, and little assistance or guidance forthcoming, they have sunk into a somewhat degraded condition, but such cases are quite exceptional. I came across none, though I have heard it asserted that there are such. On small farms, where black men work in small numbers, in company with and under the immediate control of their employers, they do exceedingly well; also when they work on their own account they do very well. It is only where they are employed in large numbers, under insufficient supervision, as on very large farms, that they are apt to take it easy and idle away their time as is the case with most such races.

Not only is the negro labour excellent, but also there is among the Southern proprietors and leading men accustomed to black labour, and not so used to whites, a disposition greatly to rely on black labour as a conservative element, securing them against the dangers and difficulties which they see arising from the combinations and violence of the white labourers in some of the Northern States; and on this ground the blacks are cherished and protected by democratic statesmen, who now hold power in the South.

As in other parts of America, wages are not so high as they were; but a common negro labourer in rural districts can generally earn about fifty cents . . . a day and that, with food so cheap as it is, and in a country which requires little fuel and no very expensive shelter, is a very good wage. Nothing so much brings home to me the poverty and lowness of living of

In the Cage

our Indian population as to hear these wages talked of as low; being as they are six or eight times the wages of a coolie in India, while food is scarcely, if at all, dearer. In truth, the negroes are very well off. . . .

From Sir George Campbell, *White and Black*, pp. 136–140, 142–146.

Ernst von Hesse-Wartegg (1854–1918), born in Vienna, was an author and world traveler as well as a diplomat. In 1909 he published his second book about the United States, *Amerika als neueste Weltmacht der Industrie* [*America as the Newest Industrial Power*]. He spent much of his later years in London. In 1879 he took a cargo boat South from St. Louis and toured the Mississippi Valley. In the selection below he describes his observations and gives impressions of Negroes at work.

We saw the so-called "Nigger" working on the piers along the Mississippi. Aboard the Steamer *Vicksburg*, dozens of ragged Negroes ran around and rolled the meal-tub about with astonishing skill. . . .

Under the weight of the goods our steamer sank deeper and deeper into the river bed of the Mississippi. The sweating, ragged Negro worked constantly on the cargo.

The chief mate drove and cursed the Negroes. They worked frantically, loading and stacking goods, their hands smelling like butter. They were a picturesque yet sorrowful sight, both for the artist and the philanthropist. . . .

Black, ragged Negroes also worked on the deck of the small steam-boats [in Louisiana]. We stood on the hurricane deck, that is, the deck above the passenger cabins, and viewed the men. Their wage is twenty cents per hour. They could work perhaps eight or ten hours per day and earn up to two dollars, but for that they are too lazy. For two hours they earn forty cents, and this was enough for them for two days. They sleep in any unoccupied house, of which currently there are so many in New Orleans. And their meals? Bananas and oranges are inexpensive, and with these they take the leftovers from the ship's meals and drink the water of the Mississippi. . . . It is amusing, at times, to see these men use their hats—and what hats!—to dip and drink the water from the dirty, muddy river. . . .

Finally, after midnight, we reached the "Magnolia Plantation," our destination. . . . Hercules, the Governor's black chauffeur, stood ready with his wagon. . . . Magnolia is the greatest sugar plantation in Louisiana. . . .

The mornings and evenings in the [Negro] "Quarters" offer a moving picture. Hardly has the big clock on the roof of the meal halls struck its second morning signal than the wide, shady square in front of the Negro houses begins to fill. As under slavery, the Negroes are grouped, counted, and marched out onto the plantation by the overseer. But now they have more gaiety and life than they formerly had. Singing, laughing, they skip gaily to the plantation. Baskets on their heads, tools on their shoulders, they dance high-spiritedly over the wide yard, past the planter's house to the fields. . . . The Negro generally shows in his daily performance a certain *tournüre*, a burlesque elegance, which contrasts sharply to the sullen, rude ways of the white plantation workers. Then, too, he performs his work laughing, chattering, singing, and even frolics back to his "Quarters." . . .

On the sugar plantation there is one Negro for every seven acres of land. He receives eighteen dollars per month

In the Cage

and free living quarters. He can work twelve hours per day, receiving fifty cents more for each hour more than eight and a half or for night work. Negro women do the same work for only fifty cents per day....

On a rice plantation [in Placquemine Parish, Louisiana] one gets a picturesque view of Negro women marching into the field. The black "Guinea wives," with thick lips, stupid faces, and bulky figures, have their aprons draping to their knees. They carry the seeds in these aprons or in little baskets, and sow them by hand in the furrow.

The rice will be cut by the Negroes with ... "rice hooks" and at the same time bundled....

The Chinese is certainly more intelligent, more agile, and more industrious than the Negro ... but he is very unpopular among Southerners, white as well as black....

From Ernst von Hesse-Wartegg, *Mississippi-Fahrten: Reisebilder aus dem amerikanischen Süden (1879–1880)* (Leipzig: Carl Reissner, 1881), pp. 18, 21–27, 61, 264–270, 291, 296, 349, translated for this volume.

T. Thomas Fortune, the Negro editor, though critical of overemphasizing professional education for blacks, was quick to applaud those members of the race who had succeeded in business and the professions. In the selection below he also saw a bright future for the Negro farmer and praised black property holders.

A few months ago I sat in the banking office of Mr. William E. Mathews and ex-Congressman Joseph H. Rainey (of S.C.), in Washington. As I sat there a stream of patrons came and went.

Making a Living

The whites were largely in the majority. They all wanted to negotiate a loan, or to meet a note just matured. Among the men were contractors, merchants, department clerks, etc. They all spoke with the utmost deference to the colored gentlemen who had money to loan upon good security and good interest.

A few months ago I dined with ex-Senator B. K. Bruce (of Mississippi), now Register of the United States Treasury. The ex-Senator has a handsome house, and a delightful family. In running my eyes over his card tray, I saw the names of some of the foremost men and women of the nation who had called upon Register and Mrs. Bruce. In passing through the Register's department with the Senator, sightseeing, I was not surprised at the marks of respect shown to Mr. Bruce by the white ladies and gentlemen, in his department. . . . Mr. Bruce is a gentleman by instinct, a diplomat by nature, and a scholar who has "burned the midnight oil." Such a person does not have to ask men and women to respect him; they do so instinctively.

I walked down F street and called at the office of Professor Richard T. Greena, a ripe scholar and a gentleman. The professor not only has a paying law practice, but is president of a new insurance company. He has all that he can do, and his patrons are both black and white.

All this and more came under my observation in the course of an hour's leisure at the capital of the nation. And the black man has not yet aroused himself to a full sense of his responsibilities or of his opportunities. . . .

In Baltimore . . . we have colored men of large wealth, who conduct extensive business operations and enjoy the confidence and esteem of their fellow citizens without regard to caste. . . .

He [the Negro] is, essentially, a man of the largest

wealth, God having given him, under tropical conditions, a powerful physique, with ample muscle and constitution to extract out of the repositories of nature her buried wealth. He only needs intelligence to use the wealth he creates. When he has intelligence, he will no longer labor to enrich men more designing and unscrupulous than he is; he will labor to enrich himself and his children. Indeed in his powerful muscle and enduring physical constitution, directed by intelligence, the black man of the South, who alone has demonstrated his capacity to labor with success in the rice swamps, the cotton, and the cornfields of the South, will ultimately turn the tables upon the unscrupulous harpies who have robbed him for more than two hundred years; and from having been the slave of these men, he in turn, will enslave them. From having been the slave, he will become the master; from having labored to enrich others, he will force others to labor to enrich him. The laws of nature are inexorable, and this is one of them. The white men of the South may turn pale with rage at this aspect of the case, but it is written on the wall. Already I have seen in the South the black and white farm laborer, working side by side for a black landlord; already I have seen in the South a black and white brick-mason (and carpenters as well) working upon a building side by side under a colored contractor. And we are not yet two decades from the surrender of Robert E. Lee and the manumission of the black slave. . . .

At this time the colored people of the South are largely in the industrial class; that is, they are the producing class. They are principally the agriculturists of the South; consequently being wedded to the soil by life-long association and interest, and being principally the laboring class, they will naturally invest their surplus earnings in the purchase of the soil. Herein lies the great hope of the future. For the man who owns the soil largely owns and dictates to the men who are com-

Making a Living

pelled to live upon it and derive their subsistence from it. The colored people of the South recognize this fact. And if there is any one idiosyncracy more marked than another among them, it is their mania for buying land. They all live and labor in the cheerful anticipation of some day owning a home, a farm of their own. As the race grows in intelligence this mania for landowning becomes more and more pronounced. At first their impecuniosity will compel them to purchase poor hilllands, but they will eventually get their grip upon the rich alluvial lands. . . .

Indeed, I confess, I strongly incline to the belief that the black men of the South will eventually become the large landholding class, and, therefore, the future tyrants of labor in that section. All the indications strongly point to such a possibility. It is estimated that, already, the colored people own, in the cotton growing states, 2,680,800 acres, the result of seventeen years of thrift, economy, and judicious management; while in the State of Georgia alone they own, it is reliably estimated, 680,000 acres of land and pay taxes on $9,000,000 worth of property. . . .

The future landlord and capitalist of the South are no longer confined to the white race; the black man has become a factor, and he must be counted. . . .

From T. Thomas Fortune, *Black and White*, pp. 181–183, 194–195, 207–211, 213, 215.

James Bryce observed Negroes in various occupations across the South. He thought that, in the main, they were improving industrially.

In the Cage

Of the economic and industrial state of the whole nine millions it is hard to speak in general terms, so different are the conditions which different parts of the country present. In one point only are those conditions uniform. Everywhere, alike in the Border States and in the farthest South, in the cities, both great and small, and in the rural districts, the coloured population constitute the poorest and socially lowest stratum, corresponding in this respect to the new immigrants, in the Northern States, although, as we shall presently observe, they are far more sharply and permanently divided than are those immigrants from the classes above them. They furnish nine-tenths of the unskilled labour, and a still larger proportion of the domestic and hotel labour. Some, a comparatively small but possibly growing number, have found their way into the skilled handicrafts, such as joinery and metal work; and many are now employed in the mines and iron foundries of Southeastern Tennessee and Northern Alabama, where they receive wages sometimes equal to those paid to the white workmen, and are even occasionally admitted to the same trade unions. In textile factories they are deemed decidedly inferior to the whites; the whirr of the machinery is said to daze them or to send them to sleep. On the other hand, they handle tobacco better than the whites, and practically monopolize the less skilled departments of this large industry, though not cigar making, for which Spaniards or Cubans are deemed best. In the cities much of the small retail trade is in their hands, as are also such occupations as that of barber (in which, however, they are said to be yielding to the whites), shoe-black, street vendor of drinks or fruit, together with the humbler kinds of railway service. In the rural districts the immense majority are either hired labourers or tenants of small farms, the latter class becoming more numerous the further south one goes into the hot and malarious regions, where the white man is less disposed

Making a Living

to work on his own land. Of these tenants many—and some are both active and thrifty—cultivate upon a system of crop-sharing, like that of the *metayers* in France. Not a few have bought plots of land, and work it for themselves. Of those who farm either their own land or that for which they pay rent, an increasing number are raising crops for the market, and steadily improving their condition. Others, however, are content with getting from the soil enough food to keep their families; and this is more especially the case in the lower lands along the coast, where the population is almost wholly black, and little affected by the influences either of commerce or of the white race. In these hot lowlands the negro lives much as he lived on the plantations in the old days, except that he works less, because a moderate amount of labour produces enough for his bare subsistence. No railway comes near him. He sees no newspaper; he is scarcely at all in contact with anyone above his own condition. Thus there are places, the cities especially, where the negro is improving industrially, because he has to work hard and comes into constant relation with the whites; and other places, where he need work very little, and where, being left to his own resources, he is in danger of relapsing into barbarism. These differences in his material progress in different parts of the country must be constantly borne in mind when one attempts to form a picture of his present intellectual and moral state. . . .

From James Bryce, *The American Commonwealth*, II, 514–515.

W. E. B. DuBois conducted a far-reaching study of the Negroes of Farmville, Virginia, for the U.S. De-

In the Cage

partment of Labor in 1897. In the selection below he describes the economic activities and condition of the town's blacks.

Agriculture is the chief occupation of the inhabitants of the county, tobacco being the leading product. Corn, wheat, oats, and potatoes are also raised, together with dairy products and poultry. . . .

On Saturday, the regular market day, the town population swells to nearly twice its normal size from the influx of country people—mostly Negroes—some in carriages, wagons and ox carts, and some on foot, and a large amount of trading is done. . . .

The chief industries of the town are: the selling of tobacco and its storage in warehouses, which is done by stock companies composed of Negro as well as white stockholders.

If we divide the total colored population above ten years of age according to the popular classifications of pursuits, we have in professional occupations, twenty-two; in domestic, 287; in commercial, forty-five; in agricultural, fifteen; in industrial, 282; not engaged in gainful occupations, 259, and not reported, fourteen. . . .

There are no colored physicians or lawyers in the town, preachers and teachers being the only representatives of the learned professions. The position of preacher is the most influential of all positions among the Negroes, and brings the largest degree of personal respect and social prestige. The two leading preachers in the town receive, the one $480 and house rent; the other, $600 a year. Both are graduates of theological seminaries and represent the younger and more progressive element. . . . Such are surely crowding out the ignorant but picturesque and, in many particulars, impressive preacher of slavery days. Types of the latter are now to be

Making a Living

found only in small churches, or in country districts where they care for two or three churches and receive salaries ranging from $75 to $300 a year.

The teacher stands next to the preacher in general esteem. An increasing number of these are now young women. . . . The teachers earn from $100 to $250 a year by teaching, and sometimes they do other work during vacation. . . .

The individual undertaker of business enterprise is a new figure among Negroes, and his rise deserves to be carefully watched, as it means much for the future of the race. The business enterprises in which Farmville Negroes are engaged on their own account are brickmaking, the grocery trade, barbering, restaurant keeping, furniture repairing, silver-smithing and clock repairing, shoemaking, wood selling and whip making, steam laundering, contracting and building, painting, blacksmithing, wheel-wrighting, hotel keeping, and farming, representing in all thirty-two separate enterprises conducted by thirty-six proprietors and employing, besides, about forty other persons. . . .

The wealthiest Negro in the town is the leading barber, who is reported worth not far from $10,000. There are five barber shops altogether—three for whites and two for blacks—and all run by Negroes. This is rather too many for the trade of the town, and one at least is being forced out. The income of barbers varies largely, probably from five dollars to fifteen dollars a week would be the average. There are five proprietors, and generally five assistants, who receive from three dollars to five dollars a week. There are two restaurants which do a good business, especially on Saturdays, with the farmers. They employ about four persons besides the proprietors. There is also a lunch business done by one of the grocery stores. . . .

The only steam laundry in the county is conducted by

two young colored men, brothers, who also own one in Richmond.... It is equipped with the latest machinery.... They probably do a business of $100 a week in Summer....

Most of the Negroes have given up farming for the industrial chances of the town. Of those living in town, three—the brick-maker, the wood merchant, and one of the barbers—own large and well-conducted farms. Besides this, nearly every family has a vegetable garden, sometimes of considerable size, from which produce is sold. Many factory hands hire out as farm laborers during the spring and summer; they receive from thirty-five to fifty cents a day and board, or, if they work by the month, from eight dollars to ten dollars....

The manufacture of tobacco strips consists in ridding the dry tobacco leaf of the woody stem. The loose tobacco is taken to the factory and placed on the floor of a room in piles, according to grade, style, and quality. Enough of a certain grade to make a hogshead of strips is then taken to another room and sprinkled and steamed, a little at a time. The bundles are then ready to be stemmed, as the leaves are supple and pliant. Women and young men, assisted by children who untie the stems, and the children tie the strips thus left into uniform bundles. The bundles are then weighed, stretched on sticks, and hung up in the drying room for from eight to twelve hours. When thoroughly dried and cooled the tobacco is again steamed as it hangs, and then cooled for two days. Finally it is steamed a third time in a steam box, straightened, and quickly packed in hogsheads.

The women and young men who stem the tobacco get fifty cents for every hundred pounds of stemmed tobacco, and can, with the aid of children, stem from 100 to 300 pounds a day, thus earning from $2.50 to $9.00 a week or more, for from five to seven months in the year.... The men who prize, steam and pack tobacco receive from seventy-five cents to one dollar a day for eight or nine months. The better classes of women do not like to work in the factories, and the surroundings are said to be unsuitable for girls. Many children are kept from school all or part of the time to enable them to help in this factory work. . . .

There is considerable dissatisfaction over the state of domestic service. The Negroes are coming to regard the work as a relic of slavery and as degrading, and only enter it from sheer necessity, and then as a temporary makeshift. . . . Negroes themselves are beginning to hire servants. Ten families among Farmville Negroes regularly hire one servant each, and several others have a woman to help occasionally. . . .

The economic importance of the black population of Farmville has brought many white men to say "mister" to the preacher and teacher and to raise their hats to their wives. . . .

From W. E. B. DuBois, "The Negroes of Farmville, Virginia: A Social Study," *Bulletin* of the United States Department of Labor (January 1898), pp. 3–6, 15–19, 21–22.

Samuel J. Barrows, the New York-born clergyman, was favorably impressed with most aspects of Southern Negro life. In the selection below he offers his impressions of the economic conditions of Southern blacks.

To know . . . what the colored man is doing for himself we must know the conditions from which he has to rise. These are hard enough, but not beyond the capacity of the Negro to break through them, as is shown in thousands of instances. Thus in Virginia and Kentucky and Tennessee the condition of things

In the Cage

is much better than further south, and the colored man, in spite of these obstacles, is rapidly becoming a farm-owner and householder. "In North Carolina," said Bishop Moore, "our people are buying land wherever they can get it." Land ranges from ten to fifteen dollars. The bishop himself has a little farm of thirty-three acres, near Salisbury, that cost thirty-four dollars an acre. "I am so anxious to see my race improve," he said, "that I should like to have a great deal more done, but in view of the small wages we get for labor we are doing pretty well." In Tennessee, experts assured me that the colored people are buying land throughout the country, and the mortgage system does not prevail extensively. As we go south and enter the Black Belt, the conditions vary with the fertility of the soil, the intelligence of the people, and the degree of education. A great difference is sometimes apparent in different counties in the same State. Thus in Lee County, Georgia, the people are laborers, working for wages. But in Marion County fifty per cent of the people own homes, and some of them have large plantations. In Sumter and Terrell counties, they likewise live mostly on farms. In the latter county, I was told that in a small city of 10,000 nearly all the colored people own their homes, and live in cabins or houses varying in size from one room to eight. The same difference is seen in Alabama. In Russell County the blacks are much behind those of Pike County, where there are better schools and more freedom from the mortgage system. In Bullock County, much government land has been preempted by the Negroes. In one section of that county the colored people are prosperous, one man of exceptional thrift owning 300 acres, twelve good mules, and four horses, and raising his own meat and potatoes. In Coffee County, the people are just beginning to rent their homes. In Elmore County, many have farms of fifty acres. In Macon County, not much land is owned. In Barbour County, land is

Making a Living

mainly rented, but there are many who have stock. In the southern part of Randolph County, about half of the blacks own their land. In one township of Lee County, nearly all the colored people own their homes. At Notasulga, about half the people have farms ranging from twenty-five to one hundred and fifty acres. Here I learned of one prosperous woman farmer, who raises three or four bales of cotton, as well as potatoes, chickens and cows. In the vicinity of Birmingham, farms are owned ranging from fifty to two hundred acres. . . .

The home-buying that is going on in the agricultural districts is going on also in the cities. In Montgomery street after street is owned by colored people. In Chattanooga, one third of the colored people own their homes. Suburban lots range in cost from $350 to $400. A cottage costs in the neighborhood of $600 to $650. In Birmingham colored people pay $10 or $12 a month rent. . . .

The Negro is also venturing as a tradesman. In all the large cities, and even in the smaller towns, in the South he is hanging out his sign. Two young men have engaged in the grocery business at Tuskegee, Alabama. Their credit is good at the bank, and I was told that they were doing more for their race by their industry and thrift than could be done by any amount of talk. . . . Near a little place where I visited in the Black Belt, a colored school-teacher, who got his education with hand and brain at Tuskegee, had bought for $225 a lot of land, and established a grocery store. At Tuscaloosa, the livery stable man who drove me owns several horses and carriages, and is doing well. Thus, in whatever direction one goes, he can find Negroes who are rising by force of education and of character. The influence of such schools as Hampton, Atlanta, and Tuskegee is felt all through the South in the stimulus given to industrial occupations. Tuskegee has turned out a number of printers who have made themselves independent,

In the Cage

and get patronage from both white and colored customers. One has a printing office in Montgomery. Another has opened an office in Texas. The growth of journalism and the gradual reduction of illiteracy among the colored people will make a way for many printers. In all the mechanical trades, colored men are finding places. . . . In Washington, colored brickmakers are earning from four to five dollars a day. Hod carriers receive $1.50. A boy trained in the industrial department of Atlanta University has built a schoolhouse in Alabama on contract. This boy can earn $2.50 a day with his hands and tools, and is besides a college graduate.

In slavery times there was no stimulus to Negro inventiveness. Before the war, an application made at the United States Patent Office for a Negro inventor was denied, on the grounds that he was a slave. With industrial education and diversified mechanical pursuits, the Negro brain is becoming adaptive and creative. The records of the United States Patent Office make no distinction between white and colored inventors. It is impossible to furnish statistics therefore, showing how much the colored man has done in this direction. The chief of the issue division surmises that there may be between five and ten thousand colored patentees, but this estimate has no reliable basis, being derived simply from the casual reports of attorneys in paying their fees. A colored assistant examiner in the Patent Office department has, however, placed at my service a list of some fifty patents taken out by colored people, which show the scope of their inventive genius. In the list of things represented are an improved gridiron, a locomotive smokestack, a cornstalk harvester, a shield for infantry and artillery, a fire extinguisher, a dough kneader, a cotton cultivator, life-preserving apparatus, a furniture caster, a biscuit cutter, a rotary engine, a printing press, a file holder, a window ventilator for railroad cars, an automatic switch for

Making a Living

railroads, and a telephone transmitter. The electric inventions are said to have a good deal of merit, and have been assigned to a prominent company. In Birmingham, a colored inventor is making money out of his patent. . . .

The result of higher education is seen in the rise of a professional class. I remember the time when a colored doctor was a curiosity even in Washington; but colored physicians, lawyers, journalists, college professors, dentists, educated clergymen, and teachers are now to be found in all the large cities of the South. In Montgomery, Dr. Dorsette has built up a thriving practice. He has erected a three-story brick building, on the lower floor of which are two stores, one of them a large and well-equipped drug store. . . . In Birmingham, there are two practicing physicians, one dentists, and one lawyer. At Selma, the practicing physician is a graduate of the university. There is also a pharmacist, owning his drug store, who studied at Howard University. There are six colored lawyers and seven colored physicians in Baltimore. The professional men command the confidence and support of their own people. . . .

Under slavery the Negroes were not organized, except in churches. The organic spirit must have time for growth. Co-operation has made no great headway. In various States and counties the Farmers' Alliance is attracting attention, many of the Negroes hoping to find relief through it from the bondage of the mortgage system. Small stock companies for various purposes exist in a number of cities. . . . A daily paper of Charlotte, North Carolina, in speaking of the loan association there, said that the colored shareholders were outstripping the white. It was noticeable that they paid more promptly. A penny savings bank, chartered under state law, was organized at Chattanooga about ten months ago. It has already one thousand depositors, the amounts ranging from two cents to one thousand dollars. The white as well as the colored children are being educated to save by this bank. In Birmingham, a similar institution was opened last October, and has about three thousand depositors. A school savings bank or postal savings bank system, as recommended by the Mohonk Negro conference, would be of great benefit to the colored people. . . .

From Samuel J. Barrows, "What the Southern Negro Is Doing for Himself," pp. 805–810, 812–815.

George K. Holmes was, like W. E. B. DuBois, born at Great Barrington, Massachusetts. Admitted to the Massachusetts bar in 1877, he was later special agent in charge, Division of Farms, Homes and Mortgages, U.S. Census of 1890, and subsequently agricultural statistician and member of the Crop Reporting Board of the U.S. Department of Agriculture, 1905–1925. Holmes toured most of the South in 1893 and reported his impressions of the tenant system.

On the Southern farm there is a neglect and a want of thrift which are a burden in themselves. The farmer is not ready to lift a hand to delay the dilapidation of his buildings. The plow is left at the end of the last furrow until the next year; a few nails or screws would save dollars of loss or of eventual credit with the merchant, in scores of places. . . . Such has been the subjection of the cotton planter to his unthrifty habits and to the system, of which the merchant is king, that not until very recent years did the production of corn in the cotton States exceed that of 1850.

But the black tenant has more to overcome. He too is living on the next crop, but he operates on so small a scale on his one-mule or two-mule holding that his net product of wealth gives him no more than a poor subsistence. The tenant system, as now managed, is economically inferior to the previous slave system, and, while he did not get a due share of the products of his labor as a slave, he gets even less now, because he receives a share of the incidence of the comparative economic loss. As a slave he was better fed and better housed than he now is, he had the best medical attendance in the county, and, if he was disposed to neglect his master's interests, which would have been his own as well, had he been free, he was restrained. Now he is almost as helpless as a child, and is still as thoughtless of the morrow. The merchant who has a lien on his share of the crop pays his taxes, buries his wife or child, buys him a mule if he needs one, and feeds and clothes him and his family to the extent that his improvidence and laziness are allowed credit. The high prices that the tenant pays for supplies are partly due to his untrustworthiness; not infrequently he is missing, after his living has been advanced to him until it is time to pick cotton, or he carries off cotton in the night without accounting for it to the merchant.

The first step in the tenants' elevation now consists in their producing their own food and, as far as possible, other supplies, which are now mostly a charge against their share of the crop. They may then have a margin for saving, if they are economical, and it is only with this fact they can elevate themselves to farm ownership and give themselves the independence that was their vision at their emancipation. That any considerable number of them will ever do this is not believed in the South.

The blacks prefer a tenancy to selling their labor for wages, and in some regions, at least, the white owners who cultivate their farms find that only the inferior laborers can

In the Cage

be hired, because the superior ones prefer tenancies. As the planters become independent of merchants, they are unfriendly to these tenancies, but, in some instances, have to grant very small ones, in order to hold the services of the blacks, who under such circumstances work for wages during a part of the year on the plantation cultivated by their landlord. If the white landlords arrive at independence from debt before the black tenants do, as it may be assumed that they will; if either class is to improve, it seems likely that the blacks will see a service for wages encroaching upon the tenant system. . . .

It rests with the plantation owners to determine whether the South shall escape from the thralldom of the crop lien. Southern farming, both large and small, needs to shun the store-keeper as much as it can. When the supplies for farm and family are derived mostly from the farm itself, it is apparent that the charges against the cotton crop will be reduced, a margin for saving established, and that peonage will be abolished. After this has been done cotton production can not be forced upon the farmer and he can begin the diversification of agricultural products and branch out into stock raising, truck farming, fruit culture and other occupations according to his opportunities and his markets. The ills of the farmers are not going to be cured by legislation; "our remedies oft in ourselves do lie, which we ascribe to heaven."

From George K. Holmes, "The Peons of the South," *Annals of the American Academy of Social and Political Science,* IV (1893), 270–274.

Matthew B. Hammond, born at South Bend, Indiana, was educated at the Universities of Michigan,

Making a Living

Wisconsin, Tübingen, and Berlin, and received a Ph.D. in economics from Columbia in 1898. He taught at the Universities of Missouri, Illinois, and Ohio State, was a member of various commissions, and was labor adviser to the U.S. Food Administration in 1918. His books include *The Cotton Industry* (1897) and *Railway Theories of the Interstate Commerce Commission* (1911). Hammond studied the agricultural situation in Georgia and Texas in 1897 and concluded that the Negro farmer was partly to blame for the current Southern farm depression.

The change of the agricultural system in the South accomplished during the years of industrial reconstruction, rendered necessary many other changes in plantation economy and in methods of living in the cotton states. Not the least important of these changes was that in the methods of obtaining credit. . . . Before the war the planters on the large estates were often obliged to seek credit of the cotton factors in the leading port cities, and to pledge their prospective cotton crops as security for these loans. The successors of these planters, the small farmers, white as well as black, who undertook to carry on cotton cultivation after the breakdown of the old plantation system, were certainly in far less favorable economic circumstances than had been the great planters whom they so largely displaced. . . . True to Southern traditions and habits, these small producers looked for their profits only to their cotton, and relied mainly on other sections of the country for their food supplies. But with little or no property to serve as security for loans, and with no business standing to recommend them to the money lenders at the distant ports, the small farmers were not able to follow in the footsteps of their predecessors by obtaining advances from the cotton factors. Their borrowing had to come, if at all, from the source nearer home. . . .

In the Cage

The extent to which the credit system prevails varies, of course, with localities. It is less common in the more western states, especially Texas, than in the older cotton states; and it is much less prevalent in communities settled chiefly by whites than in those sections of the country where negro croppers are largely employed. But it is characteristic throughout the cotton belt, and to say that three-fourths of the cotton growers are in this sort of dependence on the advancing merchants or factors would not be an extravagant estimate....

The superiority of Texas as a cotton-growing region is to be explained partly by her new and fertile lands, which without fertilizers and with relatively little labor, will produce more cotton to the acre than land east of the Mississippi on which large quantities of guano and intensive methods of cultivation are applied....

Texas has another advantage in her more reliable and efficient labor. The negroes have always been in a minority in that state; and since the war their proportion to the whites has been steadily decreasing, until now cotton is raised there chiefly by white laborers. The climate and resources of the state and the absence of negroes have made Texas an exception to the general rule in the South, and have enabled her to attract large numbers of immigrants from the North and even from Europe. Her more progressive and intelligent laborers have enabled the cotton growers to take advantage of all the improvements in implements and modes of cultivation.

The inefficiency and unreliability of the laborers have been great drags on the prosperity of the Southern states, especially of those sections where negroes are most largely employed. The Southern negro is usually a docile worker, but he lacks energy and ambition. His standard of living is low, perhaps not higher than it was in slavery days, and with this bare subsistence he seems hopelessly content. All Southerners are agreed that his efficiency as a worker is far below what it was before the days of freedom; and it is a matter of common remark in the South that the best workers among the blacks are not the younger hands, but the ex-slaves—men and women perhaps fifty or sixty years of age, who were trained to work in their days of bondage. On the big plantations along the Mississippi, where the managers exercise an authority little short of compulsion, and the plantation economy and management are not unlike those of slavery days, the negroes are fairly successful workers. There are also to be found in every community throughout the cotton belt negro farmers who are independent, industrious, thrifty and progressive agriculturists. But they are only the notable exceptions to the general rule of negro shiftlessness and idleness. Poorer farming can scarcely be found than exists in those parts of the cotton belt where the absentee proprietor has rented out his land to the negro "croppers" and has left them free to manage the plantations in their own way. . . .

As respects the share or "cropping system," it is now generally admitted that the abandonment of this method of tenure and a return to the wage-system would be a change most beneficial to agriculture in the cotton states. The causes which led to the failure of the latter at the close of the war and necessitated the adoption of the former have nearly ceased to be operative; while the results of recent investigations show plainly that in those localities where the two systems are in operation side by side, better cultivation and more prudent management result when the farming is carried on by hired laborers than when it is left to "croppers." Even where the proprietor does not occupy his own plantation and himself conduct the farming, experience, as in the "Delta region," has shown that under efficient managers, farming under the wage-system can be made fairly successful even with negro laborers....

<blockquote>From M. B. Hammond, "The Southern Farmer and the Cotton Question," *Political Science Quarterly*, XII (September 1897), 460–467, 472–475.</blockquote>

Thomas Young, a British student of the textile industry, visited South Carolina in 1902, by which time blacks were working in the cotton mill at Columbia. Young was curious to know why there were not more Negroes in the cotton mills. He concluded that blacks simply did not choose to work in these places. They preferred agricultural work or domestic service.

The wages paid for labour in the picking (opening and blowing) room were seventy-five cents per day, and the labourers in the department were all negroes. No negroes were employed for any other indoor work at this mill, and although I have heard of one or two small bagging mills run wholly by negro labour, I am told that even here, in the Black Belt, negroes are not employed in any appreciable extent in the manufacture of cotton. The negro grows the cotton, harvests it, gins it, bales it, and brings it to the mill door in a mule-waggon, and sometimes he may open the bales and put the cotton into the hopper of the first machine which treats its fibre; but after that he gives way to white labour. Why?

Not because of race feeling, as is commonly supposed in England, and even in the Northern states, for in all sorts of other occupations one finds the negro and the white working side by side on good terms.... And not because the negro is

Making a Living

driven out by competition of the whites. I am satisfied that if the negro does not work in the cotton mills it is simply because he does not choose to. He has a child's impatience of any monotonous occupation that demands constant application and continuous vigilance; he dislikes to breathe the mill air, laden with moisture and fine particles of lint cotton; he loves the sunshine and the open sky and he is loath to forsake them for indoor work unless that work ministers a little to his vanity and sense of dignity. That, I think, is why you find George (all Southern negroes are assumed by the whites to be called George, and are almost invariably addressed by that illustrious name) wearing the evening dress of a waiter or the assistant conductor on a Pullman car, and why you will not find him standing for eleven hours a day in front of a slubbing frame or a group of looms.

No doubt the negro's natural antipathy to such work would make him a poor workman if he were driven to seek employment in a cotton mill. But he seems to feel that it is not worth it so long as he can live happily working three or four days a week in the fields. "I don't think that cotton mills wuz ever meant for coloured people," was the opinion given to me quite frankly by a Columbia negro, and he expressed the general attitude of his race. . . .

From Thomas M. Young, *The American Cotton Industry: A Study of Work and Workers, Contributed to the Manchester Guardian* (London: Methuen, 1902), pp. 68–69.

Carl Kelsey was born in 1870 at Grinnell, Iowa, attended Iowa College, Andover Theological Seminary, and the Universities of Göttingen and Berlin, and received a Ph.D. from the University of Pennsylvania in 1903. Beginning his career as a high school teacher, he became a social worker and eventually a professor of sociology at the University of Pennsylvania. He went South in 1903, specifically to study the Negro farmer, but recorded his impressions of Negro life in general. With respect to farming, he found the blacks, in the main, to be poor agriculturalists.

In all parts of the South the Negro, tenant or owner, usually receives advances from white factors, and these spend a good part of their time riding about to see that the land is cultivated in order to insure repayment of their loans. If their advice and suggestions are not followed, or if the crop is not cultivated, the supplies are shut off.... The great bulk of the cotton crop is thus raised under the immediate oversight of the white man. ... It is to be further remembered that cotton raising has been the chief occupation of the Negro in America.

As a matter of fact there is not the least difficulty for the Negro farmer to get plenty of land, and he has but to show himself a good tenant to have the whites offering him inducements....

In all parts it is the custom for the Negroes to save a little garden patch about the house, which, if properly tended would supply the family with vegetables throughout the year.

As a matter of fact they care little for vegetables and seldom know how to prepare them for the table. The garden is regularly started in Spring, but seldom amounts to much. I have ridden for a day with but a glimpse of a couple of attempts. As a result there will be a few collards, turnips, gourds, sweet potatoes and beans, but the mass of the people buy the little they need from the stores.... In many regions

Making a Living

wild fruits are abundant, and blackberries during the season are quite a staple, but they are seldom canned. Some cattle are kept, but little butter is made, and milk is seldom on the bill of fare. . . . Many families keep chicken, usually of the variety known as "dunghill fowls" which forage for themselves. But the market is supplied with chickens by the small farmers. . . . Whenever opportunity offers, hunting and fishing become more than diversions, and the fondness for corn and "possum" is proverbial. . . .

Under diversified farming there would be steady employment most of the year, with a corresponding increase of production. As it is there are two busy seasons. In the Spring, planting and cultivating cotton, say from March to July, and in the Fall, cotton picking, September to December. The balance of the time the average farmer does little work. The present system entails a great loss of time. . . .

This sea coast region [Tidewater Virginia] offers peculiar facilities for gaining an easy livelihood. There are few negro families of which some member does not spend part of the year fishing or oystering. There has been a great development of the oyster industry.

The effect of this industry is twofold; a considerable sum of money is brought into the county and much of this has been invested in homes and small farms. This is the bright side; but there is a dark side. The boys are drawn out of the schools by the age of twelve to work at shucking oysters, and during the winter months near the rivers the boys will attend only on stormy days. The men are also taken away from the farms too early in the fall to gather crops, and return too late in the spring to get the best results from the farm work. The irregular character of the employment reacts on the men and they tend to drift to the cities during the summer, although many find employment in berry picking about Norfolk. Another result

In the Cage

has been to make farm labor very scarce. . . . I do not say that the bad results outweigh the good, but believe they must be considered. . . .

There are no women working in the fields, their time being spent about the house and the garden. . . .

Although so many earn money in the oyster business, there are others who have gotten ahead by sticking to the farm. T—— now owns part of the place on which he was a slave, and his slave-time cabin is now used as a shed. . . . With the help of his boys, whom he has managed to keep at home, he derives a comfortable income from his land. His daughter, now his housekeeper, teaches during the winter. What he has done others can do, he says. . . .

The absolutely essential thing is that the Negro shall learn to work regularly and intelligently. The lesson begun in slavery must be mastered.

I would not say that I thought all Negroes should be farmers, but I do feel that the farm offers the mass of the race the most favorable opportunity for the development of solid and enduring character. . . .

From Carl Kelsey, *The Negro Farmer* (Chicago: Jennings and Pye, 1903), pp. 20, 29–34, 70, 73.

Ray Stannard Baker, the Progressive journalist, observed a large number of black-owned businesses in Atlanta and was pleasantly surprised to find them prospering. He was also favorably impressed to discover successful black independent farmers in the rural South.

Making a Living

One day, walking on Broad Street, I passed a Negro shoe store. I did not know that there was such a thing in the country. I went in to make inquiries. It was neat, well kept, and evidently prosperous. I found that it was owned by a stock company, organized and controlled wholly by Negroes; the manager was a brisk young mulatto named Harper, a graduate of Atlanta University. I found him dictating to a Negro girl stenographer. There were two reasons, he said, why the store had been opened; one was because the promoters thought it a good business opportunity, and the other was because many Negroes of the better class felt that they did not get fair treatment at white stores. At some places—not all—he said, when a Negro woman went to buy a pair of shoes, the clerk would hand them to her without offering to help her try them on; and a Negro was always kept waiting until all the white people in the store had been served. Since the new business was opened, he said, it had attracted much of the Negro trade; all the leaders advising their people to patronize him. I was much interested to find out how this young man looked upon the race question. His first answer struck me forcibly, for it was the universal and typical answer of the business man the world over whether white, yellow, or black:

"All I want," he said, "is to be protected and let alone, so that I can build up this business."

"What do you mean by protection?" I asked.

"Well, justice between the races. That doesn't mean social equality. We have a society of our own, and that is all we want. If we can have justice in the courts, and fair protection, we can learn to compete with the white stores and get along all right."

Such an enterprise as this indicates the new, economic separation between the races.

In the Cage

"Here is business," says the Negro, "which I am going to do."

Considering the fact that only a few years ago, the Negro did no business at all, and had no professional men, it is really surprising to a Northerner to see what progress has been made. One of the first lines he took up was—not unnaturally—the undertaking business. Some of the most prosperous Negroes in every Southern city are undertakers, doing work exclusively, of course, for coloured people. Other early enterprises, growing naturally out of a history of personal service, were barbering and tailoring. Atlanta has many Negro tailor and clothes-cleaning shops. . . .

The wealthiest Negro in Atlanta, A. F. Herndon, operates the largest barber shop in the city; he is the president of a Negro insurance company (of which there are four in the city) and he owns and rents some fifty dwelling houses. He is said to be worth $80,000, all made, of course, since slavery. . . .

Of course only a comparatively few Negroes are able to get ahead in business. They must depend almost exclusively on the trade in their own race, and they must meet the highly organized competition of white men. But it is certainly significant that even a few are able to make progress along these unfamiliar lines. Many Southern men I met had little or no idea of the remarkable extent of this advancement among the better class of Negroes. . . .

Another point of the utmost importance—for it strikes at the selfish interest of the landlord—lies in the treatment of the Negro, who, by industry or ability, can "get ahead." A good landlord not only places no obstacles in the way of such tenants, but takes a real pride in their successes. . . .

The result is that a number of Mr. Brown's tenants have bought and own good farms near the greater plantation. The

Making a Living

plantation, indeed, becomes a sort of central sun around which revolves like planets the lesser life of the Negro landowner.... We met one farmer driving to town in a top buggy with a Negro school-teacher. His name was Robert Polhill—a good type of the self-respecting vigorous, industrious Negro. Afterward we visited his farm. He had an excellent house with four rooms. In front there were vines and decorative "chicken-corn"; a fence surrounded the place and it was really in good repair. Inside the house everything was scrupulously neat.... The wife evidently had some Indian blood in her veins; she could read and write, but Polhill himself was a full black Negro, intelligent, but illiterate.... Near the house was a one-horse syrup-mill in operation, grinding cane brought in by neighbouring farmers—white as well as black—the whites thus patronizing the enterprise of their energetic Negro neighbour....

His [Polhill's] history is the common history of the Negro farmer who "gets ahead." Starting as a wages' hand, he worked hard and steadily, saving enough finally to buy a mule—the Negro's first purchase; then he rented land, and by hard work and close calculating made money steadily.... Then he bought 100 acres of land on credit and having good crops, paid for it in six or seven years. Now he has a comfortable home, he is out of debt, and has money in the bank, a painted house, a top buggy, and a cabinet organ!....

All of this shows what a Negro who is industrious, and who comes up on a plantation where the landlord is not oppressive, can do.... Indeed, a few Negroes in the South are coming to be not inconsiderable landlords, and have many tenants....

From Ray Stannard Baker, *Following the Color Line*, pp. 39–41, 43, 89–91.

In the Cage

Albert Bushnell Hart, during his Southern tour, had several opportunities to observe the Negro at work. Despite the record of domestic servants, he did not feel that the blacks were, on the whole, unreliable laborers.

... The shiftless population living on odd jobs and the earnings of the women as domestic servants, committing petty crimes and getting into rows with the white youths, cannot be more than one tenth of the Negroes, and the poorest tenth at that. ...

Domestic service is the most exasperating point of contact between the races. It has been reduced to a system of day labor, for not one in a hundred of the house servants spend the night in the place where they are employed. Great numbers of the women are the only wage earners in their family and leave their little children at home day after day so that they may care for the children of white families. Some mistresses scold and fume and threaten, some have the patience of angels; in both cases the service is irregular and wasteful. Nobody ever feels sure that a servant will come the next morning. Most of the well-to-do families in the South feed a second family out of the baskets taken home by the cook; and in thousands of instances the basket goes to some member of a third family favored by the cook. Hence the little song taken down from a Negro's lips by a friend in Mississippi:

"I doan' has to wuk so ha'd,
'Cause I got a gal in de white folks' ya'd;
And ebry ebnin' at half past eight
I comes along to de gyarden gate;

Making a Living

She gibs me buttah an' sugah an' lard—
I doan' has to wuk so ha'd! . . ."

Other people have . . . tales of good tempered and humorous servants; and the negro question would be half solved if the people who undertake domestic service and accept wages would show reasonable interest, cleanliness, and honesty; and a million of the race might find steady employment at good wages in the South within the next six months, and another million in the North, if they would only do faithfully what they are capable of doing.

There is little hope of regeneration by that means; the difficulty is that capable Negroes do not like domestic service and seek to avoid it. The average Southerner sighs for the good old household slaves, and harks back to the colored mammy in the kitchen and stately butler in the drawing room. . . . The house servants in slavery times were chosen for their superior appearance and intelligence, and were likely to be mulattoes; the children and grandchildren of such people may now be owners of plantations, professional men, professors in colleges, negro bankers, and heads of institutions; while the domestic servant commonly now comes from the lowest Negroes, is descended from field hands, and chosen out of the most incompetent section of the present race. The problem of domestic service is chiefly one of the village and the city, in which only about a seventh of the Negroes live. . . .

From Albert Bushnell Hart, *The Southern South*, pp. 124–127.

Sir Harry Johnston saw blacks at work in the cotton and sugar cane fields of Alabama, Mississippi, and Louisiana, but also found Negro mine workers in Birmingham, business and professional men in Alabama and in Washington, and turpentine laborers in Florida. In many ways, he felt, the Southern black laborers were better off than their counterparts in England.

How often I contrasted in my mind the life of these Negroes in the Southern States with that of our English poor; how often I felt it to be greatly superior in comfort, happiness, and even in intellectuality; for many of these peasant proprietors of Alabama had a greater range of reading, or were better supplied with newspapers, than is the case with the English peasantry, except in the home counties. . . .

Of course the keeping of live-stock is a very important feature in the life of the agricultural Negroes of this and other States, and has of late been remarkably encouraged and benefited by the teaching of Tuskegee. On most of the holdings there were good milk cows descended from Guernsey or Holstein stock. Many a negro farmer kept mares and a jackass for mule breeding. I was surprised at the excellence of the poultry. There were Leghorns, Buff Orpingtons, Plymouth Rocks, and other good breeds for laying and for the table. Turkeys, of course, were kept on a very large scale; also geese and guinea-fowl. . . .

Negroes form a large proportion of the population [in Birmingham], for in the adjacent iron mines about ninety per cent of the labour is negro, while the same race furnishes fifty-five per cent of the coal miners and fifty per cent at least of the men employed in the great steel works and iron industries (it might be mentioned incidentally that throughout the Southern States seventy-five per cent of the men employed in constructing and repairing the railroads are negroes).

In Birmingham there are several negro banks. I visited

Making a Living

one of them which was lined with marble and upholstered with handsome woods. There are, as in the other towns of Alabama, negro doctors, dentists, haberdashers, modistes, shoemakers, barbers, grocers, druggists and general storekeepers. There are theatres for coloured people at which only negro actors and actresses perform. Excellent are these performances, usually in musical comedy—how excellent, amusing, and of good taste. . . . There is a Negro press, and there are numbers of young negro or mulatto men and women who are expert stenographers and typists. . . .

The field work in the vast plantations of sugar-cane [in Louisiana] is also mainly in the hands of negro men, women, and children, who toil for good wages under the supervision of negro and white overseers. A few Italians or Sicilians work alongside the black people without quarrelling, but without social inter-mixture. By negro labour the cane is attended throughout the year. In November–December it is cut, stripped of leaves, and carefully laid on the ground in parallel rows, ready to be picked up mechanically by machinery—huge iron arms and fingers cleverly directed by negroes or mules (working in a merry accord which seems unattainable between mules and white men)—and deposited in large wagons. When the cane is first laid low with great knives, it lies—with its unnecessarily luxuriant leaves—in many areas of hopeless confusion about the sturdy limbs and bulky petticoats of the negro women. But—as if by magic—it is deftly lopped, pruned, and laid in absolutely straight rows while you stand and watch. . . .

And through all this cycle with its varying cares and responsibilities, negro labour seems to be the one unfailing resource of the Louisiana planter. The white men have strikes, are called away by higher ambitions, or are stricken by occasional epidemics of disease. The Negro is there all the time.

In the Cage

He is a spendthrift, yet loves to have money to spend. There are the sugar or the rice planters and the fruit growers, the railway companies, builders, and shipping firms always ready with work at good wages. The Italians, Hungarians, and Slavs save and often transmit to Europe the payment for their labour. The Negro is at home, and spends his money locally as soon as he earns it.

Great indeed is the debt which the Industrial and Agricultural South owes to the co-operation of the Negro. . . .

In the north-western part of Florida the rougher class of negro works a good deal in the pine forests, collecting turpentine. I had a glimpse of some of these camps in the pine woods, but thanks to that blessed spread of prohibition in the South and the restrictions on the sale of alcohol, these camps seemed . . . orderly and without crime, although the country Negro of Florida, like his brother of the other Southern States, still lies under the stigma of being a petty thief, prone to carry off at night the fowls, turkeys, or vegetables of some homestead in his vicinity. . . .

It is often a grievance to the indignant Southerner that the Federal Capital should contain such a large Negro population—about one hundred thousand. The coachmen are nearly all negroes, the men who attend the streets are negroes, so, of course, are all the lesser employees on the railways and at the railway stations; many of the clerks, typists, shorthand writers; barbers and shop assistants. In addition there are numerous colored doctors, dentists, lawyers, and surveyors, engineers, electricians, builders, and architects. Not a few of the excellent officials in the great public offices, museums, galleries, are negroes. . . .

From Sir Harry H. Johnston, *The Negro in the New World*, pp. 428–429, 436, 453–455, 469, 473.

Making a Living

Rossa B. Cooley became a close friend and adviser to the blacks on the South Carolina Sea Islands. She describes here some of their financial enterprises, among which their cooperative society and Credit Union are of special interest.

And so, in turn, I will tell you about our Cooperative Society, its struggles, its near failure, its small measure of success. That little group of nine men who were the founders in 1912 went out from their meeting determined to get new members; and that first year 111 were enrolled. The average loan was $24.07, sixty-three loans were made, and ninety sacks of fertilizer were bought and sold to the members. It was a good crop year and the little society sailed through smooth waters with flags flying.

The storm that led to the birth of the society gave it its first chance to do some cooperative work for the community. Our main road was in terrible condition. The county had hauled oyster shells for its repair, and a great pile lay at the edge of the tide river near the school. There they stayed for over a year, while the island people and horses were "punished" by the poor road. This was the day before automobiles, and roads were made by the simple method of dumping shells along the way to be broken down by the carts and other vehicles. A simple system but a very perfect road resulted after an incredibly short time of discomfort.

The officers of the society saw their chance. When work was slack, the call went out, and men with their oxen, ponies, and carts responded. The merchants also helped, and in a few days our road was in good shape. This experience welded membership. It also showed who were the weak reeds in the society for not quite half of them came out for this volunteer service. Those who worked came from a great variety of plantations, from Land's End to Coffins Point, the far ends of the island. . . .

By 1918 the society had handled $13,865.44 and, with all the experiences gained, had $58.00 out in bad debts. Year by year, if we could read between the lines of its minute book, we should see the honest efforts to hold on, the difficulties met. The meetings were full of interest to all of us. I heard one of the officers say, "We must stop excusing ourselves by saying the Lord sends the rain! The Lord gives us the brains and strong arms for ditching! We say the Lord sent the drought! He gives us brains and strong arms to save every drop of moisture by cultivating right." "Stop raising nubbins! Stop being a nubbin!" was the vigorous advice of one who had paid his loan with interest promptly. One of the men who had borrowed $15 was found out as a double dealer; he had mortgaged his cow to the merchant, the same cow to the society. A committee of two was sent out "to visit him and teach him," one of them saying as he took on the job, "Things have been raggy. We members have been raggy too in our coming and going." Nine members were dismissed at one meeting because they would not meet their obligation and pay the eighty-one cents each member was taxed to cover the loans unpaid because of death or inability to collect. The total liability clause in the constitution (all the members being liable for all the loans) has worked well in keeping the society healthy and afloat. It is in the back of their minds, even if it has had to be put into practice but once.

The "Bold Evil" [boll weevil] tested the society to its marrow. If he did not prove his magnitude, the vast numbers of his family descending on our cotton fields demonstrated that "in union there is strength." Could our little cooperative

Making a Living

make headway against the scourge by the application of the same principle? The old sea-island long-staple cotton for which the region is famous seems to be beaten by the weevil. It is blighted before it is ready to gather. Early maturing seed has made the short staple a possibility. Young demonstrators are using improved seed and improved cultural methods and unless the season is entirely on the side of the weevil, cotton has its chance. But it must take its place alongside the other crops. The struggle is one, and conditions hold a threat, which serves as a spur to the young. . . .

In 1924, the St. Helena Credit Union was born, an outgrowth of the Cooperative, the same membership practically, as the "Co-ops" voted to move into the new society as a whole. Here a new element entered—shareholding—and each member bought a $5.00 share. It also made it possible for members to save through their own society, but that . . . hasn't happened either, for a Beaufort bank failure shook the confidence of these young Negroes as well as the older ones; if the white men with all their business experience could not succeed in their financial business, it looked as if the colored men had better watch their step. This is only a passing condition, I believe, and the Credit Union will eventually be functioning in a rounded way. As it is, all the loans are now in the hands of the Union, and all the buying and selling in the hands of the "Co-ops." . . .

From Rossa B. Cooley, *School Acres*, pp. 119, 121–125.

André Siegfried, the noted French political economist, thought that Negro farmers—though far from prosperous—were better off than many whites upon his return to the South in the 1920's. The competition of the Negro farm laborer, Siegfried felt, was partially responsible for the worsening condition of the "poor whites." They had sunk to "a mediocre lot, often living in squalor." Economically and physically, they were the Negro's inferior. Siegfried (1875–1959) came of an Alsatian family long noted for great political insight, and he himself enjoyed a distinguished academic and diplomatic career. He first visited the United States in 1898.

The Southerners can exploit these illiterate masses with complete impunity, since there is no court of appeal where they can receive justice. Only a short while ago it was quite common for them to take advantage of the small coloured farmer in the country districts. They deceived him about the exact area of his farm, and when he had to pay rent in kind, they gave him very little say as to what he had produced, even dictating the amount of his payment to him. His final reckoning was indefinitely delayed, and in the end he was forced to accept it, whether correct or otherwise. Such conditions no longer exist to the same extent, for war-time prosperity has even reached the small black proprietors, and in addition the wholesale immigration of the negroes to the northern cities has at last made the southern employers reflect. But the economic contest between the races is not carried on with equal weapons, for not only must the negro win the good will of the employers, but what is more difficult, he must also overcome the ferocious jealousy of the "poor white" class, who are the bitterest enemies of his race.

In a colony of "planters," a white planter controls coloured labour. This is an accepted system of production. In a colony of "settlers," however, where the population is homogeneous, the presence of a negro *bloc* is bound to be unhealthy. Owing to the competition with a race of more modest needs,

Making a Living

the white worker must reduce his standard of living down to that of his competitor. One of the residues of slavery is the "poor white," who on the one hand is unable through lack of land, to raise himself to the level of the employer class and on the other is menaced by the presence of servile labour. In spite of their purely Anglo-Saxon descent they are a mediocre lot, often living in squalor. As a result of the climate, malaria, parasites, etc., they are physically feeble; and being perpetually in debt, they constitute a reserve of cheap labour from which the employers can go on drawing indefinitely.

In the South they will tell you that all the unskilled labour is reserved for the negro, and that the skilled work is done by the superior race. If this were always so, contact between the two races would be limited and rivalry greatly diminished. In point of fact, however, there are many whites who are ready to do the lowest type of manual work, while an increasing number of negroes are attempting occupations which require considerable technique. The employers naturally do not raise any objections to such ambitions; for not only is the coloured labourer paid less, but he is more obedient. The white labourer, however, is left on the frontier between the two races, in constant fear of being dragged down and merged with the inferior one. In the wealthy families some of the old-time sentimentality still survives from the slave days, but the "poor white" sees in the negro nothing but a brutal competitor who is trying to rob him of his job. His hatred is unrelenting, merciless, and mingled with fear. To understand the South, we must realize that the lower we descend in the social scale, the more violent is the hatred of the negro. . . .

From André Siegfried, *America Comes of Age: A French Analysis*, translated by H. H. and Doris Hemming (New York: Harcourt, Brace, 1927), pp. 96–97.

3

Life and Leisure

According to Southern legend, the happy, grinning "darky" chose to spend most of his earnings on liquor and to "have a good time." His material wants and needs, including food, dress, and housing, were meager, and he paid little attention to his health and safety. He was a mediocre laborer, yet he did well enough and had few complaints. He could be counted upon to entertain not only himself but white people as well. Contemporary observers from outside the South could judge for themselves how valid this legend was.

Booker T. Washington had pledged at Atlanta in 1895 that "in all things social" Negroes and whites could remain "as separate as the fingers on the hand." For the most part they remained so throughout the first quarter of the twentieth century. The other side of Washington's coin was that the two races were to work together for mutual economic advancement. If this formula proved successful, the Negro's social condition would improve in hand with his economic advancement. The observers' reports permit a long look at health and housing, and glances at such lighter matters as dress and recreation.

Life and Leisure

William Wells Brown, the black historian, stopped in Alabama and Tennessee upon his return to the South in 1880 after a long absence. He noted some new developments in the social life of blacks, such as assemblies of cotton growers, but many of the old traditions remained. Brown was especially critical of the purchasing habits of black women.

The old love for visiting the cities and towns remained, and they [Negroes] became habituated to leaving their work on Saturdays, and going to the place nearest to them. This caused Saturday to be called "nigger day," in most of the Southern States.

On these occasions they sell their cotton or other produce, do their trading, generally having two jugs, one for the molasses, the other for whiskey, as indispensable to the visit. The store-keepers get ready on Saturday morning, putting their brightest and most gaudy-colored goods in the windows or on the front of their counters. Jew shops put their hawkers at their doors, and the drinking saloons, and other places of entertainment, kept for their especial accommodation, either by men of their own race or by whites, are all got ready for an extra run.

Being on a visit to the State of Alabama, for a while, I had a fair opportunity of seeing the colored people in that section under various circumstances. It was in the autumn and I was at Huntsville. The principal business houses of the city are situated upon a square which surrounds the court house, and at an early hour in the morning this is filled with colored people of all classes and shades. On Saturdays there are often fully two thousand of them in the streets at one time. At noon the throng was greatest, and up to that time fresh wagon-loads of men, women, and children were continually arriving. They came not only in wagons, but on horses, and mules, and on foot. Their dress and general appearance were dissimilar. Some were dressed in a queer looking garment made of pieces of old army blankets, and a few were apparelled in faded military overcoats, which were liberally supplied with patches of other material. The women, unlike their husbands and other male relations, were dressed in finery of every conceivable fashion. All of them were decked out with many-colored ribbon. They wore pinchbeck jewelry in large quantities. A few of the young girls displayed some little taste in the arrangement of their dress; and some of them wore expensive clothes. These, however, were "city niggers," and found but little favor in the eyes of the country girls. . . .

While the men are selling their effects, the women go about from store to store, looking at the many gaudy articles of wearing apparel which cunning shop-keepers have spread out to tempt their fancy. As soon as "the crop" is disposed of, and a negro farmer has money in his pocket, his first act is to pay the merchant from whom he obtained his supplies during the year. . . . When they have settled up all their accounts, and arranged for future bills, they go and hunt up their wives. . . . They then proceed to a dining saloon, call for an expensive meal, always finishing with pies, puddings, or preserves and often with all three. When they have satisfied their appetite, they go first to the dry-goods stores. Here, as in other shops, they are met by obsequious white men, who conduct them at once to a back or side room, with which most of the stores are supplied. . . . After diligent inquiry . . . I discovered that since the war, unprincipled store-keepers, some of them northern men, have established the custom of giving the country negroes, who come to buy, as much whiskey as they wish to drink. This is done in the back rooms I have mentioned, and when the unfortunate black men and women are deprived of half their wits by the vile stuff which is served to them, they are induced to purchase all sorts of useless and expensive goods.

In their soberest moments average colored women have a passion for bright, colored dresses which amounts almost to madness, and, on such occasions . . . they never stop buying until their money is exhausted. Their husbands have little or no control over them, and are obliged, whether they will or not, to see most of their hard earnings squandered upon an unserviceable jacket, or flimsy bonnet, or many-colored shawl. I saw one black woman spend upward of thirty dollars on millinery goods. . . .

Hearing the colored cotton-growers were to have a meeting that night, a few miles from the city, and being invited to attend, I embraced the opportunity. Some thirty persons were assembled, and as I entered the room, I heard them chanting—

"Sing yo' praises! Bless de Lam!
Getting plenty money!
Cotton's gwine up—'deed it am!
People, ain't it funny?
Chorus.—Rise, shine, give God the glory. [Repeat glory]
Don't you tink hit's gwine to rain?
Maybe was, a little;
Maybe one ole hurricane
'Slilin' in de kittle!—*Chorus.*
Craps done fail in Egypt lan'—
Say so in de papers;
Maybe little slight o' hand
'Mong de specerlaters.—*Chorus.* . . .
Fetch me 'roun' dat tater juice!

In the Cage

Stop dat sassy grinnin';
Turn dat stopper clear a-loose—
Keep yo' eye a skinnin'.—*Chorus.*
Here's good luck to Egypt lan'!
Hope she ain't a-failin'!
Hates to see my fellerman
Straddle ob de pailin'!—*Chorus.*"

The church filled up. The meeting was well conducted, and measures taken to protect cotton-raisers, showing that these people, newly-made free, and uneducated, were looking to their interest. . . .

From William Wells Brown, *My Southern Home*, pp. 167–170, 172–176.

Ernst von Hesse-Wartegg sailing down the Mississippi, and on the Louisiana plantations, saw blacks amusing themselves and others in a variety of ways. In the selection below he relates some of his experiences.

I saw young mulatto women in the section of the ship reserved for ladies. I also saw many old, decaying Negro women, with pipes in their mouths, their bottles on the floor, smoking and drinking and cackling. I could not understand their speech so I asked the Captain what language they were speaking. "It is French," he said. "But I don't understand any of it!" I replied. "That doesn't surprise me," he answered. "You need black ears to understand Plantation French!"

Perhaps half of the Negroes in this part of Louisiana speak only French and can barely understand a word of English. It is a curious dialect, which has lost complete touch with the original language. . . .

We tried to become acquainted with these people. There was among them a very beautiful black woman. . . . Her big eyes sparkled with a certain radiance. Her full, half-opened mouth had an odd but delightful appearance. She wore a bright green hat and long glass earrings. A scanty scarlet corset enclosed her breast. Her arms were bare and covered with cheap glass pearls and bracelets. Her name was Calypso—that was all we could find out. A dozen questions in Parisian French were answered only with smiles and shrugs.

I soon gave up my efforts to penetrate the mysteries of the Negro tongue. Not so my friend. He obviously had greater talents to understand, even though he spoke not a word of French. He apparently found a language which he, like the black, hot-blooded Calypso, could understand better than French. They stood outside together in the dark, so that both of them appeared black. But what language did they speak? Parisian it may have been, but it was not French! . . .

The laughter and jokes of the blacks are impossible to describe. . . . One woman who was irritated by the Negroes on the bank of a river cried: "O you damn Niggers! O you dirty Niggers! Oh! Oh! Oh!" The Negroes on the bank clapped their hands and stamped their feet in laughter. . . .

Not long thereafter we saw the young black boys of the steamboat giggling together and breaking out in loud laughter whenever a white person smiled at them. One of them came to the Governor (who was also an owner of great Louisiana sugar plantations) and asked if he could work for him. "I can work on your plantation in the Summer, massa," he said. "I serves there more than on the Steamer, and I am satisfied to be a roustabout." "You damned Nigger" another said as he hit him softly in the ribs, "do's do Govana Lana" (that is the

In the Cage

Governor of Louisiana)! "Dat's all same to me!" replied the first one. "I dono ke, if h'is Govana o no, is money I's vont— I dono ke!" And with that he shrugged his shoulders and strutted off nonchalantly with an aristocratic air that astonished us. But so are they all, these proud Negroes, these colored gentlemen of the South! . . .

Several stonethrows from the master's house there are a few dozen small houses. They are all in the same style and appear to be built the same size. . . . The houses are clustered together. . . . A large building is a hospital, another is a church. This is the so-called "Quarter," the dwellings of the plantation Negro, the former slaves. Here they live with their families, their children, outside behind the houses, around the rim of the fields. The Negroes show a certain pride in their dwellings, their "home," and they furnish them in strange ways with all sorts of little pictures, gay paper, old pieces of furniture, shreds of curtains and carpetry. The wives are outside on the plantation with their husbands, and only here and there one sees an old Negro woman in a brightly colored dress, a turban on her head, sitting in front of the doors. Here is a "Mammy," who feeds her small, dirty, naked grandchild. On her knees she holds a bowl with perhaps some mash (pap), and the small rascal takes it and allows it to run out of his mouth. . . . Small, but even so the young black pigs imitate the old ones and sometimes have them as playmates. The old sometimes even run with them under the house, and only here and there is there an accident . . . an idyllic picture. Further on, a couple of fine, pitch black youngsters sit on the edge of a ditch crab fishing. Since birth they have never had a stitch of clothing on their bodies and now sit calmly in the nude in the ditches. Their fishing tackle consists of a cord, with a little piece of meat tied onto it. A crab takes the bite, so they pull him quickly out of the slimy water. In this manner the rascals spend their childhood, until they are big enough to go into the field and cut sugar cane. Then they pass their juvenile leisures on to their younger brothers....

It appears somewhat strange when a couple of young Negro women meet black workers on the way home from their jobs.... It is a precious, cheerful sight. Everyone flirts with one another, tossing amorous glances and other signs of love. In the ballroom they caper and shake as they dance a cotillion. These young, fresh plantation Negro women are in lovely form. Nature, the warm sun of the South, has given them a certain sensuousness. They take it not like the whites, as a vice, but rather in such an enticing manner as to set fire to the cold hearts of the half-brown Creole planters....

From Ernst von Hesse-Wartegg, *Mississippi-Fahrten*, pp. 254–256, 262–263, 268–270.

James Bryce viewed the evolution of social classes among blacks in cities such as Baltimore, Atlanta, and New Orleans as one result of the progress of the race. Yet he seemed to think it unfortunate that there was no social intercourse between upper-class blacks and their white neighbors, and that these same blacks had been condemned by whites to perpetual inferiority.

As respects their intelligence, their character, their habits of industry, the coloured people are in most States making real progress. It is a progress very unequal as regards the different regions of the country, and perhaps may not extend to some districts of the so-called Black Belt, which stretches from the

In the Cage

coast of South Carolina across the Gulf States. It is most evident in the matter of education, less evident as respects religion and the influence of literature. Its economic results are perceptible in the accumulation of property by city workmen, in the acquisition of small farms by rural cultivators, in the slow, but steady, increase in the number of coloured people in the professions of medicine, law, and literature. Were it accompanied by a growth of good feeling between whites and negroes, and a more natural and friendly intercourse between them in business and in social matters, the horizon would be bright.... This intercourse is, however, conspicuously absent. The progress of the coloured people has been accompanied by the evolution of social classes within their own body. Wealthy and educated negroes, such as one may now find in cities like Baltimore, Louisville, Richmond, Atlanta, and New Orleans, have come to form a cultured group, who are looked up to by the poorer class. But these cultured groups are as little in contact with their white neighbours as are the humblest coloured labourers, perhaps even less so. No prospect is open to them, whatever wealth or culture they may acquire, of finding an entrance into white society, and they are made to feel in a thousand ways that they belong to a caste condemned to perpetual inferiority. Their spokesmen in the press have latterly so realized the position as to declare that they do not seek social equality with the whites, that they are quite willing to build up a separate society of their own, and seek neither intermarriage nor social intercourse, but that what they do ask is equal opportunity in business, the professions, and politics, equal recognition of the worth of their manhood, and a discontinuance of the social humiliations they are now compelled to endure....

From James Bryce, *The American Commonwealth*, II, 528–529.

Iza Duffus Hardy attended a black wedding held in a laundry at Orlando, Florida. When things became dull a Negro could always, it seemed, go to a wedding or a funeral. Whites, whether outsiders or natives, generally took more interest in funerals than in weddings, but Miss Hardy, a novelist, chose the latter.

"There's to be a nigger wedding in the laundry to-night" is our evening news. . . .

The laundry—a little wooden cottage, outside of which we are accustomed to see the various articles of our wardrobe flapping in the breeze—is modestly secluded. The entrance door leads us straight into a small room, which is so crowded from wall to wall with our coloured brethern and sisters that we cannot see how it is furnished, or whether there is any furniture at all beyond a bed, on which some of the wedding-guests have deposited their bonnets and shawls. . . . The guests all fell back and formed a circle round the bridal couple—and a very young couple they were! the bride being only about fourteen, though looking a little older.

She was clad in white muslin, with an enormous wreath, that made her look top-heavy, especially as her black face was modestly inclined on one side, turned away from the bridegroom, until it nearly rested on her shoulder.

He was attired in a beautiful brown velvet coat; he had on a pair of the biggest white gloves I ever saw; and the attitude in which he kept his left hand, laid upon his heart, with the fingers outspread, displayed the extravagant waste of ma-

In the Cage

terial in these gloves, which extended about an inch beyond the tips of his fingers. The bridegroom was as black as the bride, he could not well have been blacker and he looked rather more sheepish than she did; she in spite of her downcast face, seemed inclined to giggle until the minister—also as black as coal—clad in as glossy broadcloth and as snowy cravat as his white brethren—stepped into place, and began the service.

The only peculiarity I observed about the ceremony was that the baptismal names were omitted, and the important questions were put simply—"O man, wilt thou have this woman? and "O woman, wilt thou have this man?" The service over, the minister dropped the solemnity he had decorously assumed for the occasion; and his good-humoured ebony face broke into a broad smile that beamed from ear to ear, as he waved his hand with an air of impartial invitation to everybody, and suggested generally that they should "Salute the bride!"

Thereupon ensued a general kissing match. . . .

From Iza Duffus Hardy, *Oranges and Alligators: Sketches of South Florida Life* (London: Ward and Downey, 1886), pp. 92–97.

Samuel Barrows concluded after visiting a dozen or so cities that the social conditions of Negroes were improving markedly across the South, especially in the urban areas. Here was fresh evidence, he thought, of a new and laudable spirit among blacks.

With the purchase of homes and the accumulation of property, the colored people are gradually changing their condition of living. It is seen at its worst in the miserable one-room cabins of the country districts, and in the alley population of such cities as Washington and Baltimore. In the Black Belt, the typical home is a rude log cabin, without windows, and with one door and a stick chimney. The door is usually kept open during the day, in fair weather, to admit light, which at night is furnished by a pine knot. Into such cabins a whole family is frequently crowded. In Alabama, I heard of twenty-five persons living in three rooms. The genial climate permits a good deal of outdoor living, and the babies need no sand yards to be made for their benefit. The mother sets them out on the ground, and lets them roll. Bad as the one-room cabin is, it is not so bad as the tenement houses in the slums of the great cities. The Negro, too, can rival the Chinaman in practicing economy. Sixty cents a week, spent in pork, meal, and syrup, will keep him alive. At Athens, Georgia, a colored man testified in court that "a man can live mighty good on thirty-five cents a week."

The social evolution of the Negro can be seen even by the casual observer. A house with a window, even if closed with a shutter, is an improvement over one which has only a door, and a double-room house is an improvement over one with a single room. The influence of new ambition is seen later in the growth of the cabin into a two-story house, and at the dinner table in a more varied bill of fare. At Pensacola, where the wages received for loading vessels are unusually good, the laborer is prosperous, and a colored censor said, deprecatingly: "They live 'most too high as far as eating is concerned; some of them eat as fine food as millionaires." A Methodist bishop told me that in Montgomery $24,000 was spent annually on excursions. The Negro is surely learning how to earn his dollar, but he has not learned how to spend it. He is buying his experience dear. The patent-medicine vender and the

In the Cage

sewing machine peddler draw no distinctions in regard to color, and the black often insists on spending his money as foolishly as his white brother. In one little country cabin stood a wooden clock worth about $1.25, for which a woman had paid $10, giving new sarcasm to the proverb that "time is money." Yet the Negro's knowledge of what a dollar will buy is growing....

The social progress of the Negro is well illustrated by two historic cities,—the federal capital at Washington and the former capital of the Confederacy at Montgomery.... In Montgomery, under the guidance of Dr. Dorsette, a colored physician and a respected citizen, I had an opportunity to see the homes of the colored people at their best. In some of the streets, the whites occupy one side, and the blacks the other. Occasionally the colors alternate, like the squares on a checkerboard.... The interiors of these homes, especially of the younger and more progressive people, are comfortably and tastefully furnished. The rooms are as high as those of their white neighbors, well carpeted and papered, while the piano or the cabinet organ suggest loftier musical tastes than that of the plantation banjo....

From Samuel J. Barrows, "What the Southern Negro Is Doing for Himself," pp. 808–809, 813–815.

Charles Dudley Warner, in the course of a horseback tour of Virginia, North Carolina, and Tennessee in 1888, joined local whites in viewing the antics of "a typical nigger" at Asheville, North Carolina. To see a Negro "clown"—in this instance, "Happy John"— was of great interest to outside observers in the South. Warner (1829–1900), the well-known novelist, essayist, and editor, was born at Plainfield, Massachusetts, and educated at Hamilton College and the University of Pennsylvania.

The evening gayety of the town was well distributed. When we descended to the Court-House Square, a great crowd had collected, black, white, and yellow, about a high platform, upon which four glaring torches lighted up the novel scene, and those who could read might decipher this legend on a standard at the back of the stage:—

HAPPY JOHN.
ONE OF THE SLAVES OF WADE HAMPTON.
COME AND SEE HIM!

Happy John, who occupied the platform with Mary, a "bright" yellow girl, took the comical view of his race, which was greatly enjoyed by his audience. His face was blackened to the proper color of the stage-darky, and he wore a flaming suit of calico, the trousers and coat striped longitudinally according to Punch's idea of "Uncle Sam," the coat a swallow-tail bound and faced with scarlet, and a bell-crowned white hat. The conceit of a colored Yankee seemed to tickle all colors in the audience amazingly. Mary, the "bright" woman (this is the universal designation of the light mulatto), was a pleasing but bold yellow girl, who wore a natty cap trimmed with scarlet, and had the assured or pert manner of all traveling sawdust performers.

"Oh, yes," exclaimed a bright woman in the crowd, "Happy John was sure enough one of Wade Hampton's slaves, and he's right good looking when he's not blackened up."

Happy John sustained the promise of his name, by spontaneous gayety and enjoyment of the fleeting moment; he had a glib tongue and a ready, rude wit, and talked to his audience with a delicious mingling of impudence, deference, and pa-

In the Cage

tronage, commenting upon them generally, administering advice and correction in a strain of humor that kept his hearers in a pleased excitement. He handled the banjo and the guitar alternately, and talked all the time when he was not singing. Mary (how much harder featured and brazen a woman is in such a position than a man of the same calibre!) sang, in an untutored treble, songs of sentiment, often risque, in solo and in company with John, but with a cold indifferent air, in contrast to the rollicking enjoyment of her comrade. The favorite song, which the crowd compelled her to repeat, touched lightly the uncertainties of love, expressed in the falsetto pathetic refrain:—

"Mary's gone away wid de coon."

All this, with the moon, the soft summer night, the mixed crowd of darkies and whites, the stump eloquence of Happy John, the singing, the laughter, the flaring torches, made a wild scene. The entertainment was quite free, with a "collection" occasionally during the performance.

What most impressed us, however, was the turning to account by Happy John of the "nigger" side of the black man as a means of low comedy, and the enjoyment of it by all the people of color. They appeared to appreciate as highly as anybody the comic element in themselves, and Happy John had emphasized it by deepening his natural color and exaggerating the "nigger" peculiarities. I presume none of them analyzed the nature of his infectious gayety, nor thought of the pathos that lay so close to it, in the fact of his recent slavery, and the distinction of being one of Wade Hampton's niggers, and the melancholy mirth of this light-hearted race's burlesque of itself. . . .

From Charles Dudley Warner, *On Horseback: A Tour in Virginia, North Carolina, and Tennessee* (Boston: Houghton Mifflin, 1889), pp. 112–117.

Mifflin Wistar Gibbs, born in 1823 in Philadelphia, was at various times anti-slavery lecturer, carpenter, contractor, merchant, railroad builder, and superintendent of mines in California in the years immediately following the discovery of gold. He witnessed Reconstruction in Florida and actively took part in it in Arkansas. He held various local and federal appointments, including that of United States Consul to Madagascar. Here Gibbs writes of the kind of "industrial fair" Negroes organized and held throughout the South, as well as participating in those sponsored by whites. The Negroes exhibited, among other things, their skills as artisans and craftsmen.

... The directors of the World's Exposition held at New Orleans, Louisiana, in 1884, gave a pressing invitation to Afro-Americans to furnish exhibits of their production from farm, shop, and home. The late B. K. Bruce, having been created Chief Director, appointed commissioners for the various States to solicit and obtain the best specimens of handicraft in their respective localities for "The Department of Colored Exhibits." ...

I therefore accepted, and proceeded to canvass my State urging the great opportunity offered to show our progress in industry and culture, on the fields of nature or within the realms of art. The movement was a novel one, and the leading colored men and women in the different sections of the State had much to do to awaken the interest that resulted in a very commendable showing.

In the Cage

One of the specialties of these expositions was that designated as "Emancipation Day," or colored people's day, for the two-fold purpose of directing the attention of the general public to race advancement, and inducing a larger attendance of the class directly concerned, and thereby stimulate race pride for greater achievements. With some of our brethren this appointment of a particular day seemed derogatory to their claim of recognition and equality of citizenship, and evoked considerable discussion. In this I thought some of us were unduly sensitive. Where intention can be ascertained it should largely govern our estimate of human action. This exposition was not only open each and every day to our people, but we were constantly invited, and the few who attended were most cordially treated and our exhibits were properly placed without distinction.

The directors of the exposition were gentlemen known to be most liberal in their dealings with us, and regretted the small attendance, remarking that aside from our patronage, the exhibits would be beneficial as object lessons, educating and inspiring, and proposed a day—"Colored People's Day." It was not unlike in design and effect "Emancipation Day" at the Minneapolis Exposition, where noted colored leaders from various States attended and spoke, and were not impressed that it was derogatory to the race. . . .

Industrial fairs, promulgated and held by the colored people in different Southern States, have been exceedingly beneficial and cannot be too often repeated. Several have occurred at Pine Bluff, Arkansas, on the extensive race and fair grounds owned by Mr. Wiley Jones, who, with Dr. J. H. Smith, Ferdinand Harris, and other prominent colored men of the State by executive ability, tact and judgment made them a success. . . .

Life and Leisure

In affairs of this character the comingling of the substantial and best element of the white race, their liberal subscriptions and fraternal endeavor, give impetus and valuable assistance, emphasizing the fact along the lines of a higher industrial advancement that they are in hearty sympathy. We cannot too often have these object evidences of our progress. They speak loud and convincing far beyond oral announcement the most eloquent. It stimulates the farmer to extra exertion and more careful measures for increase of quality and quantity of his crop; it insures the artisan and mechanic for his best handiwork, and welcomes articles of the product of our cultured and refined women from the realms of the home. We need this continued stimulus, shut out as we are from most of the higher industries, the incentive born of contact, and which promotes rivalry, to us is denied; hence our inspiration must be inborn and unceasing. . . .

A feature attraction at these fairs has been the drill and martial bearing of our military companies, for while jubilant in the "pride and pomp and circumstance of glorious war," the measure of praise for precision of maneuver of the soldier is only excelled by commendation for his bravery in action. The colored citizens took quiet pride and much interest in these companies and were saddened when many were commanded by the State authorities to disband. The motives which conspired and demanded their dissolution were not commendable, but ungrateful, for the Negro soldier in every war of the Republic has been valorous, loyal, and self-denying, and has abundantly earned a reputation for discipline and obedience to every military requirement. . . .

From Mifflin Gibbs, *Shadow and Light: An Autobiography* (Washington, D.C.: published by the author, 1902), pp. 196–200, 206–210.

In the Cage

Timothy Shaler Williams (1862–1930), born in Ithaca, New York, was a graduate of Cornell. He began work on a newspaper, served as private secretary to two New York governors (1889–1894), and had his main career with the Brooklyn Rapid Transit System as secretary-treasurer, vice-president, president, and director (1895–1923). Because "the conditions of their life" were not such as to acquaint Negro children "with the sports usually enjoyed by other children," Williams was impressed with their ability to have fun with their own games. He was apparently unaware of Negro participation in such sports as football and baseball, which was occurring when Williams visited the South in 1903.

The little negro girls and boys who live in the towns or on the plantations of the South enjoy their games and sports quite as heartily as do any healthy and hearty girls and boys; but the conditions of their life are not such as to make them acquainted with the sports usually enjoyed by other children. If you were to ask one of these curly-haired, black-faced school-children of the South what games he played, he would be very likely to roll the whites of his eyes at you, and his teeth would glisten, while he answered: "Don't play any, sah!"

Most of the games which colored children play are "ring" games. These seem to furnish an outlet for the melody in the negro soul, for nearly all are accompanied by singing and dancing. The songs are extremely simple, and of course vary with every game. Very curious rhymes are sometimes thrown together. The tunes in all the games differ very little. . . . It is comical to see a circle of these happy little creatures moving hands, feet, and mouths in perfect harmony, and giving rapt attention to the game.

"Hop like de rabbit, ho!" is a favorite ring game. One player enters the circle made by the others, and chooses a partner. In a queer embrace the two clasp each other's shoulders and jump round and round. Meanwhile those in the ring, clapping their hands and beating with their feet, sing these words:

"Hop like de rabbit, ho!
Hop like de rabbit, ho boy!
De rabbit skip,
De rabbit hop,
De rabbit eat my turnip top!
Hop like de rabbit, ho!
Hop like de rabbit, ho boy! . . ."

"Shouting Josephine" is the odd name given to a peculiar game. Two of the players stand inside a ring formed by the others, and the following dialogue ensues between them:

"Josephine!"
"Ma'am?"
"Have you had your breakfast?"
"Yes, ma'am."
"How much?"
"Spoonful."
"Josephine, do you want to shout?"
"Yes, ma'am."
"How long?"
"An hour and a half."
"Then shout, Josephine!"

And so Josephine shouts as loudly as she can, and with her hands resting on her hips and her elbows bent, dances gracefully and in perfect time with her lively shouting. Meanwhile the others beat time with their hands. . . .

In the Cage

Christmas is the greatest holiday among the negroes. It lasts a whole week with them, and during this time some of them seem to think it wrong to do any work. The children believe firmly in the existence of Santa Claus. They hang their stockings beside the fireplace, and on Christmas morning imagine that they see his footprints on the hearth. One would think that old Saint Nick would leave a great many gifts in such a home, it is so easy for him to climb up and down the chimney; but he doesn't leave very many; so it is fortunate that the black children are satisfied with an orange, an apple, a doll, or a stick of candy. . . .

From Timothy Shaler Williams, "The Sports of Negro Children," *Saint Nicholas*, XXX (September 1903), 1004–1007.

Clifton Johnson (1865–1940), of Hadley, Massachusetts, wrote travel accounts for a living. He made his most extensive Southern trip from St. Augustine to Virginia during 1903–1904. Johnson was not at all impressed with Negro living conditions in the South—you could always tell a black's house by its dirt and dilapidation, he thought. Yet when it came to leisure, blacks displayed zest and "simplehearted enjoyment."

One effect of the prevalence of the negro in the South is to make it a land of cabins. To be sure the poor whites help materially to swell the number of humble dwellings of this class, but in the main they are the homes of the blacks. You see them scattered in groups or singly over the face of the country in the rural districts, and you see them huddling on the borders of every city—shabby and unpainted, all about the same size, and most of them barren and depressing. The rustic cabins often gather near the "big house" just as they did before the war, sometimes flanking it with a line on either side, sometimes only on one side in a double row, sometimes built along the road that turns into the plantation from the main highway.

It is an aphorism that you can tell a "nigger's place" by its dirt and dilapidation. Poverty, ignorance, and lack of pride or ambition are general among the colored people. They simply exist, and the amenities of life are nearly altogether disregarded. However, those who own homes are very apt to make improvements and to take at least rudimentary care of their premises. The commonest type of the rustic cabin consists of one room within, the main walls and a shed-room attachment. At one end of the house, outside, is a big chimney, sometimes of brick, sometimes of clay-daubed sticks laid up cob-house fashion. Log cabins are numerous and are still built, but they are not very lasting and need a good deal of repairing and are gradually becoming obsolete. Double cabins are occasionally seen, though they are not always occupied by two families. Two households under the same roof are bound to quarrel, and the arrangement is not satisfactory. They quickly forget their disputes, and may be on intimate terms within an hour of a genuine row, yet things are constantly occurring where one party or the other thinks its rights are infringed on.

The main room of a negro cabin is certain to have an open fire-place, and the leaping flames on chilly evenings fill the apartment with cheerful light. Two beds and a trundle-bed are likely to be included in the room furnishings, and if these do not suffice for sleeping accommodations, some of the family bunk on the floor. The ventilation is poor, the cabin is usually crowded, and it smells of eating and sleeping. The only advantage the negroes have over the dwellers in the worst tenements of our cities is that they spend most of their lives outside their hovels in the open fields.

"A nigger always has a dog, a poor nigger has two, and a desperately poor nigger has half a dozen."

Hounds and coon dogs are preferred, but any sort of a cur is acceptable. The dogs sleep in the house with the rest of the family, and they steal not a little of the household food. They are kicked and cuffed and abused, yet a dog prefers a colored master to a white one. . . .

The negroes enter into their pleasures with zest and simplehearted enjoyment. The young men take particular delight in balls and "treatin' the ladies." Evening visiting is common, and employers say that "you can work a nigger hard all day and he'll be walking off afterwards to some of the other cabins and be out till mid-night." It is this propensity which in part accounts for the numerous paths through fields and woodlands which network the country. Such paths are a sign of a pastoral, primitive people, and they never fail to be beautiful to the eyes and suggestive to the imagination. It is by these paths that the news travels, and you can depend on the negroes knowing promptly all that is going on within a radius of fifteen miles. . . .

From Clifton Johnson, *Highways and Byways of the South* (New York: Macmillan, 1904), pp. 334–337, 347–348.

Paul Auguste Marie Adam (1862–1920) was a Frenchman who won a considerable reputation for his historical and sociological novels. Publication of his first naturalist work, *Chairmolle* (1885), led to

Life and Leisure

his being prosecuted. In 1899, with *La Force*, he began a series of novels depicting French life during the period 1800–1830. He arrived in the United States in April 1904. In the selection below he describes the living conditions of Negroes in St. Louis and around New Orleans as lamentably poor. Yet the blacks, particularly in St. Louis, managed to remain cheerful and, indeed, on occasion to have a drunken good time.

The colored people live on the right bank. This is their city [St. Louis], their hell. . . . Certain of these damned people seem to be tinted with blue ink. Many of them appear to be exact models of our artistic bronze statues. They are sad devils, dressed in checkered shirts with old tattered overcoats and bagged pants. Their lamentable cigarettes are hanging between the rims of their large lips. For the most part, thin and flat, they seem to be gnawed by sadness and hatred. . . .

The most unfortunate ones grumble in the basements which serve as a house for them. Ten or twenty sleep on straw mattresses, separated by parallel walls. A solitary gas burner flickers under the common arch of these rooms. . . . Those who are not as poor live in brick tenements located on a slope. Against the façade are hung . . . long staircases that lead from the twisted corridor which passes in front of the parlor right up to the poorly plastered apartments of the boarding house. There are two stinking rooms decorated with political posters. They generally contain a tiny broken stove, a table of wood, an oil lamp, suspended, and two or three chairs. Also an iron bed and a zinc pot with its base on a tripod. One finds there also a trunk decorated with tinsel. This hovel is rented for $10.50 per month. The negro who is able to assume this expense almost immediately finds a girl friend ready to share his luck. She may be a slovenly slut with a full bosom, with

In the Cage

her head ornamented with ribbons, or she may be a bony youth, thin about the neck, whose cervical wool is twisted, knotted into three centimeter mats at the longest and adorned with green ribbon. No matter which, the son of Shem nourishes a female companion and hence becomes conscious of his dignity. He talks about her and their home in so comical a fashion that his remarks sometimes become jokes in the little, illustrated Yankee gazettes.

Talkative, indolent, quarrelsome, basically good, amoral, naive and sensitive, the negro woman can be compared to our old type of landlady, who was dear to the humanists of the 1850's. . . . In reality the negro woman is a poor housewife and a fruitful mother. Behind her skirts she drags an ensemble of little negro children. . . . Their smiling faces peek out from all the holes in the alley-ways of the special quarters reserved for them and they lean out from all the attic windows. One can understand the American terror before this African prolification. . . .

When drunk, the negroes become lewd fools. If by chance they then meet a woman or girl who is white, they do not always hesitate to commit *the crime*. And that the Yankees do not pardon. . . .

Now recently in St. Louis where the negroes usually hold their dances, the police had to close down the place because the conduct became uproarious. . . . Accompanied by detectives, I witnessed the negroes capering. The odor of unclean underwear didn't bother the dark gentlemen. One had a hat on his crumpled wool. There was a woman, skinny and puny, especially around the neck, but large around the hips and feet. This one was dirty and friendly, half nude, under a red blouse and a colorless skirt. These Devils and Jezebels moved around for about a half hour doing a square dance. . . . The heavy smoke of the cigarettes clouded the room full of round, grimacing faces. From some of them a sort of fluid was disengaged which was startling. . . . Soon the frenzy overtook them. One woman flirted with her necklace in the middle of the floor. It was something bestial. Men and women moved around like animals. . . . It took less than a quarter of an hour for these so-called civilized beings to become once again brutes, forgetful of their dresses and jackets. They were like monkeys in a zoo who suddenly abandon their posture and return once again to four paws while still in their colonel's uniforms.

If the police are not present to prevent the strip-teasing, the dancing spurred on by alcohol continues. . . .

From Paul Auguste Marie Adam, *Vues d'Amérique* (8th ed., Paris: Société d'Editions Littéraires et Artistiques, 1906), pp. 150–162.

Thomas Jesse Jones was born in Wales in 1873, came to the United States in 1884, and attended Washington and Lee University in Virginia, Marietta College in Ohio, Union Theological Seminary, and Columbia University, where he received a Ph.D. in 1904. He was a member of the faculty at Hampton Institute from 1902 to 1909; a statistician in the United States Census Bureau from 1909 to 1912; a specialist in education for the United States Bureau of Education from 1912 to 1919; and director of research for the Phelps-Stokes Fund beginning in 1913. His studies of Negro education for the Phelps-Stokes Fund and the U.S. Bureau of Education won him wide recognition. Jones conducted a study of tuberculosis among blacks in 1905–1906, and presented his findings to the second annual meeting of the National Association for the Study and Prevention of Tuberculosis in Washington in the spring of 1906. He saw environmental, rather than racial, factors accounting for the prevalence of the disease among Negroes, and called for urgent measures to combat the problem which threatened whites as well as blacks.

While it is well known that this disease is quite prevalent among negroes, few if any of us know the extent of this prevalence. . . .

The death rate for the colored people is from two to seven times that of any other race, with the exception of the Irish, whose death rate is about two-thirds that of the colored. As to the extent of consumption, . . . the negro death rate is far greater than that of any other people. . . .

The danger to the nation of tuberculosis among negroes . . . is further increased by the proximity of the colored race to the other races. . . .

In the cities of the South . . . the death rate of the negroes from consumption is two and three times that of the whites. . . .

The most striking fact . . . is the high death rate for colored children. While the rate for adults of the colored race is about twice that of the whites, the rate for colored children under fifteen years is over seven times that of the white children. The greatest mortality for colored is between the ages 16–44 years; that for the whites is at the ages 65 years and over. . . .

One class is inclining to ascribe the prevalence entirely to racial characteristics and the other class ascribing it altogether to environment. . . . The extent to which the racial element enters into the cause of tuberculosis has not yet been determined. . . . Few of us realize the great difficulties under which this race struggles. In our cities they live in the poorest houses. Even those who can pay for better homes are often compelled to occupy unsanitary dwellings. A third of the race is yet living in one-room cabins. The possible danger of such an existence is indicated by a fact which I discovered last year in a so-called two-room cabin. Two-thirds of the space in one room was filled by a stove and a table, one-half of the other room was filled by a bed. In this house thirteen children had been born since the war and twelve of the thirteen had died when they were children.

Almost one-half of the race is illiterate. The consequence of such a degree of ignorance upon the health of the race is far greater than we can realize. One ignorant father whom I know has infected his wife and nine children. Seven of these children cannot walk. The man is now dead, but the consumptive mother, at the brink of the grave, continues to wash for the white people of that city and her two sons work in barber shops. The unusual and heroic struggle for an education under adverse conditions is often also a potent cause of consumption among colored students.

The economic disadvantages of the race develop an environment which contributes much to the increase of mortality from consumption. It is well known that the majority of tuberculosis cases of all races are from the laboring and servant classes, and from that part whose weekly wage is $10 a week and under. . . . When it is remembered that over 80 per cent of the negro race belongs to these classes, their economic disadvantages assume proportions which totally eclipse any racial disposition. . . .

I have searched diligently for any evidence of activity in behalf of the negro consumptive. The result of the search is very meager . . . because the states and cities and colored physicians have neglected to answer my request for information, and . . . because the efforts in behalf of the negro are "few and far between." . . . Up to this time very little has been done for the colored consumptive aside from some free dispensaries and an outdoor department in connection with the State Insane Asylum for Negroes at Petersburg, Virginia. . . . The 1,700 colored physicians of the land must be enlisted in the cause. The negro conferences held annually at Atlanta, Hampton, Tuskegee, and other schools for negroes must be informed of the ravages of disease upon their people, and urged to speak to them about the disease. Southern states and cities must be aroused . . . so that they may provide hospital and sanatorium facilities open to negroes. . . .

From Thomas Jesse Jones, "Tuberculosis Among the Negroes," *Transactions* of the Second Annual Meeting of the National Association for the Study and Prevention of Tuberculosis (Washington, D.C., May 1906), II, 97–100, 103–107.

Sir Harry Johnston scrutinized the dress of Southern Negroes of all classes and concluded that most blacks were as well dressed as the average white American.

Who that visited Sierra Leone, say, ten years ago, or Liberia at the present day, can have failed to contrast unfavourably the Negro in high white collar, black coat and tight waistcoat, trousers, patent leather boots, and an ugly black "chimney pot" or hard-straw hat . . . with the Muhammadan people passing by, aptly clothed in costumes that were cheap, cool, dignified, and yet very picturesque.

On the other hand, I am quite ready to admit that the latest developments of European fashions for men suit the Negro's appearance remarkably well—the panama or straw hat, the Tyrolese or squash jacket, fairly loose, straight trousers on his well-shaped body. . . . All over the States now Negro men from the artisan to the college professor are as a rule not only as well dressed as the average white American, but are nicely dressed, so that they present nothing to gird at. . . .

Dr. Booker Washington and his sons dress well in appropriate clothes that are of good cut. I am almost inclined to hope and believe that he possesses no frock-coat and silk hat in his wardrobe. I certainly trust that he and other leaders of the Negro people will not fail to inveigh against these garments, which only look well on two white men out of ten, and never look other than ugly and inappropriate on a person of dark complexion.

But it is in regard to the Negro women of civilization who are not Muhammadans that some special effort should be made in the way of dictating a law of taste and suitability in costume. . . .

At a large evening party which took place at Tuskegee whilst I was there, I passed in review some two hundred female costumes. Only a few were tasteful. Some negresses of almost black skin came in dresses of snowy white, or cream colour, which simply made them unendurably grotesque. Others were in pale blue, bright pink, or vivid green. On the other hand, those that dressed . . . in varying shades of brown, dark blue, or . . . greenish blue; in grey-green . . . looked exceedingly nice. . . .

From Sir Harry Johnston, *The Negro in the New World*, pp. 413–414.

Arrah B. Evarts, a psychiatrist, was assigned to the wards for Negro females at the Government Hospital for the Insane, Washington, D.C. There, just before World War I, she examined the mental condition of a number of Southern Negro women, and concluded that insanity was "on the increase in the colored race" (James Bryce had said the same thing thirty years before). The disorder that especially interested Dr. Evarts because of its prevalence among blacks was dementia precox.

We are beginning to think of insanity as a failure on the part of the individual to adjust to the demands of his environment. In the upward spring of any race it is inevitable that many individuals will fall because of their inability to change with changing conditions. With this in mind, we can understand why insanity should be on the increase in the colored race, for of it is being demanded an adjustment much harder to make, when we consider the factors to be used in the problem, than any other race has yet been called upon to attempt. . . .

Dementia precox is essentially a deteriorating psychosis. It is protean in its manifestations, every case being a case by itself. . . .

Because the colored patient already lives upon a plane much lower than his white neighbor, actual deterioration in the individual must be differentiated from the supposed loss of a racial period he has not yet attained.

As the psychosis exists in the colored race, it differs in no essentials from the picture so well known. Its etiology is the same. The race, because of the vicissitudes of its history, is peculiarly prone to this form of mental trouble. The last 100 admissions to the female colored receiving service of the Government Hospital for the Insane have contained 37 cases of dementia precox. . . .

A strain of heredity is often found, although it is necessarily short, being invariably lost in the darkness of " 'fore de war."

The two great exciting causes, worry and emotional shock, are found repeatedly. Worry over the waywardness of a son or daughter; over the growing difficulty of making both ends meet; or over the very real neglect of a lazy husband are many times assigned as the cause. As to shock, acute excitement followed in specific instances: the sudden insanity of a beloved brother; the sudden death of a dear sister; and again of a mother; and in one patient, a deep catatonic stupor followed the institution of divorce proceedings in which she was named as co-respondent.

The pathology of this disease, so far as it is known, shows only evidences of a deteriorating process—lipoid degeneration, reticular degeneration of the ganglion cells, proliferation of neurogliar tissue, and Kornchen cells. It is axiomatic that race can have no bearing upon this. . . .

One woman, a greatly excited precox, with impulsive tendencies, when asked if she were crazy very promptly answered. " 'Deed, I ain't crazy! I can scrub as well as I ever could." She had for years earned her living by scrubbing floors; she had worked to within a short time of her admission, and even when still greatly excited in the hospital, she would come from her room and scrub the floors of the ward spotlessly clean. Again, and again in talking with the relatives of patients, do we hear, "I don't see how she can be crazy, she did her work as well as she ever did." Many colored servants come to us from white families and mistresses, in speaking of them, will say, "We knew she had been queer for a long time, but her work was not changed."

This is not to be interpreted as meaning that the precox patient of the colored race does not lose his ability to carry on that line of work which had been his before the onset of the psychosis, for he does lose it as absolutely as does one of a higher race. But it is a much later development in the course of the disease. Whereas in the Caucasian race this is often the earliest and perhaps for some time the only manifestation, in the Negro race, when the ability of the patient to carry on his daily task is impaired, the disease is no longer in its incipiency....

As the race exists in Africa, its sexual instincts are peculiarly unrestrained, and although they have learned much moderation, these desires are usually fully satisfied with no feeling of having done wrong. This will account for the fact that the ordinary sexual perversions are seen among precox patients of the colored race much less frequently than among those of the white race. A masturbator upon the female colored wards of the Government Hospital for the Insane is rare, and smearing of filth is much less common than upon the white wards. During the last eighteen months pleasure in self-mutilation has been seen in but one colored woman, and it was then a transient manifestation.... The experience of the writer has been that her patients usually will speak freely and unreservedly of this portion of their lives, and buried complexes do not seem to exist. Even their dreams are frankly wish fulfilling, and are as frankly described....

Dementia precox in the colored race is seen in its three chief forms, hebephrenic, catatonic, and paranoid, their relative frequency being in the order named, as is the case in the Caucasian race. The catatonic type is very pronounced. Its three cardinal symptoms, resistance, negativism, and mutism, exist in so extreme a degree that it seems impossible they could grow deeper. A foreign psychiatrist, well known by his work on schizophrenia, in a recent visit to some of the institutions for the care of the insane in Jamaica, was told that catatonic precox did not exist in their colored patients. This is far from the experience in the Government Hospital for the Insane. In the last hundred admissions there were eight cases of catatonic type, all quite severe. . . .

Dementia precox is dementia precox still, though present in an already primitive race. . . .

From Arrah B. Evarts, "Dementia Precox in the Colored Race," *Psychoanalytic Review*, I (1913–1914), 394–398, 403.

Henry H. Hazen, a dermatologist, undertook in 1914 a study of syphilis among black patients in the hospitals of Washington, D.C. Like tuberculosis, syphilis was often supposed to prevail among Negroes because of "racial characteristics." That the Negroes suffered the disease with greater frequency than whites, Hazen found, could not be denied, but the factor of class seemed to loom larger than that of race. Hazen (b. 1879) was a native of New Germantown, New Jersey. Educated at Johns Hopkins University, where he received his M.D. in 1906, he taught at Johns Hopkins (1910–1912) and Howard University (1911–1925), and was visiting dermatologist at Georgetown University Hospital, Freedmen's Hospital, and Columbia Hospital for Women, Washington, D.C. Hazen was special consultant to the Venereal Disease Division of the U.S. Public Health Service in 1918–1921 and 1924.

The subject of syphilis in the negro is one which has never been thoroughly studied and concerning which there are still many disputes, caused largely by prejudice and broad statements and the lack of careful investigation. Statistics on dis-

In the Cage

ease in the negro are very meager, and on the subject of syphilis are almost entirely lacking. The rule has been to publish personal opinions, often totally unaccompanied by evidence of any kind.

At the start it should be pointed out that there are two distinct classes of negroes, just as in every other race, and that the same rules cannot possibly apply to both classes. In the one class we have the colored people who are trying to make something of themselves, who have become responsible physicians, lawyers, teachers and businessmen, and who live a life not materially different from the same type of whites. In a considerable experience with these men I am convinced that syphilis is not more prevalent among them than among the whites, although there are no statistics to prove the point.

There is a poorer class of negroes, the class . . . who frequent the hospitals and dispensaries. . . . Even to-day their lot is none too good; as a rule, they are compelled to dwell under conditions that can breed neither good morals nor good health.

The negro springs from a southern race, and as such his sexual appetite is strong; all of his environments stimulate this appetite, and as a general rule his emotional type of religion certainly does not decrease it. Both Quillian . . . and Murell . . . state that they have never examined a negro girl over 16 years of age who was a virgin, and the leading negro physicians of Washington admit that virginity is very rare among the poorer members of their race. In fact virginity is as rare among this class of negresses as continence is among white men. . . . It should be stated, however, that some of the European cities have just as high a ratio of illegitimate births as the colored population of Washington. . . .

In 1907 Howard Fox . . . read an excellent paper on "Observations on Skin Diseases in the Negro" and his general statement "that syphilis in the negro is not only very prevalent, but more so than in the whites, is one point on which the majority of writers, my correspondents, and statistics agree," seems pretty generally accepted today. . . .

I have endeavored to ascertain the frequency with which syphilis occurs among the negroes of Washington, and my results have been substantially the same as those of Fox. . . . It is worth noting that practically all diagnoses were made by the white attending staff, and not by colored physicians. . . .

I cannot agree with the usual statement that the lesions of syphilis are less severe in the negro; I can see no difference in the course of the disease in the two races, either with respect to the clinical symptoms or to the Wassermann reaction. . . . As regards treatment, it is somewhat surprising to find that negroes attend the clinics as regularly as they do; they attend just as faithfully as do white patients, and the magic words "blood test" have much influence over them. Usually they are very docile patients: while they complain of the pain of intramuscular injections, they will come back for more, though they cannot be depended on to carry out the inunction treatment. The secret of treating them is to show them that you are taking an interest in them and also that you mean just what you say.

The prophylaxis of syphilis in the negro race is especially difficult, for it is impossible to persuade the poor variety of negro that sexual gratification is wrong, even when he is in the actively infectious stage. It is probable that sex hygiene lectures will not have the slightest effect on this type. . . . All male babies should be circumcised . . . for the purpose of avoiding local irritation which will increase the sexual appetite and for preventing infection. It is questionable whether adult negroes should be taught the use of prophylactic packages, which appear to have worked much good in certain quarters. . . .

The passage and enforcement of a strict curfew law might

do much good. The cocaine and alcohol problems are also urgent, for indulgence in either of these drugs usually stimulates sexual desire and renders the victim careless as to the means of gratification. . . .

From H. H. Hazen, "Syphilis in the American Negro," *Journal of the American Medical Association*, LXIII (August 8, 1914), 463–465.

Julian Street, a Chicago-born author, was especially interested in the "gulla" dialect prevalent among the rice plantation Negroes of the Sea Islands and the South Carolina Coast. He thought that gulla was almost a language in itself, and admitted his inability to comprehend most of it. Street (b. 1879) was principally a writer of magazine articles and novels. He toured the South in 1917.

The most extraordinary negro dialect I know is the "gulla" (sometimes spelled "gullah") of the rice plantation negroes of South Carolina and of the islands off the South Carolina and Georgia coast. I believe that the region of Charleston is headquarters for "gulla niggers," though I have heard the argot spoken as far south as Sepeloe Island, off the town of Darien, Georgia, near the Florida line. Gulla is such an extreme dialect as to be almost a language by itself. Whence it came I do not know, but I judge that it is a combination of English with the primitive tongues of African tribes, just as the dialect of old Creole negroes, in Louisiana, is a combination of African tribal tongues with French.

A Charleston lady tells me that negroes on different rice plantations—even on adjoining plantations—speak dialects which differ somewhat, and I know of my own knowledge that

Life and Leisure

thick gulla is almost incomprehensible to white persons who have not learned, by long practice, to understand it.

A lady sent a gulla negro with a message to a friend. This is the message as it was delivered: "Missis seh all dem turrah folk done come shum. Enty you dun gwine come shum?" (To get the gulla effect the sounds should be uttered very rapidly.)

Translated, this means: "Mistress says all them other folks have come to see her. Aren't you coming to see her?"

"Shum" is a good gulla word. It means all kinds of things having to do with seeing—*to see her, to see him, to see it.* Thus, "You shum, enty?" may mean, You see *him—her* or *it?* Or You see what he-she- or-*it is doing,* or *has done?* For gulla has no genders, and no tenses. "Enty" is a general question: *Aren't you? Didn't you? Isn't it?*, etc. Another common gulla word is "Buckra" which means a *white man of the upper class,* in contradistinction to a poor white. I have known a negro to refer to "de grame o' de bud," meaning the carcass, or frame, of a fowl. "Ay ain' day" means "They aren't (ain't) there."

A friend of mine who resided at Bluffton, South Carolina, has told me of an old gulla fisherman who spoke in parables.

A lady would ask him: "Have you any fish to-day?" To which, if replying affirmatively, he would answer: "Missis, de gate open"; meaning, "The door (of the "car," or fishbox) is open to you." If he had no fish he would reply: "Missis ebb-tide done tack (take) crick" signifying: "The tide has turned and it is too late to go to catch fish." This old man called whisky "muhgundy smash," the term evidently derived from some idea of the word "burgundy" combined with the word "mash." . . .

From Julian Street, *American Adventures* (New York: Century Co., 1917), pp. 242–247.

In the Cage

Rossa B. Cooley, while teaching and heading the Penn School in South Carolina, participated in most of the Negro social affairs. In the following selection she describes the Negroes' celebration of Christmas, the holiday of holidays for the blacks; their annual "Week of Song"; and their folklore society.

The gala time in the autumn when the old and young come together at the Farmers' Fair is matched in the wintertime by our Christmas celebrations. I remember one old Negro who said, "Oh yes, we has Christmas Eve, Christmas Eve's Eve and Christmas, Christmas Adam and Christmas Madam!" He was remembering the Christmas week of freedom from work and general jollification on the plantation in slavery days. We hold to about as many days of celebration in our community school. And meanwhile, throughout December, in anticipation of them, every child from the six-year-olds to the young people in their twenties, is making a gift that will go home for the holidays, and every school department is in league with the festival....

Sometimes I think no one has felt the real joy of Christmas who has not spent it at Penn School! Here for twenty-five years we have been awakened before "dayclean" (as the islanders call sunrise) by the singing of the old Christmas carols in our hall. Our front door key is "stolen" the night before, a mere matter of form really, for we never lock our doors and windows on this island! The singers steal in so that we hear nothing until the glad carol bursts forth, and we realize that the gift is ours again. They steal out as quietly as they enter and

Life and Leisure

we hear them go from building to building, singing. Those liquid notes in the dark of the morning usher in the Christmas week and strike the keynote for all that is to follow.

Christmas on the old plantations was the most joyful time of the whole year. It meant freedom from the routine of work, the giving out of the new clothing, more food and drink and on most plantations a "Christmas Gif'" for each slave; a time to mingle; a time for dance and song; the drab year gave up some sunshine when Christmas came!

And Christmas on St. Helena today keeps all that is best in the old tradition. There is no one-day limit. There is the school Christmas when all the pupils gather for the Christmas tree in Darrah Hall. Each class sings a carol as its joint gift to the holiday; everyone tries to bring something for the poorer folk; and these gifts, from one box of matches to a large bag of grits or potatoes, are laid on the benches below the tree before the excitement of receiving presents begins. . . .

Our Folk Lore Society with its occasional meetings and the St. Helena Quartette share the responsibility for seeing to it that these songs of the people are preserved in the midst of a faster life epitomized by the automobile and tractors. Natalie Curtis Burlin spent a few weeks here before her untimely death collecting and writing the spirituals that belong particularly to the Sea Islands. These were published later in her "Negro Folk Songs." Her death interrupted garnerings which were deeply appreciated by all of us. . . .

Once every year—and that time is chosen to light up the long pull of our real winter months when the going is the most difficult—there is one whole delirious week of song, which is opened by sermons on song given in our churches. Every day at noon a concert is arranged for chapel. Different organizations sing, the older people as well as the younger, not only spirituals but the folk songs of other peoples and national hymns. The church choirs give special music of their own choosing, and there is the quartet contest—when every grade in the school competes for recognition as "The Winning Quartet."

I can but wonder if it is not literally true that their love of singing is what has carried these people through all their experiences without bitterness. . . .

From Rossa B. Cooley, *School Acres*, pp. 74–75, 140–142.

4

Religion and Superstition

Long a victim of racial discrimination and oppression, the Negro in the United States has had to make a series of adjustments. With little or no control over his own life, he has been (and in some places still is) considered less than human. In a real sense he found it necessary to develop techniques of survival, among them what is now called American Negro religion. Very early the church gave the black man the one and only institution in which he could release his "suppressed emotions" or develop independent leadership. Outside of his own churches, he faced virtually complete suppression.[1]

At "Frogmore" shortly after the Civil War, Laura Towne, the white Sea Islands educator, heard an old black woman, newly freed, praying a simple but stirring invocation. She implored "Massa Jesus" to come down among her race and lift their heavy burdens. (He would not have to knock at the door, just come right in.)[2] This kind of simplicity and emotionalism have remained vital features of the Negro's religion. The evangelical denominations, Baptists and Methodists, with

---

[1] Benjamin Elijah Mays and Joseph William Nicholson, *The Negro's Church* (New York: Institute of Social and Religious Research, 1933), pp. 1–2.
[2] *Outlook*, XC, 431.

In the Cage

their emphasis on freedom of emotional expression and simple rites, attracted the great masses of the race—as they did the Southern whites as well.

American Negro worship has not been wholly unique. There are decided similarities between it and other forms of evangelical religion both in this country and in Europe. And it has paralleled, in many particulars, primitive worship in Asia, Africa, South America, and among North American Indians. Even the voodoo worship once seen among Louisiana Negroes, an import from Africa and Haiti, did not differ radically from the practices of snake cults and "holy rollers" later to be found among some "backward" American whites.[3]

The unique element of the Negro's religion—and one of the most attractive to outsiders—is the Negro spiritual with its dialect peculiar to the United States. The development of Negro spirituals was a part of the adjustment the Negro made to his new conditions in America. The songs were partly reactions to the oppression which their creators experienced as Southern chattels and which their descendants faced under the succeeding caste system. Basically, they represent what Mays and Nicholson call the soul of a people—their "joy and sorrow," "hope and despair," "pathos and aspiration." The race seems through them to grasp for a way to relieve its oppression and to endure.[4]

Southern whites came to look upon Negro religion as

---

[3] Mays and Nicholson, *The Negro's Church*, pp. 1-2; E. Franklin Frazier, *The Negro Church in America* (New York: Schocken Books, 1963), pp. 1-6, 82-83.

[4] Mays and Nicholson, *The Negro's Church*, pp. 1-3. Frazier vigorously dissents from these views, and questions the American origin of the spiritual. He does, however, see some continuity between the spiritual, especially as sung on the Sea Islands, and the Negro's African heritage, and gives some credence to the contention that it partly reflects the oppressed condition of the slaves. *The Negro Church in America*, pp. 12-13.

very different from theirs, so much so that they often made special visits to black churches to observe the rites there. The blacks were believed to possess "unusual," if not enchanting, superstitious practices, and to exhibit strange reactions to other supernatural phenomena. This being so, it is no surprise that visitors to the South also showed a great curiosity about the Negro's religion.

> **Mary Allan-Olney,** an English woman of letters and an extremely harsh critic of Negroes, settled on a farm near Lynchburg, Virginia, about 1880, where she remained for approximately three years. She saw Negro religion, characteristically, in an unfavorable light. One of her most serious indictments was that blacks could see no connection between morality and religion. The blacks were some sort of half-Christian heathen, which made their conversion more difficult than if they were totally heathen.

Then there are shouts and waving of arms, and cries of "Oh, I'm so happy! so happy!" from the elder brothers and sisters. Once Aunt Birthynia, in her excitement, forgot to keep her eye on her basket which she had put down when she began throwing her arms about. A nigger stole the dinner out of her basket on that occasion. So now she combines rejoicing in the Lord with an eye to business. . . .

As likely as not the chicken had been stolen from the fowl-house of Aunt Birthynia's mistress. But as I said before, the negroes cannot see any connection between morality and religion. . . .

In the Cage

People talk glibly about going out to convert the heathen. Here are we, with these few heathen at our doors, and we know not what to do. Our task would be easier, I think, if they were real heathen worshipping wooden gods. But how likely are they to listen to our teachings of the necessity of personal holiness, when their own preachers abstain from "pestering" them about "such little things," and tell them all they want is to "get 'ligion"? . . . They don't want to be told "that God is of purer eyes than to behold iniquity." If white folks' God is made like that, they prefer a God of another sort. . . .

All the negroes in the county appeared to be on their way to Mount Rock [Church]. There was to be a baptising. Most were on foot; here and there we came upon a party in a wagon, and a few were riding mules. All were provided with ample picnic-baskets. . . . A little brook . . . had been artificially widened and hollowed out, so as to form a pool.

"Oh, Almighty God, we are here before Thee this mornin', an' we's poor mis'ble critters, an' we dunno nothing." . . . The preacher stepped into the pool, feeling, as he proceeded, with a big stick. . . . The candidates, six women and one man . . . stood holding each other's hand. They wore very dirty dresses, dirty cloths around their heads, and their shirts were tied tightly round them half-way down the leg. The man had a clean handkerchief round his head. I think he was barefoot; but the women stood in their stockings.

Each woman, I noticed, had a cloth bound round her waist for the preacher to hold her by. . . . "I baptise thee in the name of the Father, the Son, and the Holy Ghost."

The first woman was a middle-aged, yellow negro. She was dipped, head backwards, and went into the dirty water with her mouth wide open. Once on her feet she gave a loud whoop, and threw her arms and legs about like one possessed. . . .

From Mary Allan-Olney, *The New Virginians* (2 vols., Edinburgh: William Blackwood and Sons, 1880), I, 244–246; II, 235–244.

William Wells Brown was another of those who attacked Negro religion. His criticisms were centered on the loud demonstrations of piety, the late revival meetings, the ignorant, self-seeking ministry, and the building of expensive houses of worship.

After settling the question with his bacon and cabbage, the next dearest thing to a colored man, in the South, is his religion. I call it a "thing," because they always speak of getting religion as if they were going to market for it. . . .

"You better go an' get religion, dat's what you better do, fer de devil will be arter you one of dees days, and den whar will yer be?" said an elderly sister, who was on her way to the "Revival," at St. Paul's in Nashville, last winter. The man to whom she addressed these words of advice stopped, raised his hat, and replied:

"Anty, I ain't quite ready to-night, but I em gwine to get it before the meetins close, kase when that getting up day comes, I want to have the witness; that I do. . . ."

The church was already well filled, and the minister had taken his text. As the speaker warmed up in his subject, the Sisters began to swing their heads and reel to and fro, and eventually began a shout. Soon, five or six were fairly at it, which threw the house into a buzz. Seats were soon vacated near the shouters, to give them more room, because the women did not wish to have their hats smashed in by the frenzied Sisters. . . .

The shouting now became general; a dozen or more entering into it most heartily. These demonstrations increased or abated, according to the movements of the leaders, who were in and about the pulpit; for the minister had closed his discourse, and first one, and then another would engage in prayer. The meeting was kept up till a late hour, during which, four or five Sisters becoming exhausted, had fallen upon the floor and lay there, or had been removed by their friends.

St. Paul is a fine structure, with its spire bathed in the clouds, and standing on the rising land in South Cherry Street, it is a building that the citizens may well be proud of.

In the evening I went to the First Baptist Church, in Spruce Street. This house is equal in size and finish to St. Paul. A large assembly was in attendance, and a young man from Cincinnati was introduced by the pastor as the preacher for the time being. He evidently felt that to set a congregation to shouting, was the highest point to be attained, and he was equal to the occasion. Failing to raise a good shout by a reasonable amount of exertion, he took from his pocket a letter, opened it, held it up and began, "When you reach the other world, you'll be hunting for your mother, and the angel will read from this paper. Yes, the angel will read from this paper."

For fully ten minutes the preacher walked the pulpit, repeating in a loud, incoherent manner, "And the angel will read from this letter." This created the wildest excitement, and not less than ten or fifteen were shouting in different parts of the house, while four or five were going from seat to seat shaking hands with the occupants of the pews. "Let dat angel come

Religion and Superstition

right down an' read dat letter," shouted a Sister, at the top of her voice. This was the signal for loud exclamations from various parts of the house. "Yes, yes, I want's to hear the letter." "Come, Jesus, come, or send an angel to read the letter." "Lord, send us the power. . . ." The pastor highly complimented the effort, as one of "great power," which the audience most cordially endorsed. . . . And this was one of the most refined congregations in Nashville. . . .

From William Wells Brown, *My Southern Home*, pp. 190–197.

> ***James Bryce*** agreed that younger black ministers were improving their theology and their morality, but he noted that wild, superstitious rites still prevailed in some parts of Louisiana and the lower Mississippi Valley.

In the days of slavery, religion was practically the only civilizing influence which told upon the plantation hands. But religion, like everything else that enters the mind, is conditioned by the mental state of the recipient. Among the negroes, it took a highly emotional and sensational form, in which there was little apprehension of doctrine and still less of virtue, while physical excitement constantly passed into ecstasy, hysterics, and the other phenomena which accompany what are called American camp-meetings. This form it has hitherto generally retained. The evils have been palpable, but the good has been greater than the evil; and one fears to conjecture what this vast mass of Africans might have been had no such influence been at work to soften and elevate them, and to create a sort of tie between them and their masters. Christianity, however, has been among the negroes as it often was in the Dark Ages and as it is in some countries even to-day, widely divorced from morality. The negro preachers, the natural and generally the only leaders of their people, are (doubtless with noble exceptions) by no means a model class, while through the population at large religious belief and even religious fervor are found not incompatible with great laxity in sexual relations and a proneness to petty thefts. Fortunately, here also there is evidence of improvement. The younger pastors are described as being more rarely lazy and licentious than were those of the older generation; their teaching appeals less to passion and more to reason. As it is only coloured preachers who reach negro congregations, the importance of such an improvement can hardly be overestimated. There is, of course, an enormous difference between the coloured churches in the cities, especially those of the Border States, where one finds a comparatively educated clergy and laity, with ideas of decorum modelled on those of their white neighbors, and the pure negro districts further south, in some of which, as in parts of Louisiana, not merely have the old superstitions been retained, but there have been relapses into the Obeah rites and serpent worship of African heathendom. How far this has gone no one can say. There are parts of the lower Mississippi valley as little explored, so far as the mental and moral condition of the masses is concerned, as are the banks of the Congo and Benue. . . .

From James Bryce, *The American Commonwealth*, II, 520–521.

José Martí witnessed some of the Negro's fervid emotionalism that showed itself beyond the church

Religion and Superstition

door, particularly in times of crisis—in this instance, the Charleston earthquake of 1886. Martí (1835–1895), Cuban poet, essayist, dramatist, and patriot, is one of his country's greatest heroes and, like Simon Bolivar, a symbol of liberty throughout Latin America. The son of a Spanish sergeant stationed in Cuba, Martí sympathized with the cause of the Cuban patriots. For this he served six months of hard labor and was finally deported to Spain in January 1871. On his third return to Cuba in 1895 he was killed fighting with the rebels.

Charleston has been destroyed by an earthquake. There is nothing but ruins where once stood a city spreading like a basket of fruit between the sandy waters of two rivers, merging inland into beautiful villages surrounded by magnolia trees, orange trees, and gardens.

Since the war, the defeated whites and the now tolerated Negroes have lived there in languid concord....

Brightly colored rugs and ornaments contrasting with the white walls, are hung out in the morning on the veranda along the upper floor gallery by smiling Negresses with red or blue bandannas covering their heads. The dust of defeat has dimmed the brick-red color of opulent residences. They live with courage in their souls and light in their minds in this peaceful, black-eyed town.

But today trains have to stop outside of the city on the twisted, broken, sunken, torn-up rails; towers have toppled; the population has been a week on their knees; Negroes and their former masters have slept under the same tent and partaken of the same bread of compassion, in front of their ruined houses, the fallen walls, the grilles wrenched from their stone supports, the broken columns!...

Certain pilgrims come and go with their tents on their backs, sit a while, then march on, then stop and sing. They do

In the Cage

not seem to find a sure place for their rags and their fear. They are Negroes: Negroes in whom is reborn, in wailing hymns and terrible dances, the primeval fear with which the phenomena of nature filled their emotional ancestors. It is as though fearful birds, unperceived by other men, had lighted on their heads and plucked at them and furiously lashed at their backs with their wings.

From the moment one had eyes to see in the night's horror, it became apparent that a strange nature began to surge out of the blurred memory of those Negroes and show on their faces: it was the constricted race; it was the Africa of their parents and grand-parents; it was that sign of ownership which every nature stamps on its man and which, regardless of accidents and human violations, lives its life and finds its way!

Every race brings with it into the world its mandate and it must be left its right of way, lest the harmony of the universe be disturbed, so that it may employ its strength and fulfill its mission with all the decorum and fruitfulness of its natural independence. Can anyone believe it possible, without incurring a logical punishment, to interrupt the spiritual harmony of the world by closing the way to one of its races, under pretext of a superiority which is but a degree in time?

It seems as though a black sun illumined those men from Africa! Their blood is fire; their passion like biting; their eyes flames, and everything in their nature has the energy of Africa's venoms, the enduring potency of her balms. The Negro has a great native goodness, which neither the martyrdom of slavery has perverted, nor his virile fierceness obscured. But he, more than the men of any other race, lives in such an intimate communion with nature, that he seems more capable than other men of shuddering and rejoicing with her changes.

In his fright and his joy there is something supernatural and marvelous which cannot be found in other primitive races.

His movements and his glance bring to mind the majesty of the lion. In his affection there is such a sweet loyalty that we do not think of dogs but of doves; and his passions are so clear, tenacious, and intense that they resemble the sun's rays. . . .

Having been taught the Bible, they utter their fright in the Bible's prophetic tongue. The Negroes' horror reached its extremity from the very start of the earthquake.

The greatest love of these disconsolate creatures in all of what they know of Christianity is Jesus, because they see him whipped and meek like themselves. Jesus is theirs, and in their prayers they call him "Jesus, my Master," "My sweet Jesus," "My blessed Christ." They implored him on their knees, beating their heads and their thighs as spires and columns came crashing down. "This Sodom and Gomorrah" they cried trembling. "Mount Horeb is opening up; it sure is!" And they wept, and opened their arms, and swayed to and fro, and begged not to be left alone until "the judgment was over."

They came and went dragging their children about crazily. When the poor elders of their caste appeared, the elders held sacred by all men but the white men, they prostrated themselves around them in great groups, listened to them on their knees with heads bowed to the ground, repeated together convulsively their mysterious exhortations, which derived from the vigor and candor of their nature and the divine character of old age such sacerdotal strength that even the white folks, the cultured white folks, rapturously joined the music of their distressed souls to that tender and ridiculous dialect.

Some six Negro children, in the night's saddest hour, rolled in a tumble on the ground, possessed with the racial frenzy in the garb of religion. They actually crawled. In their song an unutterable anxiety trembled. Their eyes were bathed in tears. "They're the little angels, the little angels, knocking on the door!" In a low voice they repeated singing the same stanza they had sung out loud. Then came the refrain, heavy with prayer, incisive, desperate: "Oh! Tell Noah to hurry and build his ark, and build his ark, and build his ark!" The elders' prayers are not joined sentences, but the short phrases proper of genuine emotions and simple races. . . .

In front of a tent we see a Negress whose extreme old age gives her a fantastic appearance. Her lips move, but we do not hear her words. She sways her body incessantly back and forth. Many blacks and whites surround her visibly anxious until the old woman takes up the hymn: "Oh let me go, Jacob, let me go!" The crowd joins her singing, swaying like her, raising their hands to heaven, clapping to express their ecstasy. One man falls to the ground imploring mercy. . . .

Then after seven and a half days of praying, people began to return to their homes. The women returned first, giving courage to their husbands. . . .

Charleston lives again, though her agony is not yet over, nor has the ground ceased to rumble under her swaying houses. The relatives and friends of the dead find that work reconstructs in the soul the roots that death has pulled out. The humble Negroes, once the fires that burnt in their eyes in the hour of fear have been spent, return to their tame chores and their abundant progeny. . . .

From José Martí, *Martí on the U.S.A.*, selected and translated by Luis A. Baralt (Carbondale, Ill.: Southern Illinois University Press, 1966), pp. 95–104.

Hezekiah Butterworth, a New England author and traveler, accompanied a small group of students to the Van Ness home in Washington, D.C., in 1892

Religion and Superstition

to investigate the adventures surrounding the place. Legend told of a plot to abduct President Lincoln, hide him in the Van Ness cellar, convey him across the Potomac, then demand a ransom for his life. Another story concerned the late Mayor Van Ness's six white horses. Butterworth (1839–1905), born at Warren, Rhode Island, was assistant editor of *Youth's Companion* from 1870 until 1894. He traveled extensively in the United States, Europe, Canada, and Latin America, and published several books of *Zig-Zag Journeys* and other works. He was conducting a private Spanish class for New Englanders in 1892 when he visited Washington, D.C., Louisiana, and Missouri. At the Van Ness residence Butterworth talked with black servants who were undoubtedly the source of the strange tales. The unlettered Negro was generally fascinated with ghosts and spooks.

The next morning Arthur repaired to the Van Ness place again. He met an old negro, with white hair, shuffling about the grounds. "An' what brings you here so early, my little man?" asked the negro. "Did you ever see the six white horses?" asked Arthur.

"Sho, now you hab got me shure." The negro sank all in a heap on one of the picnic seats. "Did I ebber see de six white horses? No, but I'se seen dem dat did. Dem horses comb across riber on Christmas nights, just as de clock strikes twelve, and smoke comes out of their necks and the smoke has the faces of the big men gone; this place used to be great on Christmas days."

"Where do the horses come from?"

"Dey belonged to old Mayor Van Ness. He thought a deal ob' 'em, as I've hern tell, and when dey returned from his funeral, dey all of dem drap right down dead. An' dey come an'

In the Cage

listen for him at the doo' ebry Christmas night just at de midnight cock-crowin'! . . . Ole Aunt Maria . . . she's seen de horses." . . .

"Seen 'em, yes, honey; I has now, shure as your bawrn. Old Si, he tell 'ye about 'em did marnin'. Well, old Si, he hain't no sense of de ting at all. Dem horses didn't fell down ded after comin' home from de funeral. Dey all went out into de medders yere, an' dey all died ob broken hearts, and de riber rose and covered 'em. . . ."

"Wasn't it the mist that you saw, Aunt Maria?"

"You go way! You came from up Nof, an' hab an unbelievin' soul. Stans to reason dem horses want no mist. . . ." Aunt Maria gave her turban several indignant nods and said, "Mist? mist?" . . .

From Hezekiah Butterworth, *Zig-Zag Journeys on the Mississippi: From Chicago to the Islands of Discovery* (Boston: Estes and Lauriat, 1892), pp. 125–127.

John Bennett has written one of the most vivid descriptions of a Southern Negro church and worship service. Born at Chillicothe, Ohio, in 1865, Bennett was educated in the town's public schools, and later at the Art Students League of New York. Having married a South Carolinian, he took up residence at Charleston in 1902. His novels included *Master Skylark* (1897) and *The Treasure of Peyre Gaillard* (1906). The sermon, music, prayers, shouting, and all that Bennett witnessed seemed to border on the hysterical, if not the insane. In the end he called it "a half-pagan frenzy."

Religion and Superstition

The church of Little St. John's, Anderson County, stands in the hollow fork of the Foxford Ridge Road, just this side of Fink's Camp-Meeting Grove. The building, formerly a ginhouse, was bought by the black men of the settlement, and converted into a sanctuary, used also as a schoolhouse for the black children. The negroes bought also the plantation bell which once rang summons to the cotton-field gang, and erected it upon the roof of the church in a crude little belfry of boards. By day the church, beaten purple-gray and lichen-green by the weather, is spotted over with orange patches of sunlight, sifted through the thin-leaved branches of the oaks surrounding it. By night the whole crossroads huddle close together in the darkening brilliance of the moonlight, which is half mystery. . . .

Along the road members of the congregation were coming, singing, not loudly, as wild airs as ever African twilight listened to. Through the faint light and the mist we could see them in the darkness and the shadow of the woods, seeming a part of it, their bodies swaying from side to side, hands upraised, with harsh, clapping sounds, their feet scarcely clearing the sandy ruts, shuffling, scuffling along, in time to the beat of the music.

Where the preacher came, by another path, with a one-armed deacon, hymnbook and Bible in their hands, there was decorous—it were not true to call it pompous—silence.

The women had not yet come. There had been a prayer meeting, led by lay brothers, exhorters, before the evangelist, preacher, and deacons came. As we paused at the edge of the little grove a man with a wonderfully soft, deep voice was praying. He seemed almost to be singing, his voice was so melodious and so evenly modulated in its tones; a bass, not of the rasping, guttural variety common among mountain whites, but deep and suave as an organ-pipe. His prayer, in its strange,

In the Cage

sweet, half-chanted intonations, seems a *Laus Perennis,* its melodious flow going steadily and musically on without a pause, like an old Ambrosian chant; old Antioch seemed to listen with us.

Suddenly, without a pause, and where I could not lay my finger, the chanted prayer turned into a song. The same deep bass voice led it. The others, with scarcely a moment's hesitation, joined in its quaint refrain. The grouped voices rolled heavily and compactly together, like distant, condensed thunder in a barrel; or, rather, like a dozen sleepy trombones making music under a window at night. The voices all were bass, or baritones, if a rather sombre cast, and all possessed the same searching, melancholy tone. The blending was close, the effect rich and full, the passionate, dramatic melody (with gradations of tone which sharps and flats are inadequate to express,—persistently minor) now and then rising in a rush of sound into the harmony of some strange, chromatic accidental chord. Individual voices could be distinguished, modulating themselves to the greater body, some a little sharp, some a little flat; all feeling, as if without knowledge or intent, for that vibrating sense which attests perfect harmony, or for the unjarring flow of perfect unison; never quite attaining either, yet, nevertheless, going on in unbroken sweep. Some were singing antiphonally, at deeper octave, some magadizing, using indifferently and irrelevantly harmonies of the third, fifth, or sixth, producing odd accidental concords of sound, strange chromatic groups of semitones, and irregular intervals such as are found in Magyar music. Yet, as they sang, dissonance and harsh intervals seemed to weed themselves away; the melody sweetened, the discordant voices fell, or wrought themselves, into a complex, unusual harmony, and ended suddenly upon a diminished chord, startling both my companion and me. . . .

Religion and Superstition

The preacher, the deacons, and the evangelist had gone up the church steps; the women of the congregation had come; the wooden flights creaked and rattled under their heavy tread. We stopped at the door to look in, not wishing to stare about the Lord's house, even if it were a shanty.

Three kitchen lamps with wrinkled tin reflectors were nailed against the wall. They shed a dim, uncertain light through the church, fading away into the darkness behind us. The doors were of unplaned, whip-sawed plank, warped and cracked. They had no locks; on one hung three rusted links of an old padlock chain. The windows were boarded up with rough plank, the congregation being too poor to purchase glass. Wide cracks in the walls everywhere let in pale streaks of the moonlight. Along the ridgepole the wind had stripped away two rows of shingles, and through the gap a line of stars peeped faintly down through the yellow lamplight. The ridgepole looked like a bare-boned spine. The lamplight, smoky at best, lost itself among the beams and shadows overhead, the room being unceiled. The wind whiffed up softly through wide cracks in the floor.

The benches were of plank and slabs, bored each with four holes into which peg-legs were driven; the seats of the benches shone, worn smooth by attrition. A small pulpit of boards with a little ledge held the dog-eared Bible; behind the pulpit, upon a rude bench, on a ruder platform sat the preacher, the evangelist, and the one-armed deacon. In front of the pulpit and its little square platform was a small table on four uneven legs. The old cotton-bale door in the end of the building, behind the pulpit platform, was planked over; the people were poor indeed, and this was their highest chancel. . . .

Postscript. Strange and grotesque as this sketch may seem, ridicule of any sort is utterly outside the writer's purpose.... As to the music: no attempt is made in the scores to give harmonies, save in one slightest instance. No score written could convey the barbaric and stirring effect of a congregation of primitive negroes singing an old-time spiritual song. Some of the airs to these spiritual songs are in the pentatonic scale, some in the compass of a tetrachord, some correspond to various of the mediaeval modes, while others are irreducible to European scales, containing as they often do, such quarter-tones or other fractional intervals as are found in the Siamese system; their harmonies are correspondingly wild and irregular, being for the greater part accidental and instinctive, except under direct white influence. The personal reproofs directed at the congregation by the preacher were all in sharp, ironic, conversational tone; but the remainder of the sermon, after the opening passages, was chanted, from first to last, upon four tones, shown in the angel's cry of "Woe, wo-oh!" The tones employed were usually those of the address: "John, O John!" used with infinite variation.... The foregoing sermon and service may be taken as typical of the primitive negro churches of the South. In contact with the whites they are less, in remoter districts and in the low country of the coast much more, primitive and strange. Such services are always highly emotional, sometimes hysterical, almost madly corybantic, combining with a half-Christian service a half-pagan frenzy....

From John Bennett, "Revival Sermon at Little St. John's," *Atlantic Monthly*, XCVIII (August 1906), 256–259, 267–268.

Jules Huret, a French journalist, witnessed the wake, funeral, and interment of two black women in

Louisiana. The fervid emotions of many blacks, probably a release of frustrations, could be most clearly seen at funerals. The loss of a loved one was likely to evoke emotional outbursts from even the most staid deacon. Huret characterized the scenes as madness and hysteria. Born in 1864 in the Boulogne-sur-Mer district of France, Huret was educated in private grammar schools and chose a career in journalism that eventually led him to the Paris *Figaro*, which he later edited. He visited Louisiana and Alabama in 1903–1904.

Someone just told us that two negro women from the plantation had died this morning and that they are going to be buried the next day. I know that the funeral customs of negroes are particularly curious. I thought of nothing else but attending the funerals of these poor souls. . . .

They led us to the house of one of the dead women. It is a box made of poorly joined planks. Old yellowed newspapers cut up into bizarre designs were pinned up from one to another on the walls serving as wallpaper. In the middle of the room stretched out on a board, completely enveloped in white calico and covered with branches of green fir was the dead woman. Someone lifted up her veil in order to show her to us and I saw the face of a mummy, completely black, dried up as one conserves them in the museums. The unfortunate woman must have suffered a lot. Her facial traits were sad enough to cry over.

Most of the Negroes in this area are Baptists, that is to say that they are in the hands of practitioners of christianity of a crude form with barbaric rites. The custom requires that the coffins of the dead people be exposed in the chapel. One cannot, however, call it a chapel, this hangar without any sign of religious symbol—Here all members of the congregation came to wake around the dead.

In the Cage

That evening, toward nine o'clock, I was led to the wake of the two departed women. The room was full right up to the door. The negroes moved away when we approached. Despite our protests they led us right up to the choir stand, behind the pulpit where the negro pastor was talking. ... As we sat down, the pastor turned his back to us. ... The two coffins were side by side, of a reddish wood, ornamented with handles and ornaments of white metal. The rather vast room was lighted with little gas lamps. All of the benches were occupied by negroes. We were the only white people in the audience. Here was the picture of the characters. But how can I explain to you what I saw and heard in those two hours while I was there?

While the pastor was speaking . . . the entire audience cried, moaned and lamented in a sorrowful tone. The women with their mouths closed pitied and complained. Others cried, sobbed, and gave out dispirited exclamations. They began saying "O, Lord! O, God." The pastor spoke to the crowd sympathetically and then began to speak rapidly and vehemently. The saliva filled his mouth. ... I didn't understand what he said. ... The audience got worked up; continued to cry, sob, and mourn. ... Some women had turbans. Others had feathered hats. ... The negro minister was dressed in a long black top coat, handkerchief around his neck. ... The negroes rocked back and forth on benches. "O, Lord, have mercy on us." They cried real tears. ... A young, beautiful negro woman prayed for the dead. Others tapped their feet as the woman prayed. The pastor then called for even stronger prayer. ... At eleven o'clock we left lest this madness might reach us. ...

The next day we attended the funeral and burial. The temple was full. Many had stayed all night. The pastor had been rejuvenated. He told the story of Job in a manner that had no relationship to the subject. The legend was delivered

Religion and Superstition

in an incoherent manner. In fact it was unrecognizable. Then he told that he had spoken to the two negro women during their agony and that they had pardoned all and wished all to pardon them. . . . He asked for prayer to God for their deliverance. They had gone to Heaven and one would never see them anymore. . . . The women were once again provoked to cries and sobs which came in floods. The families of the dead women on the first two rows began to sob and tap their feet. . . . Then the two daughters of the dead women got up, suffocated with sobs and began to pound on the covers of the wooden coffins, crying "Mother, Mother"; "God, God" and then "Jesus, Jesus, don't leave her alone." The entire room shook. The women were tapping their heels. They beat on their chests with their fists, crying out. The poor orphan girls had straw hats on their heads which didn't sit well on their short kinky hair. They had to take them out bodily, lifted up by their feet and their heads and they began resisting as though they were insane, shouting and crying. Their hats fell into the crowd. It was a frightening scene of sadness and mass confusion. One could not help but sympathize with these unfortunate souls. . . . The pastor thanked us for our offering and told the crowd to greet us. Everybody bowed and said thank you. . . . The cemetery was adjacent to the church. The holes were filled with water from the inundation of the nearby river. . . . The orphaned girls wanted to throw themselves into the holes. Some men stepped between them and were jostled. Two of them fell backward. The girls were going to jump in, but they grabbed them and held them back until the holes were filled. The girls continued to call their mothers, "Good bye, mama, mama. I hope to see you again." Now the men began to cry. They had been passive in the church. . . .

In the cemetery I had witnessed the grouping together of madmen. Finally the negro women, most in colored blouses,

In the Cage

... threw themselves into the arms of one another. ... This was the climax of maddened exasperation and of hysteria. ...

From Jules Huret, *En Amérique: De New York à La Nouvelle-Orléans* (Paris: Bibliotheque-Charpentier, 1904), pp. 360–366.

Rossa B. Cooley, principal of Penn School, witnessed a number of religious rites on the Sea Islands of South Carolina which were a combination of traditional Christian worship and superstition. The following selection contains excerpts from one of her reports on Negro religious activities.

In our praise house is found the simplest, the most real form of the Christian religion I have ever seen. That is the background which makes the Christmas Mystery a natural outflowering of the community life. On every one of the old plantations you will come across a tiny building furnished with rude backless benches and a leader's stand in front. The men and women who are acknowledged as religious leaders usually sit facing the others, and their rank does not depend upon the amount of education they may have, but on their religious fervor. The praise house leader is a man of position and receives his appointment from the church. He is in charge of the regular services held in each praise house on Tuesday, Thursday, and Sunday nights every week. These houses on the plantations are near to hand and the people can drop in as familiarly as they do at home. It is not so easy to travel over country roads in the dark and so our people use their churches only for midday Sunday services.

Religion and Superstition

The informality and simplicity of a praise house service is gripping. Men and women, boys and girls wander in, and take their seats, often wearing their overalls and work clothes. The only light is a small lamp on the leader's desk and often I have seen that used without a chimney. . . .

Here are sung the spirituals unchanged; here is the Scripture read as a lesson to the plantation family, here are prayers offered to show the poetic power of the race. "Pray on de knees ob yo' heart," is advised by the leader. One of the old "Mothers" prays, "May de bird ob love be in muh heart an' de Lamb ob Christ in muh bosom, an' oh, God, who tuk up de sun in de palm ob yo' han' an' t'rowed her out into de sky to be Queen ob de day, Listen to we." All through her prayer is heard soft murmur of the response struck in the hearts of her hearers. A musical rhythm it makes, which finally breaks forth into the singing of a spiritual as the prayer comes to a close; the voice of the "Mother" on her knees mingling with the singing which grows in power as the Amen is said. Yes, the pictures are vivid and real as we listen to the older folk in their prayers; "Now as we bend our hearts equal to our knees, Lord Jesus, wilt Thou climb up on dat milk-white steed called 'Victory,' an' ride ober de mountains and t'rough de valleys of our sins an' backslidin's." . . .

The young candidates for admission to the church must "come through" the praise house. In our community the "seeker" must "see visions and dream dreams" which are interpreted to him by a "Spiritual Father" or a "Spiritual Mother," who is chosen after having been seen in a dream.

A "seeker" is often marked by a white string tied around his head to show the world that he should not be disturbed. He must not play games nor sing, and in the old days many were not allowed to go to school during this experience for fear the distractions would interfere with their praying. . . . This meant sometimes that a pupil would miss so much in school that he lost his place in his class. Together with the ministers we worked out a plan that the "candidates" might come to school but if they desired it, they could always be excused to go home early and by themselves, and they would not be expected to take part in the games.

I have known young people to go into the woods and stay on their knees for hours; and in the night or before "day-clean," to steal out for conference with their Spiritual Mothers or Fathers who try to lead them on from step to step in this great experience. Sometimes it takes a long time to see all that is required before the candidate is examined by the praise house leaders. Sometimes a candidate gets discouraged and "turns back"—a serious thing in his career.

The final meeting with the church deacons before the baptism and communion is a formal examination. Then, if all is satisfactory, the "candidates" are ready for the great Sunday, which means to them and to all the people a newness of life and new responsibilities. The outward sign is the complete outfit of new clothes, and not even graduation at school can reach the climax attained by these young or old seekers of religion. . . .

My belief is that religion is the gift of the Negro to our American life. There is its strong dramatic expression found in the praise houses on the plantations. It wells up through the songs of the race. The spirituals are their one articulate contribution, echoing the history of a people who have come through the valley of the shadow. In their prayers no less than their music do we find poetic imagery and spiritual values. . . .

From Rossa B. Cooley, *School Acres*, pp. 148–157.

5

Manners and Morals

Most Negroes in the late nineteenth and early twentieth centuries, as today, lacked the material and physical comforts enjoyed by the bulk of the white population. Still, in the eyes of many whites, the Negroes managed to display an unusual cheerfulness. "There are no people in America as happy as the genuine blacks," declared a nineteenth-century English observer. They could always be counted upon for a "cheerful laugh." In the end even "the worst of the blacks" were "not worse than the worst of the whites."

Booker T. Washington himself—as even some of his most vociferous white opponents would admit—possessed a social character worthy of emulation by all blacks. Indeed, Washington stressed good character as a key to Negro advancement. As will be seen, not all Negroes could live up to his high standards, and not all were perennially cheerful. They might lapse into gross immorality, or they might, on occasion, exhibit rudeness and sullenness.

In the Cage

Mary Allan-Olney thought that a few of the old Negroes could be counted upon for charming manners and a respectful attitude, but the general Negro behavior reminded her of a wet dog, nestling close to his master, unaware that he was offensive.

I have spoken of the great mass of the blacks—those who were children and young people before the emancipation—not of the very few old, trained family servants, who become fewer everyday. I have seen one or two of these, charming in manners, and thoroughly respectable in appearance. They can imitate just like monkeys. . . . But nothing can be imagined more disagreeable, more repulsive, more uncouth in manner, than the negro left to his own untrammelled, untutored nature.

We had great trouble to teach the blacks that if they wanted us they must come to the door instead of the window. I do not know anything more startling than to see a black face and a pair of rolling eyes in the dusk looking in on you. . . .

The negro behaviour reminds me sometimes of a dog, who, when dripping with rain, will rush in and nestle close to his master or mistress; or he will just after being caressed, turn around and begin a vigorous scratching and biting, quite unconscious that his behaviour is offensive, and that you wish him a 100 miles off. . . .

I like having to do with the old negroes best. They are all thieves, of course, but they are civil and respectful in their manners. . . . They are generally head-waiters in the hotels, or cooks or nurses in private families. I have observed that many of these people speak English without . . . the unpleasant nasal twang that generally disfigures American speech. But the young, untaught negroes, what a trial they are! What uphill work it is to teach them manners! All this summer I have been trying to teach Grace, a girl of sixteen, with a husband and two children, to say "good morning" when she sees me first.

Manners and Morals

"What would you think of people that walked into your house and stared at you, never said a word? Is that the way you black folk behave when you go into each other's houses?" They both grinned broadly at this. . . .

I might in time have taught her [Grace] civility—who knows? But when the tobacco-season was over she ceased coming to the house at mealtimes, and it was just as well; for I found that she was afflicted with kleptomania, and had she continued coming, we should by the end of the summer not have had a single table-knife left. I still went on teaching Dan manners; and he, being younger, was not such a tough subject. It was hard to prevent him from coming into the parlour with his hat on; and harder still to prevent his spitting on the floor "when he felt like it." . . .

They have a faculty for learning by rote, and so has a parrot. They have a faculty for imitation, and so has a monkey. The wonderful progress of the negro race, so vaunted by the supporters of the Hampton Institute, begins and ends there.

And this is the race which is to be the dominant one in this enormous country known as "the South." I am only a foreigner and a bystander. I pity the blacks, and I pity (still more) the whites; but it seems to me that, were I a Southern woman, mine eyes would become dim, and my cheeks furrowed with weeping, for the desolation of my country. . . .

From Mary Allan-Olney, *The New Virginians*, I, 59–60, 228–229; II, 40–45, 261–262.

James Bryce compared the Southern Negro's character with that of the American Indian. Whereas the

In the Cage

red man's assigned traits were pride and inflexibility, the blacks were found to be, among other things, naturally affectionate, docile, pliable, and submissive.

... These differences in his material progress in different parts of the country must be constantly borne in mind when one attempts to form a picture of his present intellectual and moral state.

The phenomena he presents in this latter aspect are absolutely new in the annals of the world.... A body of savages is violently carried across the ocean and set to work as slaves on the plantations of masters who are three or four thousand years in advance of them in mental capacity and moral force. They are treated like horses or oxen, are kept at labour by the lash, are debarred from even the element of education, given no more status before the law, no more share in the thought or the culture of their owner than the sheep which he shears. The children and grandchildren of those whom the slave-ship brought to the plantation remain like their parents, save indeed that they have learnt a new and highly developed tongue and have caught up so much of a new religion as comes to them through preachers of their own blood. Those who have housework to do, or who live in the few and small towns, pick up some knowledge of white ways and imitate them to the best of their power. But the great mass remain in their notions and their habits much of what their ancestors were in the forests of the Niger or the Congo. Suddenly, even more suddenly than they were torn from Africa, they find themselves, not only freed, but made full citizens and active members of the most popular government the world has seen, treated as fit to bear an equal part in ruling, not themselves only, but also their recent masters. Rights which the agricultural labourers of England did not obtain till 1885 were in 1867 thrust upon these children of nature, whose highest form of pleasure had hitherto been to caper to the strains of a banjo. . . .

Other races have desired freedom and a share in political power. They have had to strive, and their efforts have braced and disciplined them. But these things were thrust upon the negro, who found himself embarrassed by boons he had not thought of demanding.

To understand how American ideas work in an African brain, and how American institutions are affecting African habits, one must consider what are the character and gifts of the negro himself.

He is by nature affectionate, docile, pliable, submissive, and in these respects most unlike the Red Indian, whose conspicuous traits are pride and a certain dogged inflexibility. He is seldom cruel or vindictive,—which the Indian often is,—nor is he prone to violence, except when spurred by lust or drink. His intelligence is rather quick than solid; and though not wanting in a sort of shrewdness, he shows the childishness as well as the lack of self-control which belongs to the primitive peoples. A nature highly impressionable, emotional, and unstable is in him appropriately accompanied by a love of music, while for art he has—unlike the Red Indian—no taste or turn whatever. Such talent as he has runs to words; he learns languages easily and speaks fluently, but shows no capacity for abstract thinking, for scientific inquiry, or for any kind of invention. It is, however, not so conspicuously on the intellectual side that his weakness lies, as in the sphere of will and action. Having neither foresight nor "roundsight," he is heedless and unthrifty, easily elated and depressed, with little tenacity of purpose, and but a feeble wish to better his condition. Sloth, like that into which the negroes of the Antilles have sunk, cannot be generally charged upon the American col-

In the Cage

oured man, partly perhaps because the climate is less enervating and nature less bountiful. Although not so steady a workman as is the white, he is less troublesome to his employers, because less disposed to strike. It is by his toil that a large part of the cotton, rice, and sugar crop of the South is now raised. But any one who knows the laborious ryot or coolie of the East Indies is struck by the difference between a race on which ages of patient industry have left their stamp and the volatile children of Africa....

From James Bryce, *The American Commonwealth*, II, 515-518.

W. E. B. DuBois found that laziness and sexual promiscuity were common among the "slum elements" of Farmville, Virginia, but that these elements were yet quite small. The larger class of industrious, and presumably morally upright, blacks best represented the general tendencies of the race.

A considerable number of idlers and loafers shows that the industrial situation in Farmville is not altogether satisfactory and that the moral tone of the Negroes has room for great betterment. One of the principal causes of idleness is the irregular employment. A really industrious man who desires work is apt to be thrown out of employment from one-third to one-half of the year.... The great demand is for steady employment which is not menial, at fair wages....

There is undoubtedly in Farmville the usual substratum of loafers and semi-criminals who will not work. There are probably five or six regular prostitutes, who ply their trade chiefly on Saturday nights. There are also some able-bodied men who gamble, and fish, and drink. Then there are the men who work, but who spend their time and money in company with the lowest classes. These people live in a few crowded tenements . . . and are regarded by whites and blacks as beneath notice. Occasional serious crime is perpetrated by this class, but their depredations are generally petty and annoying rather than dangerous.

The slum elements of Farmville are as yet small in number, but they are destined to grow with the town. They receive recruits from the lazy, shiftless and dissolute of the country around. . . .

These slum elements are not particularly vicious and quarrelsome, but rather shiftless and debauched. Laziness and promiscuous sexual intercourse are their besetting sins. Considerable whiskey and cider are consumed, but there is not much open drunkenness. . . .

The whole group life of Farmville Negroes is pervaded by a peculiar hopefulness on the part of the people themselves. No one of them doubts in the least but that one day black people will have all rights they are now striving for, and that the Negro will be recognized among the earth's great peoples. Perhaps this simple faith is, of all products of emancipation, the one of the greatest social economic value.

It seems fair to conclude, after an impartial study of Farmville conditions, that the industrious and property accumulating class of Negro citizens best represents, on the whole, the general tendencies of the group. At the same time, the mass of sloth and immorality is still large and threatening. . . .

How far Farmville conditions are true elsewhere in Virginia the present investigator has no means of determining.

In the Cage

... But it is a town which should in large degree typify the conditions of the Virginia Negro to-day. ...

From W. E. B. DuBois, "The Negroes of Farmville, Virginia: A Social Study," pp. 22–23, 37–38.

Ray Stannard Baker concluded that the problem of Negro immorality in the South was really that of a small group of "worthless," uneducated blacks. Unfortunately this small group had given a bad name to the entire race.

I tried to see as much as I could of this "worthless Negro," who is about the lowest stratum of humanity, it seems to me, of any in our American life. He is usually densely ignorant, often a wanderer, working to-day with a railroad gang, tomorrow on some city works, the next day picking cotton. He has lost his white friends—his "white folks," as he calls them—and he has not attained the training or self-direction to stand alone. He works only when he is hungry, and he is as much a criminal as he dares to be. Many such Negroes are supported by their wives or by women with whom they live—for morality and the home virtues among this class are unknown. A woman who works as a cook in a white family will often take enough from the kitchen to feed a worthless vagabond of a man and keep him in idleness—or worse. ...

This worthless Negro, without training or education, grown up from the neglected children I have already spoken of, evident in his idleness around saloons and depots—this Negro provokes the just wrath of the people, and gives a bad

Manners and Morals

name to the entire Negro race. In numbers he is, of course, small, compared with the 8,000,000 Negroes in the South, who perform the enormous bulk of hard manual labour upon which rests Southern prosperity. . . .

It is remarkable, indeed, that the Negroes should have begun to develop moral standards as rapidly as they have. For in the South few people *expect* the coloured girl to be moral: everything is against her morality. In the first place, the home life of the great mass of Negroes is still primitive. They are crowded together in one or two rooms, they get no ideas of privacy, or of decency. The girls are the prey not only of white men but of men of their own race. The highest ideal before their eyes in many cases is the finely dressed, prosperous concubine of a white man. Moreover, in nearly all Southern towns, houses of prostitution are relegated to the Negro quarter. At Montgomery, Alabama, I saw such places in respectable Negro neighbourhoods, against which the Negro people had repeatedly and bitterly objected to the city authorities, to no purpose. The example of such a place of vice on Negro children is exactly what it would be on white children. In the same way, although it seems unbelievable, Negro schools in several cities have been built in vice districts. I saw a fine brick school for coloured children at Louisville placed in one of the very nastiest streets of the city. The same conditions surround at least one coloured school which I saw at New Orleans.

And yet the South, permitting such training in vice, wonders at Negro immorality and is convulsed over the crime of rape. Demanding that the Negro be self-restrained, white men set the example in every way from concubinage down, of immorality and lack of restraint. They sow the whirlwind and look for no crop! . . .

It may be imagined how difficult it is in such an atmosphere for Negroes to build up moral standards, or to live de-

In the Cage

cently. If there ever was a human tragedy in this world it is the tragedy of the Negro girl. . . .

From Ray Stannard Baker, *Following the Color Line*, pp. 60–61, 169–170.

Albert Bushnell Hart, an avowed sympathizer with Negroes, nonetheless found little to praise in the social position of the masses of the race. A relatively large minority—many of them mulattoes—measured up to white standards of character. But the "great majority" were ignorant, childlike, liquor drinkers and drug users.

A favorite Southern phrase is: "The Negro is a child," and many considerable people accord him a child's privileges. The ignorant black certainly has a child's fondness for fun, freedom from care for the morrow, incapacity to keep money in his pocket; but some planters will talk to you all day about the shrewdness with which he manages to get money out of the unsuspecting white man; and when it comes to serious crime, it is not every judge who makes allowance for childishness in the race. The theory that the negro mind ceases to develop after adolescence perhaps has something in it; but there are too many hardheaded and farsighted persons, both full bloods and mulattoes, who have unusual minds, to permit the problem to be settled by the phrase, "The Negro is a child."

Genuine friends and well-wishers of the Negro feel intensely the irresponsibility of the race. A business man who all his life has been associated with them says: "He has all the good qualities of the lazy, thriftless person, he is amiable, gen-

Manners and Morals

erous and tractable. He has no activity in wrongdoing. He has the imitative gift in a remarkable degree, and always I love him for his faults, he is without craftiness, without greed. . . ."

The main issue must be fairly faced by the friends as well as the enemies of the colored race. Measuring it by the white people of the South, or by the correspondingly low populations of Southern or Northern cities, the Negroes as a people appear to be considerably below the whites in mental and moral status. There are a million or two exceptions, but they do not break the force of the eight or nine millions of average Negroes. A larger proportion of the mulattoes than of the pure bloods come up to the white race in ability; but if fifty thousand people in the negro quarter of New Orleans or on the central Alabama plantations be set apart and compared with a similar number of the least promising Whites in the same city or counties, fewer remarkable individuals and less average capacity would be found. Race measured by race, the Negro is inferior. . . .

It would do no good to anybody to minimize the terrible truth that the Negroes as a race are in personal morality far below the Anglo-Saxons as a race, that the heaviest dead weight upon them is their own passions; but it would be equally futile to blink at the fact that the Whites do not set them in this respect a convincing example. . . . Great numbers of the Negroes are immoral, and great numbers of white men can testify to their immorality, for the building up of character is a long and weary process in both races.

So far as the future of the Negro is concerned, the real problem is whether he can suppress his bad traits and emphasize his higher nature, but that is a question with regard to all other races. The blacks are ignorant, not only of books, but of the world, of life, of the experience of the race. They are untrustworthy, but at the same time faithful; as one of their own number says: "They'll loaf before your face and work behind your back with good-natured honesty. They'll steal a watermelon, and hand you back your lost purse intact." . . .

From Albert Bushnell Hart, *The Southern South*, pp. 104–105, 136–138.

Sir Harry Johnston, wanting to see the Negro at his worst, visited a section of ill repute in New Orleans. He came away more affected by the shamelessness of the whites than by the immorality of the blacks.

Neither men nor women give the impression of idleness: true, I encountered one wandering minstrel playing plaintive airs on a guitar; but even he was working for a living.

As to drunkenness, there was little or no sign of it, possibly because the new prohibition laws were producing their effect.

I believe, however, that the men gamble excessively; but although this is very regrettable from their own point of view, it is a stimulus to industry rather than otherwise, since the loss of their money compels them to keep steadily at work, while if they gain in lotteries, by betting, or at cards, they spend their gains on smart clothes and good living, which is beneficial to trade.

To see the Negro at his worst, I visited those parts of the vast city and suburban area of New Orleans where the coloured people of the lower classes mostly congregate. I was escorted by an official of the police force; no restrictions were placed on where I went, but no doubt I was unconsciously guided, and possibly the worst parts of the town were withheld

Manners and Morals

from my view, though as a matter of fact, my very obliging guide seemed anxious to give me a truthful impression, and to show me the worst aspects he could find of Negro life.

I came out from this inspection of "bad" New Orleans scandalized at what I had seen, but not so far as it affected the negroes; I was merely amazed at the shamelessness of the whites. Here and there, it is true, I saw a tipsy negro. In one saloon they were playing cards, but every one seemed to be in good humour. There were no angry voices (there was a marked absence of obscenity in speech, I should state), and no one complained of being cheated. In another saloon, to the music of a gramophone, some twenty Negro men were dancing, but not indecorously. Here there was not the slightest sign of drunkenness. Moreover, all these "bad" places seemed to be far cleaner than similar haunts in England.

But at last we reached the streets of strange sights. We passed through a quarter of the town inhabited by negro and coloured prostitutes, and entered some of their houses; but none of the black or yellow women thus encountered gave any sign in their outward appearance of the manner in which they earned their living. There was nothing immodest in their speech, gesture, or clothing. In fact, they might all have been the keepers or tenants of respectable lodgings . . . but for the information of the police officer that they were women of the town, and visited, by the by, by white men as well as black. . . .

From Sir Harry Johnston, *The Negro in the New World*, pp. 457–458.

Rossa B. Cooley, as principal of Penn School on St. Helena Island, saw none of the retrogression in man-

In the Cage

ners and morals among the blacks alleged by other outside observers. Even as late as 1908 Miss Cooley was impressed by the courtesy and respect Negroes showed one another and whites.

Manners, customs, and dialect were little touched by contact with a strange race, for the black children could grow to maturity without seeing a white face. To go to the nearest town means even now for most of them a long drive and a row across one or two tide rivers, so these Sea Island negro farmers have retained a certain geographical isolation which doubtless accounts for their differences from the well-known of the mainland.

The greetings on the road express their feelings simply and clearly. "How is you, sister?" "Up, I tank you," or, "Tank God for' dis Evening Chance!" or, "Able to grunt and gwine, tank you," may be the answers, and one day the following conversation was heard:

"Well! how is you, brudder?"

"Movin', tank you, but not very fas'. How is you?"

"I'm kickin', but not very high."

More often than not the replies are negative in character. "Painful tank you," or "Jes' out of bed, tank de Lord," are the answers often given, very cheerfully too. When asked why she never replied that she was perfectly well, one old "sister" said: "You ain't gwine to say you fust straight! You gwine again de Lord," and that is the explanation for this habit of mind, which in the earlier days they doubtless had because of the fear of the Evil Spirit who would be on the lookout to attack the one free from pain.

When you know that a young white woman can drive in the evening over any part of St. Helena Island, which is one of the Sea Island group, and the one about which this article is mainly written, and that she feels safer than she could feel in

Savannah or New York, you can see that these people are gentle. It is natural for the negro to be gentle and to be a caretaker. Many instances of these characteristics have been given in history and literature, but usually these are told of the "old-time negro," and people say there are no such negroes now. On the Sea Islands there are many, and those of a different type are usually found to be some who have recently returned from the slums of one of our cities. When visiting Aunt Jane's cabin one morning, the horse ran off to her stable, leaving the rider to walk the five miles home. Both Aunt Jane and Uncle Billy were much distressed to have their friend take the long walk, and eagerly offered to borrow an ox-cart for the journey. That night about eight o'clock a knock was heard, and there stood Uncle Billy, who had walked the five miles after his hard day's work in the field because "We couldn't sleep till we knew you was safe."

On these Sea Islands with their marshes, live-oaks, and palmettoes, in the fields of long staple cotton you will find these negroes, these few thousands of their race who have never been outnumbered by people of a different race, for on St. Helena Island there are about eight thousand blacks to about fifty whites, and on some of the islands even a smaller proportion of whites. Here are the real negroes of our country, whom contact with the white race has only made better because it has not meant hard conditions and fierce competition, but kind treatment and education.

In some ways these negroes are behind their people on the mainland, but in the real ways they have an advantage, and here on the Sea Islands is an exceptional opportunity to develop negro communities which shall be of service to both races. . . .

From Rossa B. Cooley, "Aunt Jane and Her People: The Real Negroes of the Sea Islands," *Outlook*, XC (October 1908), 425–426, 432.

In the Cage

> ***André Siegfried*** granted that some of the more intelligent Negroes had changed their manners since 1898. But he thought the number to be small. Then, too, only a small elite showed any sign of bitterness about, or any desire to agitate against, discrimination.

In the South, at any rate, the negroes have passively resigned themselves to existing conditions. Their attitude is that of parasites, gravitating around the whites, whom they consider their patrons. The title "Boss," which they often use for the whites, reflects their instinctive recognition of their ethnic position, and when they classify themselves into their own social categories, their viewpoint is much the same. To be the descendant of a slave is humiliating. At Charleston, Richmond, etc., certain groups from the West Indies whose ancestors were free are regarded as superior, and therefore they do not mix with the others. By much the same snobbery that we find among the domestics of old British families, it is considered the thing to be descended from the slaves who belonged to one of the first families of Virginia. Therefore it is not astonishing that a relatively fair skin is appreciated by the negroes themselves. They distinguish all sorts of shades of colour which escape us—black, brown, deep brown, yellow, reddish brown, deep yellow, dark brown, chocolate, gingerbread, fair, light brown, red, pink, tan, olive, copper colour, blue, cream, pale black, dead black, bronze, banana. . . . Pale complexions, which are more common among the educated negroes, are more frequently met in North Carolina and Virginia than in the extreme South. It is interesting to note that in the smart negro churches the best pews are reserved for the palest of the faithful. On the contrary, among the lower classes of negro the really black man inspires greater confidence, an observation which applies, for example, to the minister of a low-class Baptist community, whose colour renders disloyalty to his race impossible. Coloured people actually exist whose tint is so pale that they can be mistaken for whites. They can "pass" (a sacred expression among the negroes); that is to say, they move undetected into the superior race, where they are lost.

With the possible exception of a small *élite*, humility is the dominant trait of the southern negroes. They are docile, passive, and accept their subjugation without a murmur. A Spartacist revolt is the last thing to be feared, for their efforts are directed rather toward adaptation. Circumstances have developed in them an extraordinary instinct for judging people and knowing what they can get out of them. They have a keen perception of social differences among the whites. With the rich they quickly adopt a flattering attitude, but they utterly despise the "poor whites." So long as they keep their place and are willing to sign, as it were, a declaration of everlasting inferiority, the South will admit that they are part of the family, and indeed more truly American than the New York Jew or the Boston Italian. But let them try to climb socially, and they are looked on as dangerous beasts. In reality the South fears their *progress even* more than their brutality. . . .

From André Siegfried, *America Comes of Age*, pp. 100–101.

Frank Tannenbaum did not encounter many old-line "good niggers" on his tour of the South after

In the Cage

World War I. Instead this Columbia professor found "a newer type of negro"—a black man who had achieved a cultural outlook radically different from that of the ex-slaves. Tannenbaum, born in Poland, came to the United States at an early age. Educated at Columbia University and at the New School for Social Research, he received a Ph.D. from the Brookings Institution in 1927. He devoted much of his career to the study of Mexico and Puerto Rico, and began teaching Latin American history at Columbia in 1935. Tannenbaum examined the American South in 1923–1924.

The changing status of the negro may be illustrated in many ways. It is sufficient to mention the following facts. In 1863 there were only two newspapers published by colored persons, while at present there are some 400 publications published by or for the negro, most of them appearing in the South. In 1865 negroes engaged in forty different kinds of business undertakings, now there are more than 200 varieties of businesses conducted by negroes. . . . There were reported in 1922 seventy-four negro banks with a total capital of $6,250,000 and resources amounting to $20,000,000. . . . Exclusive of public schools, there are some five hundred secondary and higher training schools for negroes, with an enrollment of more than 28,000 secondary, 3,324 collegiate, and some 2,000 professional students. In 1921 four hundred and sixty-one students received the degree of B.A. There are nearly 8,000 college graduates and some twenty-five colored students who have received the degree of Ph.D. from standard American universities. Over fifty negroes have made Phi Beta Kappa, and the 1910 census reports seven hundred and seventy-nine negro lawyers. These are but a very few of the facts that could be listed. They have brought a new type of negro into being. He is different because he does difficult things. He assumes positions of leadership in his own group, occupies positions of responsibility, and has achieved a cultural outlook which differentiates him sharply from the type of negro who served as a slave. In fact, the bitterness of the educated negro may, in part, be attributed to the craving for distinction from the men in his own race who are far below in the scale of achievements. The imposed association with the least advanced in his own group in all things is partly responsible for the resentment at being denied the privilege of acceptance on his merits from the white people. For it must be remembered that the distinction is so drawn as to place the poorest equipped, the least reputable white man above the most capable and fully developed negro.

These forces are inevitable. The colored man is not in a position to escape their consequence; they tend to make the negro feel, think, and be different. He is caught in the whirl of a flood that is sweeping away old moorings, old relations, old loyalties, and is developing newer cravings, ideals, and habits—habits that are strange and incongruous to the white people in the South with their memories and traditions of a static world. They want him to be, as he was of old, "a good nigger." They blame him, forgetting that he is the victim of a changing world as much as the white man.

From Frank Tannenbaum, *Darker Phases of the South* (New York: G. P. Putnam's Sons, 1924), pp. 10–13.

6

Crime and Punishment

Gross immorality no doubt existed among some blacks, as among all other groups, in the post-Reconstruction era. On many occasions Negroes also became involved in crime, which often led to a kind of latter-day slavery—Southern imprisonment.

In the matter of crime and punishment the outside observer could witness and react to one of the most critical areas of Negro life and Southern race relations. The importance of the subject is demonstrated by the attention paid to it by such noted scholars as Cesare Lombroso and Frances Kellor, whose observations appear among the following selections.

The consensus in the post-Reconstruction period was that the race was prone to petty theft, which could often be overlooked, but that for crimes of a more serious nature, especially "the crime of crimes"—a physical assault on a white woman —heavy penalties would be drawn. Tragically, these penalties might not be the result of "due process of law" but the executions of lynch mobs. Outsiders had an opportunity to see it all.

Crime and Punishment

Sir George Campbell found blacks disproportionately represented in Southern prisons and saw more than Negro criminality as the contributing factor. The absence of Negroes on juries, particularly in Virginia, and the severity of punishments meted out to blacks, including flogging and lynching, drew the suspicions of this British M.P. In the final analysis, he concluded, blacks were not prone to vicious crimes but were subject to the severest penalties for offenses which they committed.

It is certain that the prison populations are composed of blacks in a proportion greater than the general population to an overwhelming degree. Whatever the degree of their criminality, there is a disposition to cure it by a strictness in penal management which requires watching, seeing how much the administration of justice is now in the hands of the whites. The magistrates and judges are either elected or nominated by the white rulers. English law is the basis of most American institutions, and the English law regulating the selection of juries has always been very lax. I found that in the Southern States there is little regard to the principle of selecting *de medietate linguae* in cases between black and white. Very few blacks are admitted on juries; in Virginia, I believe, none at all.

Then, as regards punishment, flogging is very freely used in Virginia; but further South the system of *chain-gangs*,— i.e., *extra-mural* labour—is universal. The convicts are not only employed on public works, railways, and the like, but are very usually let out to private speculators, and they are made a source of profit instead of an expense. It comes simply to this, that the punishment for crime is reduction to the old state of slavery in a form not very widely differing from the old form. I am told that the people most often convicted and sent to the chain-gang are the undisciplined young negroes who have grown up since the days of slavery. I have even heard it said by reliable men that they employ no man so readily as one who has come out of the chain-gangs, because he has there learnt discipline.

In nothing have I encountered greater discrepancies of statement than in regard to the criminality of negroes. Many people represent them as most inveterate thieves, whom nothing but severity will reform. Others say they have lived among them for years and never had occasion to lock a door; and of this last I have had personal experience. I tried very hard to sift the truth, and I believe it to be this. The negro is not much given to violent, and very little to what I may call vicious, crime. In this respect he really stands above most other races. But he has brought from slavery times a sort of childish want of respect for property in certain things. It is hardly deemed a theft, but merely a misconduct, when a child is caught taking a spoonful of jam. . . . I gather, however, that some things thought very venial in slave times are now severely dealt with. On the whole I am inclined to think that there is some foundation for the assertion sometimes put forward by friends of the blacks, that a much harder justice is dealt to one class than to another: that for all the outrages and murders committed by the whites in the troubled years after the war very little condign punishment has been executed, while justice and something more is done on the blacks. One thing did astonish me during my tour, and that is, to find how much "Judge Lynch" survives, especially when the accused are blacks. I imagined he was a thing of the past, but I found that several lynching cases of atrocity occurred before I had been many weeks in the States; that is, hanging by popular movement without the intervention of judge and jury. This is generally the case when there is any alleged assault of any kind by a black on a white woman. The blacks are popularly said to be prone to that kind of crime; with what justice I cannot say. An experienced judge told me that he had known many accused and many hanged, but none convicted on trial. The mere suggestion that a black man would like to do something of the kind if he could seems enough to hang him. . . .

From Sir George Campbell, *White and Black*, pp. 169-172.

William Wells Brown, in the following selection, sees Southern peonage and antiquated methods of punishment as contributing to black dissatisfaction and, hence, to an exodus from the region.

Among the causes of that dissatisfaction of the colored people in the South which has produced the exodus therefrom, there is one that lies beneath the surface and is concealed from even an astute observer, if he is a stranger to that section. This cause consists in certain legislative enactments that have been passed in most of the cotton States, ostensibly for other purposes, but really for the purpose of establishing in those States a system of peonage similar to, if not worse than, that which prevails in Mexico. . . .

The act [Mississippi statute of March 1878] provides that "all persons convicted and committed to jail for contempt of court, and except those sentenced to imprisonment in the Penitentiary, shall be delivered to a contractor, to be by him

In the Cage

kept and worked under the provisions of this act; and all persons committed to jail, except those not entitled to bail, may also, with their consent, be committed to said contractor, and worked under this act before conviction," . . . [and] "if any person committed to jail for an offense that is bailable shall not consent to be committed to the safe keeping and custody of said contractor, and to work for said contractor, and to work for the same under this act, the prisoner shall be entitled to receive only six ounces of bacon or ten ounces of beef, and one pound of bread and water. . . ."

The negro knows how little it will take to commit him to jail, and that then he must half starve on a pound of bread and water and six ounces of bacon a day, or work for the contractor for nothing until he can be tried; and when tried he must run the risk of conviction, which is not slight, though he may be ever so innocent. Avarice . . . is pursuing him, and with little power to resist, there being no healthy public sentiment in favor of fair play to encourage him, he yields, and becomes the peon of the oppressor.

I found the whipping post in full operation in Virginia, and heard of its being enforced in other states. I inquired of a black man what he thought of the revival of that mode of punishment. He replied, "Well, sar, I don't ker for it, kase dey treats us all alike; dey whips whites at de poss jes as dey do de blacks, an' dat's what I calls equality before de law. . . ."

From William Wells Brown, *My Southern Home*, pp. 219–222.

James Bryce discusses the matter of crime and punishment and its connection with black-white re-

Crime and Punishment

lations in the South. While admitting that it was difficult to get to the truth about lynchings, Bryce concluded that they affected whites as well as blacks.

Against the industrial progress of the negro there must be set two depressing phenomena. One is the increase of insanity, marked since emancipation, and probably attributable to the increased facilities which freedom has given for obtaining liquor, and the stress which independence and education have imposed on the undeveloped brain of a backward race. The other, not unconnected with the former, is the large amount of crime. Most of it is petty crime, chiefly thefts of hogs and poultry, but there are also a good many crimes against women. Seventy per cent of the convicts in Southern jails are negroes; and though one must allow for the fact that they are the poorest part of the population and that the law is probably more strictly enforced against them than against the whites, this is a proportion double that of their numbers. Even in the District of Columbia more than half the arrests are among the coloured people, though they are only one-third of the inhabitants. . . .

The lower class are also often unfriendly, prone to suspicion and violence. In this situation there lie possibilities of danger. The strained relations of the races appear most frequently in the lynchings of negroes. It is extremely hard to ascertain the truth of the reports regarding these lawless acts. But there can be no doubt that over the South . . . negroes accused of assassinating white men, or of outraging white women or children are frequently seized by white mobs and summarily killed; that occasionally, though probably not often, an innocent man perishes, and that the killing is sometimes accompanied by circumstances of revolting cruelty. Now and then the culprit is burned alive. Often his body, after he has been

In the Cage

hanged, is riddled with bullets, a piece of barbarism akin to the Eastern habit of mutilating the corpses of the slain. The excuses offered for these acts are that white women, especially in sparsely inhabited regions, are in considerable danger from the lust of brutal negroes, and that the swift apprehension and slaughter of the culprit not only strikes greater dread than the regular process of justice, but does not gratify the negro's enjoyment of the pomp and ceremony of a formal trial before a judge. It is also declared, and with truth, that whites also are lynched though not so frequently and in a less atrocious way, that the negroes themselves occasionally lynch a negro, that it is hard for the executive authority, with no force except the militia at its command, to protect prisoners and repress disorder, and that the lynchings are the work of a comparatively small and rude part of the white population; the better citizens disapproving, but being unable or unwilling to interfere.

Whatever palliations may be found in these circumstances,—and it is quite true that in a thinly peopled and unpoliced country white women do stand in serious risk—there can be no doubt that the practice of lynching has a pernicious effect on the whites themselves, accustoming them to cruelty, and fostering a spirit of lawlessness which tells for evil on every branch of government and public life. Were the negroes less cowed by the superior strength and numbers of the whites, reprisals, now rare, would be more frequent. Yet even in a race with so little vindictiveness or temper, terrible mischief is done. . . . The humble negro shuns contact with the whites, not knowing when some band of roughs may mishandle him; and sometimes a lynching is followed by a sudden rush of coloured emigration from the State or district where it has happened. The educated and aspiring negro resents the savage spirit shown towards his colour, though he feels his helplessness too keenly to attempt any action which could check it. . . .

From James Bryce, *The American Commonwealth*, II, 522–523, 526–528.

Cesare Lombroso, "founder of the science of criminology," studied the rising homicide rate in the United States and concluded that it was the Negro population which kept homicide from being "almost as rare" in the United States as in "the most civilized countries of Europe." Lombroso (1836–1909), an Italian Jew, became widely known through his investigations of abnormal behavior and his minute measurements of criminal types. He looked upon criminality as marking a reversion to an earlier type and as largely the product of nervous disease. Lombroso does not seem to have gone any further South than Virginia.

In the United States, as elsewhere, the southern regions by reason of their warm climate are prone to engender violence; hence the greater number of homicides in such sections. . . .

But a much greater cause of homicide in the United States is the vast number of colored people in that country. If immigration tends to the increase of crime even among the descendants of immigrants who may have become assimilated, how much greater is it increased by the presence of a race which finds itself in a state of civil inferiority. If we are to accept the statement that 60 per cent of the homicides are furnished by the whites and the remaining 40 per cent by the colored

In the Cage

race, it must be remembered that the former constitute 88 per cent of the population and the latter but 12 per cent; it is clear that were it not for the negro population the crime of homicide would be almost as rare in the United States as it is in the most civilized countries of Europe. The colored race furnishes to the statistics of this crime, proportionately, more than five times as many cases as the whites; in other words, among the former there are forty-five homicides to every 100,000 inhabitants, while among the latter there are but eight to every 100,000. It should not be forgotten, however, that the proportion of colored criminals, according to population, is apparently always greater because the average term of imprisonment is frequently longer than for the white criminal. This tends to increase the number of those in prison in proportion to the colored population. Moreover, such is the prejudice against the negro, especially in the Southern States, that it is reflected even in the administration of justice, with the result that the colored offender against the law is judged and condemned with greater severity than the white offender. If we add to this disadvantage the negro's greater shiftlessness, his greater carelessness to conceal his crime, his greater proneness to confess, we can understand how much his chances of conviction are increased.

But the greatest obstacle to the negro's progress is the fact that there remain latent within him the primitive instincts of the savage; for notwithstanding that the garb and the habits of the white man may have given him a veneer of modern civilization, he is still too often indifferent to and careless of the lives of others; and he betrays that lack of the sentiment of pity, commonly observed among savage races, which causes them to regard homicide as a mere incident, and as glorious in case it is the outcome of revenge. To this latter the negro is frequently impelled by a spirit of resentment of the prejudices of his white fellow-citizens; and just as frequently the motive for his crimes may be found in the gratification of his brutal instincts.

Further, there may be adduced in explanation of the negro's tendency to crime the fact that he is still practically in servitude; for while the law has emancipated him, it cannot be denied that the law in this respect is to a great extent a dead letter. It has been amply demonstrated that from a servile condition spring the greatest of criminals.

Again, a supreme cause of the homicidal tendency found in the negro race of the United States may be sought in their moral and material conditions, which in some respects are rendered worse by the abolition of slavery, producing, as it did a ferment in the minds of the colored people and exposing them to social problems in the presence of which even a stronger race would have stood appalled and powerless. With a diminished surveillance, and an increased antagonism between whites and blacks, rendered inevitable by an emancipation which was not due to but in spite of the Southern whites, it is not difficult to conceive that the law decreeing equality of the two races must inevitably have become practically ineffective, the negro still remaining morally, if not bodily, the white man's slave. Even in the British West Indies where the negroes have long enjoyed ample liberty, they still preserve their primitive habits, with a marked tendency to homicide and a rarity of suicides.

From Cesare Lombroso, "Why Homicide Has Increased in the United States," *North American Review*, CLXV (December 1897), 644, 647–648.

Frances Alice Kellor, in a study of the Negro that took her as far south as Alabama, reached conclusions about Negro criminality quite different from those of Cesare Lombroso—and probably more accurate. Miss Kellor, a sociologist, was born in 1873 at Columbus, Ohio, and received her education at the University of Chicago, the New York School of Philanthropy, and Cornell Law School. She served as general director of the Inter-Municipal Research Committee and was a member of the New York State Immigration Commission. At the time of her year-long study of Negro criminals she was on the faculty of the University of Chicago.

There is no denying the fact that negro criminality is out of proportion to the population, the proportion being greater than among the foreign whites. The census gives this fact without further analysis; but any one who will consider the agencies that produce crimes, and will then study the negroes' position, will see the inevitableness of this statement. Briefly, we may glance at these factors and the negroes' relation to them:

1. *Climate.*—In the North, for the greater part of the year, it induces activity; in the South it is detrimental to continued labor, and it affects both negroes and whites. There are but few large cities in the South, and occupation has a more intimate relation to, and is more dependent upon, the climate. When the white finds labor difficult, he relies upon his inheritance or goes into business in the city. The poor white and negro must labor, starve, or steal, for he has not a plantation, nor credit or opportunities in the city. The Southern climate is less rigorous, and there is less forethought required—it is not an incentive to frugality and forethought, but rather encourages thriftlessness, thus providing an opening for vice and crime. Leffingwell has shown that in warm seasons of the year crimes of passion and licentiousness are more numerous. These form

a very considerable number of the crimes of both negroes and whites in the South. Thus the climate predisposes to idleness, which is seen to furnish an opportunity for crime.

2. *Soil.*—This yields greater returns for a small expenditure of energy than in most sections. In the North the labor must be unceasing to secure similar returns. The negro rarely labors a full week, even if he knows the necessity exists; for he feels assured of a livelihood. Every race for whom Nature provides lavishly, and in whom there have not been developed desires aside from those incident to self-preservation, will not exert itself. The necessity does not exist. It is the obstacles that have assisted the Anglo-Saxon race in its upward course. When this test comes, the race will rise or disappear. The negroes' near ancestry to races lavishly provided for, and the lack of these obstacles during slavery and now, have not tended to develop thrift and forethought. Certainly the indolence of the white Southerner is equally notable, and is disappearing only as he enters urban life and is drawn into the current of sharp competition. With the extension of city populations there is increasing criminality, but this is also assuming a more professional character and lacks the simplicity that characterizes so many negroes' crimes. Thus a soil yielding lavishly predisposes to crime through idleness.

3. *Food.*—The food that the negro uses, whether by preference or necessity, is not of such a quality and is not so prepared as to give the greatest vitality. The death-rate of the negroes is often high because of the foods given during illness. In fevers and similar diseases this is important. The negro's daily food is ill-prepared, and his meals are irregular. Food in the North sustains an important place in the social and domestic life. Many cultural influences cluster about the meal hour. In the South there is none of the emphasis that makes it

so important a factor in developing or cementing a closer family life. . . .

4. *Labor.*—In the North, prison statistics show that where the criminal claims an occupation it is usually that of unskilled labor or of an artisan. Labor idleness may not be a cause of crime, but they are closely associated with it. . . . It may be argued that a man chooses his occupation according to his tastes and capabilities, and it is a result rather than a precedent. In a limited sense this is true, but among the classes from which the criminals come, and in the age of fierce competition, a man cannot more often choose his occupation than he can direct his training and education. Necessity may force him into work long before he is capable of choosing, or the parents' limited education and desires and lack of influence may keep him down in the scale. In all occupations in which the individual remains he in time develops the congeniality for it and shows the limited or undeveloped capacity characterizing it; for if he fails to keep the pace he drifts into a lower labor grade or into idleness, and if he exceeds the pace he grows out of it into new opportunities. These facts are especially true of the negro. But through his own experience and the desire of the whites his labor remains largely agricultural. Only a small per cent are skilled laborers, and still fewer are in the professional class. The whites need him in the agricultural work and offer but little incentive for him to rise in this. When he drifts into the city it is often into idleness, unless he is a skilled laborer and can endure the competition.

With regard to women, the criminals come almost exclusively from the servant class. . . . There is practically no problem of criminality among Southern white women, and this is primarily true because there is no white servant class. The few white women in the workhouses who are intemperate or immoral come from the poor white class or drift in from North-

Crime and Punishment

ern cities. . . . Thus labor in the South predisposes to crime because it favors both idleness and ignorance. It favors ignorance because education is difficult, and the school year is more often three months than six. The far removal from centers of activity makes the use of libraries and all forms of general instruction impossible. The negro is more dependent upon his master, and upon traditions and customs, for his cultural influences—and these are meager enough. . . . The negro laborers compare more nearly with unskilled labor in the North—a fluctuating mass, having no stable roots or personal interest in work except the remuneration. It is a noteworthy fact that the occupations in the Northern cities that yield a large percentage of criminals also yield a number of negro criminals in Southern cities. The negro needs that training which will take him out of the class of unskilled labor and put him in a position to attain the interests and success of the small farmer in the North. . . .

From Frances A. Kellor, "The Criminal Negro," *Arena*, XXV (January–June 1901), 60, 65–68.

Albert Bushnell Hart recognized that crimes by Negroes against other blacks constituted a serious problem, perhaps more common than violence across racial lines. Liquor, the lack of home influence, and the brutalizing effects of Southern prisons helped, he thought, to foment black crime.

Not so genial is the usual relation of Negro with Negro; both in town and city there is an amount of crude and savage vio-

In the Cage

lence of which the outside world knows little, and in which women freely engage. Jealousy is a frequent cause of fights and murders; and whisky is so potent an excitement that many competent observers assert that whisky and cocaine are at the bottom of almost all serious negro crimes. Practically every negro man carries a revolver and many of them bear knives or razors; hence, once engaged in a fracas, nobody knows what will happen. A woman describing a trouble in which a man shot her brother was chiefly aggrieved because "Two ladies jumped on me and one lady bit me." There is constant negro violence against the whites, and they occasionally engage in pitched battles with white gangs. . . .

The experience . . . shows that the Negroes are not drawn to crimes requiring previous organization and preparation; no slave insurrection has ever been a success within the boundaries of the United States; and blacks are rarely found in gangs of bandits. . . . The Negroes, according to the testimony of those nearest to them, are inveterate gamblers, and many affrays result from consequent quarrels, so that murders may be most frequent where there is the best employment and largest wages and greatest prosperity among the thrifty. Murder, manslaughter, and attempts to kill make up three quarters of the recorded crimes of blacks in the Mississippi Delta. Murders of Negroes by Negroes are very common and many of the criminals escape altogether. . . .

The allegation frequently made that these crimes are committed by highly educated Negroes, graduates of Hampton and Tuskegee, is absolutely without foundation. Most of them are by men of the lowest type, some undoubtedly maniacs. Most of these occurrences take place where the whites and Negroes are most clearly brought into juxtaposition, sometimes where they are both working in the fields. Hence they are of rare occurrence where the Whites are fewest and the Ne-

Crime and Punishment

groes most numerous. In many places in the Black Belt, white people have no fear of leaving their families, because they are sure that their negro neighbors would give their lives, if necessary, for the protection of the white women. The Northern white teachers, who are accused of arousing in the Negro's mind the belief that he is the equal of the Whites, have never in a single instance been attacked; and in the communities where the Negroes are literally fifty to one, have not the slightest fear of going about alone at any necessary hour of day or night....

The great majority of negro convicts are sentenced for petty crimes, stealing, vagrancy, and the like, and for rather short terms; but the name for this punishment, "the chain gang," points to a system practically unknown in the North. There are literal chain gangs, with real shackles and balls, working in the streets of cities, white and black together; and large bodies of convicts are worked in the open, stockaded, and perhaps literally chained at night. Right here comes in one of the worst features of the Southern convict system. The men on the chain gang are perhaps employed on city or county work, and if their terms expire too fast, the authorities will run out of labor; hence, the Negroes believe, perhaps rightly, that judges and juries are convinced of their guilt just in proportion to the falling off of the number of men in confinement; and that if necessary, innocent people will be arrested for that purpose. This is probably one reason why Negroes feel so little shame at having been in prison. "Did you know that I was in the barracks last night?" is a remark that you may hear at any railroad station in Georgia....

On the whole, one would rather not be a negro convict in a Southern state or even a white convict, for many state and county prisons are simply left-over examples of the worst side of slavery.

In the Cage

The first trouble with the Southern convict system is that it still retains the notion, from which other communities began to diverge nearly a century ago, that the prisoner is the slave of the state, existing only for the convenience and profit of those whom he serves. In the second place, it has been difficult to find indoor employment for the men, and most of them are worked out of doors. . . . In the third place, whipping is still an ordinary penalty, and very frequently applied. . . .

From Albert Bushnell Hart, *The Southern South*, pp. 187–190, 192, 200–201.

Julian Street of Chicago, spurred by tales from local Negroes, attended a session of the police court in Richmond. Street found the whole affair amusing.

My companion and I had not traveled far into the South before we discovered that our comfort was likely to be considerably enhanced if, in hotels, we singled out an intelligent bell boy and, as far as possible, let this one boy serve us. Our mainstay in the Jefferson Hotel was Charles Jackson. . . .

Having one day noticed a negro in convict's stripes, but without a guard, raking up leaves in Capitol Square, I asked Charles about the matter.

"Do they let the convicts go around unguarded?" I inquired.

"They's some of 'em can," said he. "Those is trustees."

This talk of "trustees" led to other things and finally to a strong recommendation by Charles, of the Richmond Police Court, as a place of entertainment.

"Is it interesting?" I asked.

Crime and Punishment

"Inter-*resting?* Yes, *suh!* Judge Crutchfield he suttinly is. He done charge me twenty-six dollahs and fo'ty cents. My brothah, he got in fight down street, heah. Some niggers set on him. I went to he'p him an' p'leeceman got me. He say I was resistin' p'leece. I ain't resisted no p'leece! No, suh! Not me! But Judge Crutchfield, you can't tell him nothin'. Tain't no use to have a lawyer, nuther. Judge Crutchfield don't want no lawyers in his co't. Then you got pay lawyers, too." . . .

Encouraged by this account of police court justice as meted out to the Richmond negro, my companion and I did visit Justice Crutchfield's court.

The room in the basement of the City Hall was crowded. All the benches were occupied and many persons, white and black, were standing up. . . .

At the back of the room, in what appeared to be a sort of steel cage, were assembled the prisoners, all of them, on this occasion, negroes; while at the head of the chamber . . . sat the judge—a white-haired, hook-nosed man of more than seventy, peering over the top of his eyeglasses with a look of shrewd, merciless divination.

"William Taylor!" calls a court officer.

A negro is brought from the cage to the bar of justice. He is a sad spectacle, his face adorned with a long strip of surgeon's plaster. The judge looks at him over his glasses.

The hearing proceeds as follows:

COURT OFFICER (to prisoner)—Get over there! (Prisoner obeys.)

JUDGE CRUTCHFIELD—Sunday drunk—Five dollars.

It is over.

The next prisoner is already on his way to the bar. He is a short, wide negro, very black and tattered. A large black negress, evidently his consort, arises as witness against him. The case goes as follows:

In the Cage

JUDGE CRUTCHFIELD—Drunk?

THE WIFE (looking contemptuously at her spouse)—Drunk? Yassr, Jedge, drunk. *Always* drunk.

THE PRISONER (meekly)—I ain't been drunk, Jedge.

THE JUDGE—Yes, you have. I can see you've got your sign up this morning. (Looking toward the cage at back of room): Make them niggers stop talkin' back there! (To the wife): What did he do, Mandy?

THE WIFE (angrily)—Jedge, he come bustin' in, and he come so fast he untook the do' off'n hinges; den' 'e begins.

THE JUDGE (to the prisoner, sarcastically)—You wasn't drunk, eh?

THE PRISONER (weakly)—I might of had a drink oh two.

THE JUDGE (severely)—Was—you—*drunk?*

THE PRISONER—No, suh, Jedge. Ah wasn't drunk. Ah don't think no man's drunk s' long's he can navigate, Jedge. I don't—

THE JUDGE—Oh, yes, he can be! He can navigate and navigate mighty mean!—Ten dollars. . . . If it ain't worth ten dollars to get drunk, it ain't worth nothing at all.

(While the next prisoner is being brought up, the judge entertains his audience with one of the humorous monologues for which he is famous. . . .) "I'm going to get drunk myself, someday, and see what it does to me. [Laughter] Mebbe I'll take a little cocaine, too."

A NEGRO VOICE (from back of room, deep bass and very fervent)—Oh, *no-o-o!* Don't do dat, Jedge! [More laughter]

THE JUDGE—Wher's that prisoner? If he was a Baptist, he wouldn't be so slow.

(The prisoner, a yellow negro, is brought to the bar. His trousers are mended with a large safety pin. . . .)

THE JUDGE (inspecting the prisoner sharply)—You ain't a Richmond nigger. I can tell that to look at you.

Crime and Punishment

THE PRISONER—No, suh, Jedge. That's right.

THE JUDGE—Where you from? You're from N'th Ca'lina, ain't you?

THE PRISONER—Yas, suh, Jedge.

THE JUDGE—Six months!

(A great laugh rises from the courtroom at this. On inquiry we learn that the "joke" depends upon the judge's well-known aversion for negroes from North Carolina.) . . .

From Julian Street, *American Adventures*, pp. 242–247.

Frank Tannenbaum viewed the recurring claim that black men were notoriously prone to attack white women as largely the product of imagination and emotion. "Fear and expectancy" more than Negro immorality or criminality accounted for most of the reports of Negro attacks on white women. Tannenbaum also examined the segregated Southern prisons and found the population predominantly black while the management was all white. The result was ill-tempered treatment of the black inmates —a temper and a mood that the white convicts could not entirely escape.

Every community has its weaklings, its perverts, its starved, unsatisfied, subjective members. The negroes have their share. What happens is something like this. Some poor weak-minded negro is subjected to the influences which are generated by the hysteria of defense against sex irregularity. The thing is advertised, whispered about, talked of in undertones; there are hunts, raids, lynchings, persecutions, fear, terror; a constant flood of stimuli are pressed in upon him. The very terror generated may lead to delusions of bravery, of heroism, of powers of greatness. The very cruelty may stimulate a craving for participation in the thing pervasive in the community. The poor weak-minded negro becomes haunted by delusions, by an irresistible craving to exhibit his powers, to participate in the forbidden thing. He dreams of committing the crime, of beating off a dozen white men, of ultimate escape. If he accepts the possibility of capture, the zest of the chase, of the excitation, and even of the final burning may become irresistible and attractive, and he does something that he would ordinarily never have done. This is one explanation for the fact that a community which has the most lynchings, the most terror, has also the most crimes to deal with. The very terror generates them. It is not suggested here that these are the only influences that lead to crimes or that they are not real and substantial fears. All that is emphasized is the influence which the Klan generates toward increasing their number.

There is also the fact that the things which influence the weak-minded negro influence the weak-minded over-sexed girl, and every community has its share of those. All doctors know that. The whole pressure on the subject of sex tends to stimulate delusions, fear, imaginations and hysteria. They are in an expectant mood. They imagine all kinds of possible things that they would do. They would fight, scream, run, yell; they, too, as well as the poor negro, become heroic in their own imagination. Enough is known about such things to understand that a girl over-stimulated by suggestion might imagine advances being made without their ever occurring. But more likely than that is that the expectant, strained, persistent mood of fear of attack tends to give significance to unintentional, meaningless incidents. An accidental meeting on a lonely road with a negro, a look, a chance contact, and the whole mechanism of fear and expectancy is set in motion. The girl screams; the negro runs. In the excitement that follows the thing that actually happened is forgotten. A story gets itself built up; all the emotions that have been aroused come to the front. Only one thing will pacify the community; the emotions demand their full satisfaction. They will not be denied. . . .

It is difficult to write about Southern prisons in one article. When one deals with the penal institutions of the rest of the country one thinks primarily of the prison. . . . In the South there is more diversity, the thing is more complicated. . . . Instead of one penal system there are at least three. There is the prison building which resembles that of the North. Then there is the County Chain Gang in a number of Southern States. . . . In addition to that there is the State prison farm, a huge tract of land employing hundreds of men and raising cotton, rice, or tobacco. . . . To all of this one must add the coal mines in one of the States—a system of penal administration all by itself. . . .

This diversity is still further complicated by the fact that the color line exists in the prison. The colored population of the Southern prison is predominant. The management is white. It has certain notions of discipline and control of the colored prisoner which come from experiences outside the prison walls. But the white prisoners do not escape the mood and the temper which the treatment of the colored generates—and so they suffer with their darker fellows. . . .

I was climbing the stairs in an old prison building. A prison officer without uniform and unshaven, with club in hand, and a batch of heavy keys on a large iron ring, preceded me up the stairs. "You will be interested in these fellows—and they are happy too," he added, confidentially. As we were going across the yard he told me that if I gave them a quarter they would sing for me—"and they sure can warble if you

In the Cage

only get them right." Up the stairs, darkened by barred and shadowed windows, I climbed. At each landing—and there were three of these—the guard opened a heavy iron door with one of his heavy keys. Just before reaching the top—before our heads could be seen—the guard hurriedly touched me by the arm, and placing a finger over his lips, said, "sh—listen." Slowly, mournfully, with gathering force and fervor the strains of "Nearer, my God, to Thee" reached me. There was a pathos and a sadness in those tones, a melodious and passionate self-surrender that melted and softened the greatest of all fears—the fear of death. For these men who sang were all condemned to die—and there were about fifteen of them. . . . Inside of a large iron cage—occupying the greater part of a bare loft—we saw some fifteen kneeling figures lost in the strains of their own singing. Their hands crossed, their eyes lifted to heaven, their bodies swaying in harmony with the tones, their voices mellow, passionate, tearful, gathering strength from each other, verse after verse, till the end. We broke their mood by appearing on the scene. "Here is a stranger who would like to talk to you," said the guard. Like children, a little bashful, suspicious, they slowly came forward and looked out of the cage, their white teeth shining against their dark faces. They were ready to tell their story and to ask for information. I had no information to give—no advice to offer. I gave them what I could for little things and they sang for me—I protested, but they paid back the only way they could, by singing some songs of the South. . . .

From Frank Tannenbaum, *Darker Phases of the South*, pp. 34–36, 82–83, 94–96.

7

Politics

The specter of black political domination supposedly has long haunted Southern whites. The reaction against black participation in Southern political life that arose during the critical post–Civil War period is, in many areas, still with us. Although outside observers have not left us systematic information on the Negro in politics, it is interesting to learn whether they viewed post-Reconstruction Negroes as ill-equipped, corrupt, tobacco-chewing, and whiskey-drinking lawmakers and vote-sellers or as constructive black voters and statesmen.

Those who observed black political participation in the South after 1877 had, of course, to look quickly. After the turn of the century, as a result of the disfranchisement legislation of the 1890's, effective Negro participation in Southern politics was ended, not to be revived for almost a half-century.

Laura Towne observed Negro participation in state and congressional elections in 1877 and 1878 on St. Helena Island, South Carolina, where blacks

In the Cage

were an overwhelming majority. The election of 1878 was especially distressing for Negroes because of the defeat for re-election of Robert Smalls, a Civil War hero and Negro Congressman. The defeat also saddened Mrs. Towne, for Smalls was one of her favorites.

[December 16, 1877] The election here passed off quietly, and all through the county wherever the Republican vote was large, there was perfect peace. The Democrats were not molested, but voted as they pleased, but up-country, where the Democrats were in a majority, the Republicans were driven from the polls with knives and clubs. Some of them were badly wounded and came down to Beaufort for protection and legal redress. . . .

[December 30, 1877] Our county is divided in two, thank goodness. It is now the old Beaufort County, and the upper part is Palmetto County. Though the election here went all one way, they say it will be disputed in Columbia and up at Sumter, where the majority of votes were Republican; the ballot boxes were stolen, opened, stuffed, and everything done to make a new election necessary, when intimidation could be brought to bear, so as to get a different result. The *News and Courier* of Charleston, a Hampton paper, says it is disgusting to hear of Republican victories in these two places, but that as they are undoubted victories, let the elected men take their seats.

[November 6, 1878] The election was a most quiet one. It was opposite our school, but so still that we said it was impossible to believe that hundreds of people were just outside. The Democratic Commissioner of Elections appointed none but Democratic managers throughout this whole county. Our three were C., B., and one of the drunken C.'s,—the one who

Politics

used to be so cruel and burn the people with pine tar dropped blazing on their backs. They were all watched by the people, who appointed a committee for the purpose, and numbers of them stayed to see the votes counted at night. On Saturday I went to a Republican meeting at the church. Robert Smalls told of his mobbing at Gillisonville. He was announced to speak there, and when ten o'clock—the hour—came, he was on the spot and with him about forty men. The stand was in front of a store in the street, and men and women were coming up the street to attend the meeting, when eight hundred red-shirt men, led by colonels, generals, and many leading men of the state, came dashing into the town, giving the "real rebel yell," the newspaper said. Robert Smalls called it "whooping like Indians." They drew up, and as a body stood still, but every few minutes a squad of three or four would scour down street on their horses, and reaching out would "lick off the hats" of the colored men or slap the faces of the colored women coming to the meeting, whooping and yelling and scattering the people on all sides. This made the colored men so mad that they wanted to pitch right into a fight with the eight hundred, but Robert Smalls restrained them, telling them what folly it was. Then the leader, Colonel somebody, came up and demanded half-time. Robert S. said there would be no meeting. Then they said he should have a meeting and should speak. He refused to say a word at a Democratic meeting, and as there was no Republican one, he said he would not speak at all. They gave him ten minutes to make up his mind. Then he withdrew into the store with his forty men and drew them all up around it behind the counters. They had guns. He told them to aim at the door, and stand with finger on trigger, but on no account to shoot unless the red-shirts broke in. Meantime, when the ten minutes were over, the outsiders began to try to

In the Cage

break down the door. They called Smalls and told him they would set fire to the house and burn him up in it. They fired repeatedly through the windows and walls. He showed us two balls he had picked up inside. He would not come out, and the leaders led off part of the red-shirts and began to make speeches, leaving the store surrounded, however, for fear Smalls should escape.

The people who had come to the meeting meanwhile ran to raise the alarm in every direction, and in an incredibly short time the most distant parts of the county heard that their truly beloved leader was trapped in a house surrounded by red-shirts, and that his life was in danger. Every colored man and woman seized whatever was at hand—guns, axes, hoes, etc., and ran to the rescue. By six o'clock afternoon a thousand negroes were approaching the town, and the red-shirts thought best to gallop away. They left twenty armed men to meet the train upon which Smalls was to return to Beaufort and to "attend to him." He had to go away ahead of the train and jump on the tender in the dark, and so he got back safely. At every station they met troops of negroes, one and two hundred together, all on their way to Gillisonville to the rescue. Smalls thinks this attack was caused by Hampton's saying in a public speech that there was but one man he now thought ought to be out of the way, and that man was Robert Smalls, who, by giving the Republicans one more vote in the House, would strengthen them in the choice of the next President, which would probably take place in the House of Representatives. I think if Robert S. does meet with any violence there will be hot times between blacks and rebs, but of course it is not likely they will touch him, after election,—unless he is elected,—when I do not think his life would be worth a button.

Our poor county was chuzzled out of one of its greatest

Politics

privileges last week by that rascally old turncoat, Judge M. By a trick, Dr. White was put into the Board of County Commissioners. That was the beginning of the train. Then, Renty Greaves, chairman, and the other county commissioners were all arrested for not keeping the roads and bridges on St. Helena in order, and were held on $5000 bond for Renty, and $2000 for the others, including even the clerk—our school commissioner, Wheeler. Besides this, they arrested them late on Saturday night so that they should have to spend Sunday in jail. But they found bondsmen,—Mr. Waterhouse and Mr. Collins going bail for them,—that is, for all but Dr. White, who was, of course, bailed by his Democratic friends. Then the Judge bulldozed Renty Greaves—told him he would have a term in jail, but that if he would resign his chairmanship to Dr. White, he should be set at liberty at once, and his bondsmen released. Renty, by virtue of his office, was one of the Board of Jury Commissioners, and the only Republican on it. If he resigned to Dr. White, all would be Democrats and the juries chosen by them. He was scared into doing it, and so we have three Democrats in that office, where the whole county is Republican! I see danger to the lands in this move, for one of the papers said last winter that now that they had all Democratic judges on the bench, it was time to bring the titles to these lands before "an intelligent jury of the former residents of the islands!"

The people at the election yesterday seemed much impressed by the importance of this election, and there was no sky-larking. They meant business. Only nine Democratic voters here, and all but one of these white men!

[November 10, 1878] Our election was quiet, of course. The people seemed thoroughly in earnest, and voted steadily and silently without the usual play and laughter. The four

In the Cage

Democratic managers were well watched by various parties, among others by a committee appointed for the purpose by vote of the people. The count of the vote at night was specially attended to. The result on this island was nine hundred and eighteen votes, only nine of them Democratic and only one of the nine a colored man's vote. This is much fewer than at the election two years ago, and shows that here Democracy does not gain ground. Of course, Robert Smalls was defeated, and the people are greatly grieved about it, and are not reconciled to the result.

[November 17, 1878] We had another "chiel, takin' notes" on Friday, but I do not know whether he intends to "prent 'em." It was no less a personage than Sir George Campbell, member of the English Parliament, who is here on a "tour of inspection," the papers say. Robert Smalls brought him over, and we had a good lunch together—we three, Sir G. C., Robert S., and I. I had stayed at home on account of the raw, damp day, and had a cold in my head, which is now much better. Sir G. stopped at the school, and made some remarks at the church convention, which was being held at the brick church opposite. He was a pleasing and very gentlemanly person. What he came to inspect I do not know. He questioned me chiefly about the people, and their rate of progress. Robert S. is very cheerful, and says the outrageous bulldozing and cheating in this last election is the best thing that could have happened for the Republican Party, for it has been so barefaced and open that it cannot be denied, and so much depends upon having Republicans in Congress now that he thinks it will not be negligently passed over, as it has been before.

From Rupert Sargent Holland, ed., *Letters and Diary of Laura M. Towne*, pp. 271, 283–284, 289, 292–293.

Politics

Rutherford B. Hayes, nineteenth President of the United States, made a "good will" tour to Alabama, Georgia, Kentucky, and Tennessee in September 1877, partly to see how the Negro was faring in the hands of "the intelligent" white people of the South. It is ironic that Hayes should have been the architect of the policy which, if Rayford Logan's estimate is correct, helped to send the Negroes to their nadir. Hayes favored a "hands-off" policy with respect to Southern race relations: the federal government would not interfere with local and state authorities in their handling of the "Negro problem." Hayes was confident that the mass of "intelligent" white people in the South would treat the blacks fairly. Before and after his tour, Hayes viewed, from Washington, the worsening political situation for Southern blacks, finally supporting a black exodus from the region as one way to protect their rights.

[Diary of March 16, 1877]

Stanley Matthews was yesterday night nominated for Senator at Columbus. This is an endorsement of the policy of peace and home rule—of local self-government. A number of Southern Republican members are reported ready to go over to the Democrats. On the other hand, the bar of this District [of Columbia] are in a state of mind because Fred Douglass, the most distinguished and able colored man in the Nation, has been nominated marshal for the District. If a liberal policy towards the late Rebels is adopted, the ultra Republicans are opposed to it; if the colored people are honored, the extremists of the other wing cry out against it. I suspect I am right in both cases. . . .

In the Cage

[Diary of April 22, 1877]

We have got through with the South Carolina and Louisiana [problems]. At any rate, the troops are ordered away, and I now hope for peace, and what is equally important security and prosperity for the colored people. The result of my plans is to get from those States by their governors, legislatures, press and people pledges that the 13th, 14th, and 15th Amendments shall be faithfully observed; that the colored people shall have equal rights to labor, education, and the privilege of citizenship. I am confident this is a good work. Time will tell. . . .

[Letter dated May 7, 1877, to John E. King, Collector, New Orleans]

The appointment of colored men to places under you for which they are qualified will tend to secure to people of their race consideration and will diminish race prejudice. Other elements of your population are, of course not to be overlooked. . . . Please consult with Colonel Wharton and endeavor to arrange your subordinate appointments so as to harmonize and meet the wishes and approval of all classes of good citizens, and at the same time to promote the efficiency of the service. . . .

[Diary of June 1878]

The notable political event of the month is the adjournment of Congress the nineteenth (at 7. A.M., 20th). I went with all the Cabinet to the President's room in the Capitol at 12 M., 19th. Remained a few hours when the date of adjournment was changed from 19th, 6 P.M., to 19th, 10 P.M. We returned at 8 P.M. Time changed to 1 A.M., again to 3 A.M., then to 5 A.M., and finally to 7 A.M., 20th! Too many of the Enrollment Committee of the House were drunk! So of the clerks! The colored member, Rainey, of South Carolina, kept sober and alone secured attention to the Sundry Civil Service Bill, appropriating

Politics

many millions and perhaps eighteen million dollars! At the last one or two important pages relating to the Hot Springs were omitted or stolen from the bill. *It should be investigated.* . . .

[Diary of October 5, 1878]

I am told by Mr. Rainey, colored Congressman from South Carolina, that in Sumter and other counties the whites are resorting to intimidation and violence to prevent the colored people from organizing for the elections. The division there is still on the color line. Substantially all the whites are Democrats and all the colored people are Republicans. There is no political principle in dispute between them. The whites have the intelligence, the property, and the courage which make power. The negroes are for the most part ignorant, poor, and timid. My view is that the whites must be divided there before a better state of things will prevail. . . .

[Diary of October 26, 1878]

I must make a clear, firm, and accurate statement of the facts as to Southern outrages, and reiterate the sound opinions I have long held on the subject. What good people demand is exact justice, equality before the law . . . and no denial of rights to any citizen on account of color or race—the same to colored as to whites. . . .

[Diary of November 6, 1878]

The elections of yesterday show very gratifying results. The States of New England are solid for sound principles. . . .

Everywhere in the North we are stronger than in any off year since the war, except possibly in 1866 when Johnson was overwhelmed. The South is substantially solid against us. Their vote is light; our side was unorganized, a host of people of both colors took no part. The blacks, poor, ignorant, and timid, can't stand alone against the whites. . . .

[Diary of November 12, 1878]

In the Cage

In South Carolina and Louisiana, and perhaps in some other cotton States, grave charges are made that the constitutional provisions which guarantee equal citizenship have been practically nullified; that by fraud or force of intimidation, colored citizens have been disfranchised.

[Diary of November 12, 1878]

By state legislation, by frauds, by intimidation, and by violence of the most atrocious character, colored citizens have been deprived of the right of suffrage—a right guaranteed by the Constitution, and to the protection of which the people of those States have been solemnly pledged. . . .

[Diary of May 25, 1879]

The exodus of colored people from the South still attracts some attention. Its effect is altogether favorable. The tendency will be to force the better class of Southern people to suppress the violence of the ruffian class, and to protect colored people in their rights. Let the emigrants be scattered throughout the Northwest; let them be encouraged to get homes and settled employment. . . .

[Letter to unidentified person, August 16, 1884]

. . . Wherever universal education prevails in the United States, the results of the war are cheerfully accepted and the constitutional amendments embodying the results are inviolable. Ignorance is the enemy most to be dreaded by the friends of free government. Ignorant voters are powder and ball for the demagogues. The right to vote will lose its value in our country if ignorance is permitted permanently to prevail in any considerable portion of it. The schoolmaster alone can abolish the evils which slavery has left in the South. Universal education is the only safe foundation for universal suffrage. . . .

From Charles Richard Williams, ed., *Diary and Letters of Rutherford Birchard Hayes, Nineteenth President of the United States* (3 vols., Columbus,

Politics

Ohio: Ohio State Archaeological and Historical Society, 1924), III, 427, 430, 433, 488, 501–502, 505, 509–510, 522, 553–554, 621.

George Augustus Sala saw Negro legislators in the Louisiana House in 1879–1880 who were still "in an infantile condition," and great allowances, in fairness, had to be made for them. Sala (1828–1895), born of slaveholding parentage in the West Indies, "an ardent sympathizer with the South" when he visited the United States in 1863–1864, declared in 1880, "My heart is still in the South." Sala first wrote of his experiences in letters to the *London Daily Telegraph*.

The Senate Chamber at the disestablished hotel had adjourned, and all that my guide could do was to take me into the Chamber and introduce me to some of the Senators. But the House of Representatives, or Delegates—I am not quite certain as to which is the precise legislative designation of the Louisianian House of Commons—was in full session. The hall of debate was a capacious apartment which had once been either the ball-room or the dining-room of the defunct hotel. Pale phantoms of once elegant frescoes loomed faintly on the walls. I glanced instinctively at the floor, as though expecting to find it littered with the champagne corks of Piper, Heidsieck or Veuve Clicquot—with faded bouquets, time-worn satin slippers, cards of invitation to radiant belles long since widowed and childless, to gallant gentlemen whose bones have mouldered these seventeen years past in the graveyards of the Confederate Dead. But I was aroused from my reverie by the voice of a gentleman who was addressing the House. It was somewhat of a variable and capricious voice—at one time hoarse and rasping, at another shrilly treble, and the orator ended his periods now with a sound resembling a chuckle, and now with one as closely akin to a grunt. So far—being rather hard of hearing—as I could make out, the Honourable Legislator was remarking "dat de gen'lm'n from de Parish of St. Quelquechose was developing assertions and expurgating ratiocinations clean agin de fuss principles of law and equity. What was law and equity? Was dey verities or was dey frauds? Kin yer go behind the records of law and equity? Kin de gen'lm'n from St. Quelquechose lay his hand on his heart and the Constitooshun of de Yurnited States and say dat dese votes had been counted out rightfully? An' if dese votes had not been counted out rightfully, where, he asked the gen'lm'n from St. Quelquechose, were de fuss principles of law and equity? Where was dey? From de lumberlands of Maine to de morse-clad banks of de Chefunetee Ecker answered dat de hull ting was contrairy to de standing order of dis House." Upon which the orator sat down. There were no cheers nor counter cheers—only a rippling murmur of voices such as you hear at a public dinner between the port and sherry ceasing and the champagne beginning to go round. What was the precise mode of catching the Speaker's eye I could not exactly discern, but more than one honourable gentleman seemed to be on his legs at the same time. When the contingency appeared to be imminent of everybody addressing the House at once, the dull, measured sounds of the Presidential hammer, or "gavel," as, in masonic parlance, the implement of order is called, was audible. It would be a vain task to strive textually to report what the legislators said; but the debate, so far as I understood its purport, related to a contested election.

Ere the orator who had apostrophised the gentleman from

Politics

the parish of St. Quelquechose resumed his seat, I had ample leisure to make a study of his facial outline, for there was a window close behind him, against which his profile was defined as sharply as in one of those old black silhouette portraits which they used to take for sixpence on the old Chain Pier at Brighton. The honourable legislator had a fully-developed Ethiopian physiognomy; but when he sat down I found that in hue he was only a mulatto. There were more coloured members in the House:—some of them "bright" mulattoes and quadroons, very handsome and distinguished looking individuals. As yet our dark brother as a legislator must to most intents and purposes be considered as in an infantile condition, and great allowances must in fairness be made for him. A Southern gentleman pointed out to me one of the coloured Representatives or Delegates who, prior to the war, had been his, the gentleman's slave and body servant. He was a very useful member of the House, my informant said, especially on questions of finance. As regards Parliamentary procedure, the coloured members are very often not only on a par with, but superior to, their white colleagues. They set themselves with grim earnestness to study and learn by heart all the rules and regulations of the House, concerning which the white members are often careless; and they are continually rising to that which they term "p'ints of order." When they address themselves to set speech making, they usually gabble a quantity of intolerable verbiage; but please to bear in mind that the majority of the coloured members in the Southern legislatures have either been slaves, or are the sons of men who once were slaves.

What the coloured sons of freemen may do in the next generation is the grand problem. At present they are eagerly availing themselves of the educational advantages offered by the common schools; and it remains in the future to be seen whether there be any truth in the assertion that it is possible only to educate the negro up to a certain point, but no further. He cannot be taught, so many say, to argue reasonably. This assertion applies of course to the full-blooded negro. As regards the coloured man with only a slight admixture of black blood in his veins, I see no reason why he should not—if he avail himself of the facilities for culture now open to him—become as intellectually distinguished as Alexandre Dumas. But the ranks of the "bright" mulattoes and quadroons will not be recruited. The abolition of slavery arrested the continuity of the offspring of the children of white fathers and coloured mothers; and what is known or rather darkly whispered about as "miscegenation" is only a dream, and a very wild dream of the coming era. For the present it is simply a social impossibility; and the coloured man who is audacious enough to practise "miscegenation" by cohabiting with a white woman is immediately and ruthlessly lynched. Two such "miscegenators" have been hanged by the mob in Virginia within the last month. . . .

In the Louisianian as in the Federal capital every member has a comfortable arm-chair and a desk before him, with lockers and drawers for his books and papers. One of the honourable gentlemen in the New Orleans Legislature was so obliging as to give me up his desk and arm-chair, which I occupied with great inward fear and trembling for some five-and-twenty minutes. Several divisions took place during that space of time, the House dividing on the "aye" and "no" principle; and I can only express a conscientious hope that I did not vote. The entire proceedings were, I have not the slightest doubt, quite tranquil and orderly; but, to the eye of a stranger, the scene was one of curious confusion. The citizens of the State of Louisiana en masse, white and coloured, had standing-room at the back of the apartment, which was only

Politics

separated from the House itself by a wooden barrier; but on the floor of the House there seemed to be as many strangers as legislators, and there was a continual running to and fro of messengers and telegraph boys. . . .

To return to the picture in the State House. . . . This brief sketch of a Southern Parliament should not be concluded without note being taken of the fact that the great majority of the honourable members were vigorously smoking cigars or cigarettes throughout the debate. Why not? . . .

From George Augustus Sala, *America Revisited* (New York: I. K. Funk and Co., 1880), pp. 313–318.

Sir George Campbell studied Negro political participation in South Carolina and Virginia shortly after his arrival in the South in 1878. After talking with white and black politicians in South Carolina, he discovered that blacks were cheated and intimidated at the polls. The political situation in Virginia, at least in the Petersburg congressional district, was much better for the Negro than it was in South Carolina. The Negro majority in the district had elected their candidates to federal and state offices.

Mr. Y—— [formerly a Confederate officer, now an insurance man] does not confirm the statement that a certain number of seats in the State Assemblies are allowed to the blacks by way of conciliation and minority representation. He says that whatever seats they have they only get by hard voting, and he admits that when the Democrats are hard put to it they sometimes manipulate a good deal in the counting of votes. The negroes are in a very decided majority in the Petersburg Congressional District; and, besides returning some members to the State Assembly, they have hitherto succeeded in returning a Republican member to Congress, a Norwegian, who seems generally admitted to be a very able man, and who has much influence with the negroes. The blacks have great faith in General Grant, as the man who gave them their freedom, and they go to the poll as his supporters. There are several companies of black militia volunteers in this State, with their own black officers; there is one such company at Petersburg, said to be much better drilled than the white companies. . . .

As a general result of all that I have been able to learn about the elections in this part of the country, I may say that there does not seem to be the least doubt that they were won by the most wholesale cheating. That is avowed in the most open way. Most people seem to praise the negroes, and to be on very good terms with them; but they all admit that, while the blacks will do almost anything else for them, when it comes to voting they cannot be influenced, and insist on voting with their party. . . . The blacks seem to have accepted their defeat as a foregone conclusion, and therefore it is that they are quite good-natured over it. Perhaps, too, they really have to some degree accepted Wade Hampton and his policy, and are not so anxious to fight as they otherwise might be. . . . The Democrats of Charleston have done something to conciliate those blacks who accept the Democratic ticket. In this district seventeen members are sent up to the State Assembly, and of these three are Democratic blacks. The county officers are whites, but there are some blacks in the Charleston municipality. . . .

I also made the acquaintance of General S———, the negro congressman for this district [Beaufort], who has just been ousted in the recent election, or rather will be ousted in consequence. . . . General S——— is the hero who carried off

Politics

the gun-boat *Planter* from the Confederates. He is a robust, burly, dark man, now in the prime of life and very popular with the blacks. After the war he became a General of the National Guards, a Congressman, and a considerable person. He attributes the loss of the present election entirely to fraud and intimidation. He denies that any considerable number of blacks went over to the enemy. In these lower districts there was not much actual violence at the time of the poll, but there had been intimidation and serious obstruction to his canvass and his meetings before the election. The Republicans, he says, have an enormous majority in this and the adjoining districts, if they only got fair play. Now the Democrats have elected the bitterest of their party; there has rarely been any compromise. They are sending two or three black Democrats to the State Legislature from the Charleston district; but that is quite an exception. As to the remedy for the frauds which have deprived him of his seat he says he might lodge a petition in Congress; but, if he does, he must bear all the expense of the petition and the witnesses to support his case, and then he would not have a chance as long as the Democrats have the majority in Congress. He does not seem to be supported by any party organization in or out of the State. He takes a favourable view of the condition of the coloured people, and is against Liberia.... Though they have been so unfairly treated in the elections, they are the best-natured people in the world, and bear no malice. He complains very much of the want of justice. There were eight hundred political murders committed by the Ku-Klux and other Democratic organizations, but not a single white has been hanged nor a single one sent to the Penitentiary by the States Courts—only a few imprisoned by the United States Courts. He attributed the difficulty to the rule requiring unanimity of the jury, which still prevails. The whites, he says, have sworn to their clubs never to convict. As

In the Cage

long as there is one of them on the jury they never will. . . . General S—— admits that there was very much abuse during the eight years of Radical rule in the State. They were led astray by bad men. He declares, however, that the black members now sent to the State Assembly from this county are good men; two of them are well educated, and the third, though illiterate, is a good Christian farmer. I like what I have seen of General S——. . . .

From Sir George Campbell, *White and Black*, pp. 282, 331, 341–342.

Ernst von Hesse-Wartegg, the German Consul, was amused to see Negro lawmakers in the Louisiana legislature. He would admit that blacks had established themselves as excellent field workers, but as legislators they played "a right dismal role."

The blacks, the former slaves, have a part of the reins of state government in their hands; once they were the last, now they are the first, and bitterly many of the former "firsts" have fallen back into poverty and misery. Sambo from Africa; Sambo, the black, sweaty, . . . grinning slave . . . sits in the old, high position of his former master! . . .

In the sessions of the Representatives there is much amusement when one of the many black gentlemen, in dirty shirt and stained coat, moves to speak in the debates, with the defective English of his once humble race. Shallow, pompous phraseology is repeated in each occasion. There are interruptions and confusion. The honourable Speaker helps the gentleman through it amid various motions and propositions. . . .

Politics

One yet must certainly not forget that these "Gentlemen of the House" were once slaves, that many had just learned to read and write when they acquired power. Yet I hesitate to express my legitimate doubt concerning the coming generation. The black "gentlemen" (because the word "Nigger" is despised by them) are big, strong people, who have established themselves excellently as workers in the field; but in the House of Representatives of a million people, whose capital city is an international city, they, however, certainly play a right dismal role.

The parliamentary institutions of the northern states are also in force here, only they are not passed over just a little by the blacks here; they will intentionally smoke and chew tobacco, sleep, and eat during the debates. Well, why not? Don't these black legislators live in a free country? . . .

From Ernst von Hesse-Wartegg, *Mississippi-Fahrten*, pp. 213–214, 223–226.

James Bryce, in the following selection, discusses the philosophy and practice of Negro disfranchisement, and analyzes the blacks' responses to it.

So keen is their recollection of the carpet-bag days, so intense the alarm at any possibility of their return, that internal dissensions, such as those which the growth of the Farmers' Alliance party and (later) of the Populist party evoked, were seldom permitted to give Republican candidates a chance of a seat in Congress or of any considerable State office.

These remarks apply to the true South, and neither to the mountain regions, where, owing to the absence of the negro

In the Cage

element, there is, save in the wider valleys, still a strong Republican party, nor to the Border States, Maryland, West Virginia, Kentucky and Missouri, in which the coloured voters are not numerous enough to excite alarm. When it is desired to eliminate their influence on elections, a common plan is to bribe them. In Louisville one is told that quite a small payment secures abstention. To induce them to vote for a Democrat is, to their credit be it said, much more costly. . . .

The methods whereby the negroes have been prevented from exercising the rights of suffrage vested in them by law have been described. . . . These means become less violent as the negroes more and more acquiesced in their exclusion; but whether violent or pacific, they were almost uniformly successful. In the so-called Border States, the whites have been in so great a majority that they do not care to interfere with the coloured vote, except now and then by the use of money. Through the rest of the South the negro came to realize that he would not be permitted to exercise any influence on the government; and his interest in coming to the polls declined accordingly. The main cause of the resolve of the whites to keep power entirely in their own hands is the alarm they feel at the possibility of negro domination. A stranger, whether from the North or from Europe, thinks this alarm groundless. He perceives that the whites have not only the habit of command, but also nearly all the property, the intelligence, and the force of character which exists in the country. He reminds his Southern hosts that the balance even of numbers is inclining more and more in their favour. . . .

Among the leaders of the negroes themselves there is a difference of views and policy on the matter. Some, bitterly resenting the disfranchising provisions, try to keep up an opposition to them, although they see little or no prospect of get-

Politics

ting them repealed. Others think it is better to accept facts which they are powerless to alter, consoling themselves by the reflection that provisions which make the suffrage depend on education and property tend to stimulate the negro to raise himself to the tests prescribed for active citizenship. The bulk of the coloured people who live on the plantations take no interest in the matter. Among the more educated, the authority of Dr. Booker Washington has gone some way to commend the policy of preferring industrial progress to political agitation; nor to add that it is hard to see what agitation could accomplish. . . .

No person of colour has for a long time past sat in Congress, nor in the legislature of any Southern State, though now and then one may find his way into a Northern state legislature. A few hold small county offices in the South, and a few have been appointed by Presidents to Federal posts, such as collectors of ports or postmasters, in the South. . . .

From James Bryce, *The American Commonwealth,* II, 506–507, 529, 547–549.

William Laird Clowes, chiefly remembered as a naval historian, was educated at King's College, London. He prepared for the bar, but never practiced. Beginning newspaper work in 1885 as special correspondent for the *Standard,* he was with the *Times* of London from 1890 to 1895. He wrote *The Navy and the Empire* (1892) and *The Royal Navy* (7 vols., 1897–1903). Clowes was sent to the South in the fall of 1890 by the *Times* to study the South-

In the Cage

ern scene. In this selection he describes the iniquitous practice of Negro disfranchisement—a practice which he found on the whole reprehensible.

In the "tissue-ballot" days fraudulent party leaders caused it to be printed upon the very thinnest of tissue-paper, so that the thickness of, say, twenty-five tissue-tickets did not much exceed that of an ordinary piece of writing-paper. These tickets were entrusted to unscrupulous voters of the right political complexion. The ballots, before being deposited, had to be folded, but only lightly folded; and thus, when an expert fraudulent voter folded his twenty-five tissue-tickets together and gave them a gentle flip as he dropped them into the box, the papers flew open and apart, and at once assumed a comparatively innocent appearance. Upon the close of the poll the ballots were counted and their number was compared with that of the registered electors who had voted at that booth. There was found to be a large excess of ballots; whereupon all the papers were returned to the box, and an election manager, in accordance with precedent, undertook the duty of withdrawing sufficient ballots to make the remainder tally with the number of voters who had polled. If, as was generally the case, the manager was fraudulent, he took care to draw out only thick tickets. If, as may have sometimes happened, he was honest, he took the tickets as they came, thick and thin indifferently. But in either event the party that used "tissue-ballots" naturally gained an immense advantage. If the negroes—against whom almost exclusively this device was employed—suspected and protested, revolvers were exhibited by the other side.

Such a revelation as this may appear incredible to British readers, but it by no means exhausts the villainies of American politics as they are displayed at the polls, even at this

Politics

day; and Americans themselves seem to accept such things as matters of course. . . . A normally respectable Southern newspaper, the Charleston *News and Courier,* during the last campaign, cooly gave to its readers the following advice:—"Go to the polls to-day. Vote early, vote often, vote Straight." (November 4, 1890). And I am bound to admit that the counsel was acted upon. . . .

On November 4th, 1890, I was present at a voting place at Mount Pleasant in South Carolina. The whites were voting for [Pitchfork Ben] Tillman, the Farmers' Alliance Candidate, for Governor. A small dissentient body of whites and the whole body of negroes were voting for Haskell, the Democratic-Republican Coalition candidate. The District is a very black one, one of the blackest in the State, and its vote was much counted upon by the Haskell party. Overnight, therefore, the Tillmanites tried, but in vain, to destroy the booth; and on the day of the election they adopted a modification of the old "tissue-ballot" trick, using, however, ordinary instead of tissue-ballots. Two hundred and forty-four persons voted at this particular booth. When one of the boxes was opened it was found to contain a largely excessive number of ballots; the exact number was, if I recollect rightly, 477. The surplus 233 papers were cast out by the managers, some of whom were shrewdly suspected of being parties to the conspiracy, and the result of the poll in that precinct was decided by the verdict of the remainder. Nor was this the only villainy that was perpetrated on that day in the neighbourhood. In an adjoining precinct a Tillman champion named Gaillard seized and destroyed the registration books, thus rendering the polling impossible in default of duplicate books. Ballot boxes, too, are sometimes destroyed or made away with. Indeed, there is no conceivable scoundrelism that is not, or has not been, practiced in the South to neutralise the negro vote.

In the Cage

From what I have written it will be clear that the extension of the suffrage to the coloured race in the Southern States by no means ensures the representation of the black man. The situation is a very disgraceful one for the Southern whites; but even the better class of Southern politicians with whom I have conversed upon the subject tacitly, if not expressly, defend, as with one voice, the iniquitous system. "We cannot," they say, "be ruled by the negroes; we must protect ourselves. It is very lamentable; but what is the alternative?"

It is hard to suggest a practicable one, for the fatal and irretrievable mistake of bestowing the suffrage upon every male citizen of full age has already been made....

From W. Laird Clowes, *Black America: Study of the Ex-Slave and His Late Master* (London: Cassell, 1891), pp. 78–85.

André Siegfried concluded after his Southern tour that the politics of the South were based on force. The blacks were virtually denied all political rights.

At present the blacks are crushed under the heel. In the first place, all political rights are denied them. According to the Fifteenth Amendment to the Constitution, ratified on March 30, 1870, "the right of the citizen of the United States to vote shall not be denied or abridged by the United States, or by any State, on account of race, colour, or previous conditions of servitude." The southern States refused to ratify it, but the measure went through in spite of them. After 1890 laws were passed in all the southern States which, without actually designating the blacks, excluded them from the suffrage. Sometimes

Politics

it is done by establishing electoral lists; sometimes the applicants are asked to give a "reasonable interpretation" of the Constitution, and naturally a negro never succeeds. A clause called "the Grandfather Act" automatically allows the whites, even though poor and illiterate, to vote without this examination, provided they are ex-soldiers or the descendants of those who voted in 1867. The fraud is evident and is contrary to the spirit of the Constitution, but the North winks at it; for to interfere would mean another war. If by chance a negro were to slip through the meshes of the net, he would not dare present himself at the polling booth; for he would be beaten off with clubs, and his very life would be in danger. In the eastern border States of Virginia and North Carolina this severity has been somewhat relaxed, but in the South as a whole practically all the negroes are treated as pariahs. No negro has ever been appointed or elected to a public position, although in certain rare exceptions, the Customs for example, they have been employed, owing entirely to Federal influence. Otherwise the whites maintain a united front without a single break. There is no doubt that southern politics are based not on equality, but on force....

From André Siegfried, *America Comes of Age*, pp. 93–94.

Retrospect

The views presented in this book have come from a rather select group of observers. They include novelists, journalists, economists, sociologists, historians, lawyers, politicians, diplomats, physicians, theologians—men and women with the facility to record their impressions. Clearly, they had their share of biases and preconceptions, stemming in part from contemporary ethnology and psychology.

A most important and striking conclusion to be drawn from these impressions of outsiders is that they did not differ radically from those usually attributed to Southern whites. If the Southern white saw the Negro as a physical and mental inferior, generally lazy, untidy, prone to immorality and crime, politically inept, excessively pious, but fun-loving, so did a good many outsiders. Some of these views were even shared by the four black observers included in this book, though all of the blacks denied any natural inferiority. They were more likely to see environmental, rather than racial, factors as determining Negro characteristics.

The sum of the observations presented here appears to confirm the view, now widely held, that the mass of blacks enjoyed no radical advances in social and economic conditions during the half-century from the end of Reconstruction to the eve of the New Deal. The rural black masses remained bound to the soil and its meager financial rewards, enduring destitution, dilapidated housing, ragged dress, and ill health. Dispro-

Retrospect

portionate involvement in crime was an inevitable result. The situation among urban blacks was sometimes improved, but often worse. Generally speaking, the relatively small group of artisans and professional and business people were the only ones who escaped poverty.

The political status of the blacks actually deteriorated. In 1877 large numbers of them still voted, and Negroes were to be seen in state assemblies from Virginia to Louisiana, in the United States House of Representatives, and in lesser elective and appointive positions at local, state, and national levels. But Negro disfranchisement—of which outsiders generally disapproved—became so severe by the early 1900's that it virtually ended effective participation by blacks in Southern politics until long after the New Deal.

The Negro church was a place where the blacks could find respite from their daily frustrations, whether social, economic, or political. From Reconstruction to the New Deal its simple and emotional services attracted large numbers of the race and, indeed, became the blacks' most important social institution. Only the more astute observers, however, could see this larger role of the black church—its potentials for social, and even economic and political, cohesion, and its function as a laboratory for leadership. For too many outsiders, these possibilities were drowned out by fervent preaching, wild shouts, and loud singing.

A good many outsiders made less than judicious reports of black life because they failed to realize that three centuries of slavery and discrimination had obscured the social, cultural, economic, and political capacities of the Negro and in many instances actually distorted his personality. Any outsider, any native, white or black, who drew his impressions of the Southern Negro without considering the dominating role

In the Cage

of racial discrimination, which placed the race in a straitjacket, in a cage, probably did not see the Negro at all. Such an observer, in other words, could hardly be expected to report judiciously on the lives of the blacks, or to evaluate their past, or to look toward their future.

Index

Adam, Paul August Marie, 150–153
Africa, 160, 196, 198
Age of Booker T. Washington, 7. *See also* Washington, Booker T.
"Age of recovery," 7
Agrarian Revolution in Georgia, The (Brooks), 84
Alabama, 5, 57–58, 187; rural area social conditions, 139
Alabama State Normal School, 71
Allan-Olney, Mary, 171–173, 194–195
America Comes of Age: A French Analysis (Siegfried), 127, 209, 259. *See also* Siegfried, André.
America Revisited (Sala), 249
American Adventures (Street), 165, 231. *See also* Street, Julian.
American Commonwealth, The (Bryce), 31, 33, 36, 95, 176, 198, 219, 231, 255. *See also* Bryce, James.
American Cotton Industry: A Study of Work and Workers, The (Young), 111
American Dilemma: The Negro Problem and Modern Democracy, An (Myrdal), 4
American Eugenics: Heredity and Social Thought 1870–1930 (Haller), 11

American Magazine, 41
American Nation (Hart, ed.), 45
American Negro Slavery (Phillips), 84
Amerika als neueste Weltmacht der Industrie (America as the Newest Industrial Power) (Hesse-Wartegg), 88. *See also* Hesse-Wartegg, Ernst von, 88.
"Anatomical Characters of the Human Brain" (Mall), 14
Antilles, Negroes, 197–198
Archer, William, 56–64
Arena, 225
Arkansas, 5
Arkansas, reconstruction, 143. *See also* Reconstruction.
Armstrong, General S. C., 21, 30, 33, 39, 73. *See also* Hampton Normal and Agricultural Institute.
Asheville, North Carolina, 140–142
Atlanta, Georgia: black-owned business prospering in, 7; riots, 115–117
"Atlanta Compromise" (Washington), 6–8, 16–17, 25, 75, 128. *See also* Washington, Booker T.
Atlanta University, 38–44, 56, 62; first president of, 70; Negro conferences, 102, 116, 156

Atlanta University Studies (DuBois), 34. *See also* DuBois, William Edward Burghardt.
"Aunt Jane and Her People: The Real Negroes of the Sea Islands" (Cooley), 207. *See also* Cooley, Rossa Belle.

Baker, Ray Stannard, 41–45, 117, 200–202
Baltimore: alley population, 139; Negro businessmen, 91; public schools for Negroes, 48. *See also* Education; Negroes.
Banks, E. M., 84
Baptists, 169–170, 187
Bardin, Joseph, 14–15
Barrows, Samuel J., 37–41, 99–104, 138–140
Benedict Institute, 23–24
Bennett, John, 182–186
Berea College, Kentucky, 49. *See also* Education.
Bible, the, 179–180
Birmingham, 101; iron mines, 120
Black America: Study of the Ex-Slave and His Late Master (Clowes), 258
Black Belt, 48, 135–139; safe for whites, 227
Black Man: His Antecedents, His Genius, and His Achievements, The (Brown), 24. *See also* Brown, William Wells.
Black nationalism, 10
Black Reconstruction (DuBois), 34. *See also* DuBois, William Edward Burghardt.
Black and White: Land, Labor, and Politics in the South (Fortune), 30, 93

Bluffton, South Carolina, 165
Boas, Franz, 12–14
Border States, 31, 176, 254
Brain, weight differences, Negro and Caucasian, 13–14
Brinton, Daniel G., 11, 12
Brooks, Robert Preston, 84
Brown, William Wells, 24–27, 129–132, 215–216
Brownsville, Texas, riots, 7, 58
Bruce, B. K., 91
Bryce, James, 30–33, 93–95, 135–136, 173–176, 195–198, 216–219, 253, 255
Bureau of Education. *See* United States Bureau of Education.
Burlin, Natalie Curtis, 167
Butterworth, Hezekiah, 180–182

Campbell, Sir George, 20–24, 85–88, 213–215, 249–252
Carnegie Foundation, 4
Carnegie Library, 59
Carpet-bag days, 253
Carver, Professor, 53, 56
Caste and Class in a Southern Town (Dollard), 4–5
Caucasian race, insanity, 160. *See also* Insanity.
Chain gangs, 213–214, 227–228, 233
Chairmolle (Adam), 150
Charleston earthquake, 164–165, 176–180
Chattanooga, 101
Chicago Record, 41
Christian Register, 37
Christianity: crude form of, 187; divorced from morality, 175–176; half-Christian service, 183–186; Jesus, 179; most real

Index

form of Christian religion, 190–192. *See also* Morality.
Christmas celebrations, St. Helena, 166–167
Clark University, 44
Clowes, William Laird, 255–258
Coal mines as system of penal administration, 233
Commission on Interracial Cooperation, in South, 10
Community Power Structure: A Study of Decision Makers (Hunter), 4
"Comparative Worth of Different Races, The" (Galton), 12
Cooley, Rossa Belle, 64–70, 123–125, 166–168, 190–192, 205–207
Cotton belt, 108
Cotton Industry, The (Hammond), 83–84, 107. *See also* Hammond, Matthew B.
Cotton States International Exposition (1895), 6–7
Creole planter, 135
Crime and punishment: chain gangs worst feature of Southern convict system, 227–228; factors contributing to criminality of Negro, 222–225; post-Reconstruction era, 212, 217–219
"Criminal Negro, The" (Kellor), 225. *See also* Kellor, Frances A.
Crisis, 34
"Cropping system," 109

Darien, Georgia, "gulla" dialect, 164
Darker Phases of the South (Tannenbaum), 4, 211, 234. *See also* Tannenbaum, Frank.

Death of Adam: Evolution and Its Impact on Western Thought, The (Greene), 11
Delaware, 5
"Delta region," 109–110
Dementia precox. *See* Insanity.
"Dementia Precox in the Colored Race" (Evarts), 161
Democrats, 236–240, 241, 243, 249–251, 254
Department of Agriculture, 70
Department of Labor, 96
Diary and Letters of Rutherford Birchard Hayes, Nineteenth President of the United States (Williams, ed.), 244–245
Discrimination, racial, 4–6, 261–263
Disfranchisement of Negro: legislation, 1890, 235, 244; philosophy and practice, 258–259, 261
Dollard, John, 4
Douglass, Frederick, 33, 241
DuBois, William Edward Burghardt, 7–8, 56, 62–64, 104, 198–200; first teaching assignment, 33–37; study of Negroes of Farmville, Virginia, 95–99, 198–200
Dumas, Alexander, 248

Economic exploitation, 6; plantation economy, 107; separatism, 115–117
Economics of Land Tenure in Georgia (Banks), 84
Edinburgh Evening News, 56
Education: attack on schools of academic classical variety, 27–29; Barrows impressed with progress in education, 37–39;

265

Education—*(Cont.)*
compulsory education in South not enforced, 42, 46; contributions of Northerners, 20, 23–26; criticism of, by Bryce, 31–33; elementary, 29, 31; inferiority of Negro schools, 47–51; no schools for Negro women, 26–27; primary education stimulated, 39–40; public schools, 20–22, 26; recognition of academic and industrial training for Negroes, 71–74; rise of professional class, 103–104; state schools for Negroes in Montgomery, 57; teachers, Northern, 44–45. *See also* Barrows, Samuel J.; DuBois, William Edward Burghardt; Negroes.
"Emancipation Day," 144
Emergence of the New South, The (Tindall), 9–10
En Amérique: De New York a La Nouvelle-Orléans (Huret), 190
Evarts, Arrah B., 157–161

Farmer's Last Frontier, The (Shannon), 84
Farmers' Alliance party, 253
Farmers' Fair, 166
Farmville, Virginia, 95–99, 198–200. *See also* DuBois, William Edward Burghardt.
Ferguson, George Oscar, Jr., 11–12, 13–14
Fifteenth Amendment, 258–259
Fisk, 25, 34
Florida, 5; Reconstruction, 143. *See also* Reconstruction.
Florida Agricultural and Mechanical College, 71

Following the Color Line: American Negro Citizenship in the Progressive Era (Baker), 45, 117, 202. *See also* Baker, Ray Stannard.
Foraker, Senator, 58
Fortune, T. Thomas, 27–30, 90–93
Fox, Howard, 162–163
France in World War I, 9
Franklin, John Hope, 7, 9, 10
Freedman's Colleges, 25–26
Freedmen, 27
Freedmen's Bureau Schools, 16
French. *See* Plantation French language.
From Slavery to Freedom (Franklin), 9, 10

Galton, Francis, 12
Garvey, Marcus, 10, 27
"Gate City of the South." *See* Atlanta, Georgia.
Georgia, 5, 42; Atlanta riots, 7; economic conditions, 100–104; owning of land by Negroes, 93; Statesboro lynchings, 7
Georgia State Industrial College, 71
Gibbs, Mifflin Wistar, 143–145
Gordon, Jan and Cora, 74–78
Gossett, Thomas F., 11
Government Hospital for the Insane, Washington, D.C., 157–161
"Grandfather Act," 259
Great Depression, 10, 84
Greene, John C., 11
Gulf States, 136. *See also* Black Belt.
"Gulla" dialect, 164

Index

Hall, G. Stanley, 13–14
Haller, Mark, 11
Hammond, Matthew B., 83, 84, 106–110
Hampton Normal and Agricultural Institute, 8, 21–27, 30–33, 39–40, 48, 51, 61–62, 67, 72, 79, 84, 101, 195, 226; Amerindians, 52; music, 52; Negro conferences, 156; Whittier School for Children. *See also* Education.
Handlin, Oscar, 11
"Happy John," clown, 140–142
Hardy, Iza Duffus, 137–138
Hart, Albert Bushnell, 45–51, 118–119, 202–204, 225–228
Harvard College, 34, 38, 45
Harvard Divinity School, 37
Hayes, Rutherford B., 241–245
Hazen, Henry H., 161–164
Hesse-Wartegg, Ernst von, 88–90, 132–135, 252–253
"Higher Education of Negroes in the United States" (Ware), 74
Highways and Byways of the South (Johnson), 150
Holland, Rupert Sargent, 20, 240
Holmes, George K., 104–106
Howard University, 6, 25, 27, 37
"Human Faculty as Determined by Race" (Boas), 13
Hunter, Floyd, 4
Huntsville, Alabama, new social life of Negroes, 129–131
Huret, Jules, 186–190

Illiteracy, 155
Indian, American, 20, 52; compared with Southern Negro, 195–197

Industrial education, 29. *See also* Hampton Normal and Agricultural Institute, 30
"Industrial fair," 143–145
Industrial and technological revolution, 6
Insanity, 158–161; increased since emancipation, 217
Integration, racial, 8
Interracial strife, greatest period of, 10

Jamaica, 160–161
Jeanes, Anna T., 79
Jeanes Fund, 79
Jeanes Teacher in the United States, 1908–1933: An Account of Twenty-Five Years' Experience in the Supervision of Negro Rural Schools, The (Jones), 82
Jeanes Teachers, 79–82
Johnson, Clifton, 148–150
Johnson, James Weldon, 10
Johnston, Sir Harry, 51–56, 119–122, 156–157, 204–205
Jones, Lance G. E., 79–82
Jones, Thomas Jesse, 153–156
"Judge Lynch" survives for blacks, 214–215, 217–219

Kellor, Frances A., 212, 221–225
Kelsey, Carl, 111–114
Kentucky, 5; economic conditions, 99–104
Ku Klux Klan, 232, 251

La Force (Adam), 151
LeBon, Gustave, 13
Lee, Robert E., 92

267

Letters and Diary of Laura M. Towne: Written from the Sea Islands of South Carolina, 1862–1884 (Holland, ed.), 20, 240
Liberia, 156, 251
Life and Labor in the Old South (Phillips), 84
Lincoln, President Abraham, 181
Livingston Institute, Salisbury, North Carolina, 39
Logan, W. Rayford, 6–7, 241
Lombroso, Cesare, 212; founder of the science of criminology, 219–221
Louisiana, 5; field hands in sugar cane plantations, 121, 133–135; Negro legislators, 245–249, 252–253; superstition, 176; wake, funeral, and internment of two black women, 186
Lynchburg, Virginia, 173

Mall, F. P., 14
Martí, José, 176–180
Martí on the U.S.A. (Martí), 180
Maryland, 5
Master Skylark (Bennett), 182
Mays, Benjamin Elijah, 169–170
Methodists, 169–170
Minneapolis Exposition, 144
"Miscegenation," 248
Mississippi Fahrten: Reisebilder aus dem amerikanischen süden (Hesse-Wartegg), 90, 253. See also Hesse-Wartegg, Ernst von.
Mississippi River, 5, 132–135; Negroes at work on, 88–90
Mississippi statute of March 1878, 215–216
Missouri, 5
Mollie McCue's school, 43

Montgomery, 52–58, 60; social progress, 139–140
Morality, 171–173; among Negroes as compared with Anglo-Saxons, 203–204; Christianity divorced from morality, 175–176, 193; development of moral standards, 201–202; homicide among Negroes due to moral and material conditions, 221; uprightness and industry of Farmville Negroes, 198–200
Morehouse College, 74
Morris Brown College, 43
Music, Negro, 76, 78
My Southern Home, or the South and Its People (Brown), 27, 132, 175, 216. See also Brown, William Wells.
Myrdal, Gunnar, 4

Nashville, 173–175
National Association for the Advancement of Colored People, 10
National Association for the Study and Prevention of Tuberculosis, 153–154
"The Negro in Africa and America" (Hall), 14
Negro in American Life and Thought: The Nadir, The (Logan), 6. See also Logan, W. Rayford.
Negro in the American Rebellion (Brown), 24
Negro Farmer, The (Kelsey), 114
"Negro Folk Songs" (Burlin), 167

Index

Negro in the New World, The (Johnston), 56, 122, 157, 205. See also Johnston, Sir Harry.
Negro Population, 1790–1915 (United States Bureau of the Census), 7
"Negro Schoolmaster in the New South, A" (DuBois), 37. See also DuBois, William Edward Burghardt.
Negroes: Black Belt, 135–136, 139; in Border States, 94; children's games and sports, 146–148; cocaine and alcohol problems, 164; dress, 156–157; economic fortunes, 83–84; exodus from South to protect rights, 241; fair skin desirable, 208–209; half-pagan frenzy, 183–186; inefficiency as workers, 108–110; insanity on the increase, 158–161; in iron mines, 120; Negro against Negro, 225–226; offensive behavior, 194–195; prefer agricultural or domestic service to cotton mills, 110–111; population, 1870–1900, 7; religion and superstition, 169–171; rise of professional class, 103–104; sexuality, 162–164; social evolution, 139–140; studies of education, 153; syphilis predominant, 161–164; tuberculosis, 153–156; wedding, 137–138; World War I, 92, 210–211. See also Education; Sea Islands.
Negroes in the United States, 1920–1932 (United States Bureau of the Census), 8, 10, 84
"Negroes of Farmville, Virginia: A Social Study, The" (DuBois), 99, 200
Negro's Church (Mays and Nicholson), 169, 170
New Deal, 5, 10, 260–261
New Orleans, 204–205; living conditions, 151; World's Exposition, 1884, 143–145
New Virginians, The (Allan-Olney), 173, 195. See also Allan-Olney, Mary.
New York Globe, 27
New York Sun, 27
News and Courier, Charleston, Hampton Institute paper, 236
Nicholson, Joseph William, 169–170
North Carolina, 5, 100, 208

Obeah rites, 176
"Observations on Skin Diseases in the Negro" (paper read by Howard Fox), 162–163
On Horseback: A Tour in Virginia, North Carolina, and Tennessee (Warner), 142
On Wandering Wheels (Gordon), 78
Oranges and Alligators: Sketches of South Florida Life (Hardy), 138
Outlook, 169, 207

Payne Institute, South Carolina, 26
Penn School, Sea Islands, 17–20, 48, 64–70, 166, 205. See also Education.
Pennsylvania, 17
"Peons of the South, The" (Holmes), 106
Phelps-Stokes Fund, 153

Philadelphia Negro (DuBois), 34. *See also* DuBois, William Edward Burghardt.
Phillips, U. B., 84
Pine Bluff, Arkansas, 144
Plantation French language, 132–134
Politics, 235–249, 252–259, 261
"Poor whites," 126–127, 209
Population, 1870–1900, 7–8, 84
Populist party, 253
Post-Reconstruction Era, 212, 235
Prisons, Southern, segregated, 227–228, 231–234; state farm prison, 233
Proclamation of Freedom, 24
Progressive Era, 7, 41, 84
"Psychological Factor in Southern Race Problems, The" (Bardin), 15
"Psychology of the Negro: An Experimental Study, The" (Ferguson, George Oscar, Jr.), 11, 14
Psychology of Peoples (LeBon), 13

Race, 5, 10; analysts of race relations, 4, 6; differences, 13–14; traits, 15
Race and Nationality in American Life (Handlin), 11
Race: The History of an Idea in America (Gossett), 11
Races and Peoples: Lectures on the Science of Ethnography (Brinton), 11, 12
Railway Theories of the Interstate Commerce Commission (Hammond), 83

Rainey, Joseph H., 90
Reconstruction, 5, 10, 16, 57, 84, 260–261; in Arkansas and Florida, 143
"Red Summer" (Johnson), 10
Relations of the Advanced and Backward Races of Mankind, The (Bryce), 31. *See also* Bryce, James.
Republicans, 6, 236–240, 241, 243, 251–254
"Revival Sermon at Little St. John's (Bennett), 186
Richmond Institute, 22, 23
Richmond Police Court, 228–231
Roosevelt, President Theodore, 58

St. Augustine, 148
St. Helena Island, South Carolina, 64–70, 205–207, 235–240. *See also* Penn School; Sea Islands.
St. Louis, living conditions, 151–153
Sala, George Augustus, 245–249
Salisbury, North Carolina, 39
School Acres: An Adventure in Rural Education (Cooley), 70, 125, 168, 192. *See also* Cooley, Rossa Belle; St. Helena; Sea Islands.
Schools. *See* Education.
Sea Islands, 17, 48, 169, 123–125, 164–165, 167, 190–192
Segregation, 4, 6
Serpent worship, 176
Shadow and Light: An Autobiography (Gibbs), 145
Shannon, Fred A., 84
Sharecropper, 83–84
Shaw Institute, 23

Index

Shellbank, 51, 61
Sherman's Invasion, 32
Shugg, Roger W., 84
Siegfried, André, 125–127, 208–209, 258–259
Sierra Leone, 156
Slavery, 3–4, 175, 212
Smalls, Robert, 18, 236–240
Souls of Black Folk (DuBois), 34, 63. See also DuBois, William Edward Burghardt.
South Carolina, 5, 17, 136, 164–165, 249
Southern farm depression, 107
"Southern Farmer and the Cotton Question, The" (Hammond), 110
Southern South, The (Hart), 51, 119, 204, 228
Spellman Seminary, 44
Spelman College, 74
"Sports of Negro Children, The" (Williams), 148
States, slaveholding, 1860, 5
Statesboro lynchings, 7
Storer College, 26
Street, Julian, 164–165, 228–231
Suffrage, universal, 244
Sundry Civil Service Bill, 242–243
Suppression of the African Slave-Trade to America, The (DuBois), 34
"Survival of the Plantation System in Louisiana" (Shugg), 84
"Syphilis in the American Negro" (Hazen), 164

Tannenbaum, Frank, 4, 209–211, 231–234
Tenant farming, 83–84, 104–106

Tennessee, 5, 99–104
Thorndike, Edward L., 14
Through Afro-America: An English Reading of the Race Problem (Archer), 64
Tindall, George B., 9–10
Towne, Laura M., 17–20, 65, 169, 235–240
Treasure of Peyre Gaillard, The (Bennett), 182
Tuberculosis among Negroes, 153–156
Tuskegee Institute, 17, 33, 56–72, 79, 84, 101, 120, 226; kindergarten, 54; music, 52; Negro conferences, 156; Normal school, 39–40; research in botany, 53; school of agriculture, 54–55. See also Education; Washington, Booker T.
"Tuskegee Machine," 7. See also Washington, Booker T.
Tyler, E. B., 13

United States Bureau of the Census, 7–10, 84
United States Bureau of Education, 153

Van Ness Home, 180–182
Virginia Central, 26
Vues d'Amérique (Adam), 153

Waco College, 26
Ware, Edward T., 70–74
Warner, Charles Dudley, 140–142
Washington, J. H., 54
Washington, Mrs. Booker T., 58–59
Washington, D.C., 139–140, 157, 162, 164

271

"What the Southern Negro Is Doing for Himself" (Barrows), 41, 104, 140. *See also* Barrows, Samuel J.

White and Black: The Outcome of a Visit to the United States (Campbell), 24, 88, 215, 252. *See also* Campbell, Sir George.

Whittier Preparatory School, 61

Whittier School for children, 53

"Why Homicide Has Increased in the United States" (Lombroso), 221

Williams, Charles Richard, 244

Williams, Timothy Shaler, 146–148

Woman's Medical College, 17

World War I, 9, 210–211

World's Exposition, 1884, 143–145

Yale, 70

Young, Thomas M., 110–111

Zig-Zag Journeys on the Mississippi: From Chicago to the Islands of Discovery (Butterworth), 181–182

A Note on the Editor

Alton Hornsby, Jr., was born in Atlanta, Georgia, in 1940 and studied at Morehouse College there. Awarded a Woodrow Wilson fellowship, followed by two other graduate fellowships, he earned his M.A. and Ph.D. degrees at the University of Texas. He has taught at Tuskegee Institute and is now Assistant Professor of History at Morehouse College.